# The Sisters
# of Auschwitz

# The Sisters of Auschwitz

## The True Story of Two Jewish Sisters' Resistance in the Heart of Nazi Territory

## Roxane van Iperen

Translated from the Dutch by Joni Zwart

HARPER LARGE PRINT

*An Imprint of HarperCollinsPublishers*

Originally published as *'t Hooge Nest* in Dutch in 2018. First English edition published in Great Britain in 2019 by Seven Dials, an imprint of the Orion Publishing Group Ltd.

HarperCollins books may be purchased for educational, business, or sales promotional use. For information, please e-mail the Special Markets Department at SPsales@harpercollins.com.

FIRST HARPER LARGE PRINT EDITION

ISBN: 978-0-06-311933-8

Library of Congress Cataloging-in-Publication Data is available upon request.

21 22 23 24 25   LSC   10 9 8 7 6 5 4 3 2 1

# Contents

# Preface

The moment we drive onto the woodland path and the house emerges between the trees, we fall in love. It is not quite the 'little cottage in the country' we were looking for – this house is enormous and even has a name: *The High Nest*. Our eyes travel across the majestic façade, brick walls covered with ivy, windows framed by old shutters. It has an air of history and grandeur, but without any of the usual detachment or pretence. On the contrary: the wild woodland garden, tall grass, the rope ladders dangling here and there and the orchard at the back – they call us to come run, play, light fires and spend endless nights talking underneath the stars, undisturbed by civilization. We look at each other and think exactly the same. How lucky we would be to live here.

The inconceivable happens. In the late summer of

2012, my husband and I, our three young children, an Old German Shepherd dog and three cats move into a caravan in the garden of The High Nest, and we embark on the long journey of restoring this extraordinary place to its former glory. Walls are renovated and stairs sanded, panels are removed, revealing ceilings with ingenious beam structures. With our bare hands we tear away the carpets and in almost each room we discover trapdoors in the wooden floors, hiding places behind old panelling. There we find candle stumps, sheet music, old resistance newspapers. And so, along with the renovation of The High Nest, begins the reconstruction of its history. A perplexing history which, as it turns out, includes an important part of the Dutch war years, unknown to most people – even within the vicinity of the house.

I sound out the previous owner, locals, shopkeepers in neighbouring villages, I dive into land registers and archives, and go from one surprise to the next. At the height of the Second World War, as the trains towards concentration camps are driving at full capacity and the *Endlösung der Judenfrage*, the 'Final Solution to the Jewish Question', is well on its way, The High Nest was a large hiding and resistance centre, run by two Jewish sisters. In the following years I become acquainted with the descendants of those who lived in The High Nest.

Those who hid there as children return to the house. They offer me their memories and personal documents, so I can give this story colour and the sisters a voice.

Slowly but surely, room by room, the pieces of the puzzle start to form the unbelievable story which now, six years later, is committed to paper. It is a history that confirms my very first feeling: this house is bigger than we are. We are merely the passers-by, lucky enough to live here.

# The Sisters
# of Auschwitz

# Part One
# War

'When we have to fight, so be it. One cannot become untrue to oneself. One cannot fool oneself either. This is what we believed in. We did what we had to do, what we could do. No more and no less.'

Janny Brandes-Brilleslijper

# 1

# The Battle of Nieuwmarkt

Amsterdam, 1912. Had the Battle of the Nieuw-markt been settled differently, the Brilleslijper family would probably never have existed. There, on the square in the heart of the Jewish Quarter, at the foot of the ancient city gate, young Joseph Brilleslijper fought for the hand of Fietje Gerritse.

Their families are perfect opposites: Joseph descends from a circus family of travelling, Yiddish-speaking musicians, and although his father has become a fruit importer, the Brilleslijpers still host exuberant Friday evenings at their home on Jodenbreestraat, where all family members gather to act and sing. Fietje Gerritse, on the other hand, is from a family of devout Frisian Jews; tall, sullen people with ginger hair, raising their six children with strict discipline among the godlessness of the Red Light District, with its dock workers, sailors and whores. From a young age, Fietje worked in her parents' late-night shop on Zeedijk, standing on a crate behind the till, her three brothers, acting as bouncers, by her side. She has fallen madly in love with ever cheerful Joseph, but her parents will have none of him; a good-for-nothing, out-of-work boy, constantly running off to visit his travelling grandfather at the circus.

The three Gerritse brothers have, more than once, mercilessly beaten Joseph up, and when he comes to their parents' house to ask for Fietje's hand, they even throw him out, his face flat on the clinkers. Joseph realises there is but one option left. He invites the un-beaten giants of Zeedijk to descend from their throne so he can, once and for all, show the Gerritse family his mettle. With his older brother Ruben, he drums up some friends from the neighbourhood, including Dumb Öpie, the boy who has never spoken a word but is as strong as an ox, so no one comments on that, and with their fists and jaws clenched, they head towards the old city gate. In front of the fish stalls on Nieuw-markt, a spectacular fist fight breaks loose. For the first time in their lives, the Gerritse brothers are brought to their knees. Joseph wipes the blood from his knuckles, picks his Fietje up at her parents' store and together they move in with Ruben and his wife.

Whether it was strategic insight, brute force or good fortune, the victory marks the beginning of a loving relationship. They marry on 1 May 1912 and Joseph's father finds the young couple a small place to live in the poorest part of the Jewish Quarter. And there, on 13 December 1912, their daughter Rebekka, 'Lientje', Brilleslijper first sees the light of day.

The family is penniless but happy. A few lean years later and with a little help from Opa (Grandpa) Jaap, Joseph's father, they take over a small shop on Nieuwe Kerkstraat, where they move into the apartment above the store with young Lien. While Fietje works in the shop day and night, Joseph helps out in Opa Jaap's wholesale business. It will take another four years before Fietje's parents – two squares away but worlds apart – reach out to their daughter. The occasion is the birth of Fietje's second daughter, Marianne, 'Janny', named after her maternal grandmother. Five years later, in the summer of 1921, the long-awaited son, Jacob, 'Japie', is born, and the family is complete.

While Joseph and Fietje work around the clock to make ends meet, the Jewish Quarter raises their children. Large families live in long, narrow rooms, with children sleeping underneath the sink or along the skirting board in the hall, so most of their life happens out on the street. Just around the corner from the Brilleslijper home is Royal Theater Carré where Lien and Janny spend hours, staring at the stream of beautifully dressed people who come to see the revue. Further down Jodenbreestraat is the Tip Top Theater, a popular meeting place where silent movies are shown and famous artists like Louis and Heintje Davids perform.

Everyone in the area knows each other; brothers help earn a living, sisters help raise the children and in the streets around the house it always smells of food. From Waterlooplein to Jodenbreestraat, stalls are selling roast chestnuts, fresh fish, hot spices and pickled gherkins. On Fridays, Fietje and other women in the neighbourhood always keep a large pan of soup on the stove for the poor. In the war years of 1914 to 1915, when Belgian refugees turn up in the shop, Fietje gives worried mothers their groceries even if they can't pay. 'I'll write it down,' she says, sending them away with a smile.

On Friday night the family joins the rest of the Brilleslijper lot in Opa Jaap's house on Jodenbreestraat. They have chicken soup, play music and act with all the uncles, aunts and cousins – a tradition Joseph, after his father passes away, will continue with his own wife and children.

And so the early childhood of the Brilleslijper children unfolds in the penniless but sheltered surroundings of the Amsterdam Jewish Quarter, in a family full of love and music. But life gets harder as the 1920s progress. Unemployment is on the rise, families run out of food and when Fietje visits her neighbour one Friday, her traditional pan of soup for the poor is nothing but a pot filled with steaming hot water.

The building where they have their shop and their home is sold to a large firm and they are forced to move to Rapenburgerstraat. It is just one block away from their old house, but the loss of her shop weighs heavy on Fietje. On his own, Joseph does not make enough money to pay the rent, and the family moves again, ending up in two small rooms around the corner of Marnixstraat, on the fringes of the Jordaan area. Each morning at the crack of dawn, Fietje and Joseph leave the house together to earn their keep in the fruit and vegetable trade.

In 1925 the tide slowly turns when, to their sorrow, Opa Jaap dies. With the help of his brother Ruben, Joseph takes over the wholesale business and moves his family into a house filled with other family members on Marnixstraat. They live on the first floor, where Janny and Lien get to share a beautiful room together. But the familiar Jewish Quarter feels miles away; the girls miss their old neighbourhood, the people, the familiar Yiddish–Amsterdam sound with its lisped S. Cut off from the Jewish Quarter, the girls begin to understand why the evergrowing stream of Jewish refugees from Russia and Poland stick together in narrow houses the way they do. Around the streets of the Nieuwe Prinsengracht, close to their former shop where many of the Eastern Jews bought fresh fish from Fietje, they form a tight unit – the women wearing headscarves, the men with their long corkscrew curls in black caftans.

The sisters are inseparable and look so much alike that it's very difficult to tell them apart. They enjoy the freedom offered by their parents' loving neglect. In the morning, when Joseph and Fietje have left for the market in the dark and Japie is still fast asleep, they get their bicycles out of the shed and pedal to the Olympic Stadium, their shoulders forward, race across Amstelveenseweg and then turn right onto IJsbaanpad. At the wooden footbridge across the railway towards Aalsmeer they must get off because the bridge is too steep and high. They have to brace themselves, push their bicycles up with outstretched arms, squinting so as not to see the rails below.

And there, where the Schinkel river streams into

Nieuwe Meer, resting on high piles, is Schinkelbad, an outdoor pool built with wood, filled with city water. All sweaty from cycling and their final climb, they jump into the cold water quickly and always swim just a little too long, so they have to hurry back to make sure Jaap, who they sometimes lovingly call Japie, gets to school on time.

Janny and Lien grow into two beautiful young girls. They are petite and dark, with a straight nose and high cheekbones, eyebrows like fox tails and a wealth of black hair tied low on their neck. At the end of primary school their education is finished; Father and Mother have no money for further studies – and they can do with their help. It doesn't matter; the sisters are inquisitive and have a sharp eye for the world around them. Amsterdam offers them everything they need to learn.

They help Fietje with the housekeeping, work full time as seamstresses and look after their younger brother. As they grow older, the age difference seems to shrink, but the differences in their nature become more apparent. Lien is spontaneous, outgoing, lighthearted like her father and a dreamer. Janny is down-to-earth, at times reserved, and has a strong will, like her mother.

Lien turns out to have a great talent for music. At a young age she sings in a children's choir and at Opa

Jaap's soirées she is always at the front of the stage. In her early teens she takes classes at Florrie Rodrigo's dancing school. Florrie is a Jewish–Portuguese dancer who first made a name for herself in Jean-Louis Pisuisse's shows and then as an expressionistic dancer in Berlin. She started her dancing school in the Amsterdam Jewish Quarter after fleeing an increasingly anti-Semitic Germany.

Joseph does not think much of his daughter's frivolous hobby and forbids her to take any more classes. But Joseph's stubborn genes are stronger than his authority; through Florrie, Lien ends up with the choreographer Lili Green, and around her sixteenth birthday, she secretly starts to take lessons from her. Lili is a pioneer in the world of dance, someone who modernizes the techniques of classical ballet. She sees a serious future as a dancer in store for Lien.

And so, little Lien works as a seamstress during the day, rushes to Lili Green's studio on Pieter Pauwstraat to practice in the evening and performs in the clubs around Rembrandtplein at night. When yet another morning she returns home at the crack of dawn and she runs into her worried mother on the stairs, Fietje quickly steers Lien to her room before Joseph sees her.

Janny, the younger sister, doesn't last more than six months at the sewing studio. She is impatient and rebellious, just as she was at school. She calls herself spiritual but not religious. She grew up in the heart of the Jewish Quarter, but never goes to the synagogue. She's from a family of grocers, but she joins the Zionist organization Hatzair, where most members are children of doctors and lawyers. As soon as she notices people being treated differently, she fiercely protests – inspired, obviously, by the history of her grandparents Gerritse, who didn't think her father good enough to marry her mother.

After the unsuccessful adventure at the sewing studio, Janny goes through a range of jobs before ending up at a laboratory. With the money she earns at the lab she occasionally takes courses, learns to speak a bit of English, French and German, and takes a first-aid course; something that might ultimately save her and Lien's life.

She leaves the Zionist movement, because she believes they must fight for a better society for everyone, not to secure the rights of the upper middle class only. She immerses herself in communism, in Marx, in social democratic principles – at home, both of her parents read the socialist newspaper *Het Volk* – and engages in debate with everyone, on everything. It worries her to see the number of Eastern Europeans and other emigrants in the Jewish Quarter rising, even though it has become increasingly difficult for them to cross the border. Janny tries to convince her father of the brown threat: fascism. Joseph thinks it won't get that bad, but Janny sees a real danger in the alliance between Hitler, Mussolini and Franco, and when in the summer of 1936, the Spanish Civil War begins, Janny, nineteen years old, becomes an active member of the resistance.

She mainly works for the International Red Aid, who support Dutch volunteers fighting in Spain with various activities. Janny is also a member of the committee Help for Spain, and works with a group of young people living in a community centre on 522 Keizersgracht, who Lien introduced her to – journalist Mik van Gilse, photographers Eva Besnyö and Carel Blazer, and filmmaker Joris Ivens. From Amsterdam, Janny contributes by collecting money for bandages and other scarce items, she smuggles an ambulance across the border and helps find homes for the growing number of refugees from Germany. They tell her stories of increasing hatred against Jews and 'Bolsheviks'. The German defeat in the First World War, the Wall Street Crash of 1929 causing the worldwide crisis that hit Germany hard and the increasingly openly anti-Semitic atmosphere – all these factors have led to the overwhelming victory of Hitler's Nazi Party, the NSDAP.

The situation in the Netherlands deteriorates as

well. The economic downturn reduces many to impoverishment, unemployment rises and Prime Minister Colijn has implemented a tough austerity policy. The Brilleslijper family are facing setbacks at home too: Joseph has had a number of major eye operations and he is not recovering well. Fietje and the three children bring in the money, until Mother too falls ill and ends up in hospital.

There is, however, one light at the end of those troubled thirties: both sisters meet a man who will change their life.

**Lien, in** the meantime, has moved out, mainly to escape Joseph's wrath about her dancing activities. Now twenty-four years old, she lives in an artist's commune with a colourful group of students on Bankastraat in The Hague, the largest Dutch city on the North Sea coast and the seat of parliament, around forty-three miles south of Amsterdam. There is a shared kitchen, a kitty to cover expenses and a blackboard for residents, room numbers and administrative announcements in the hall. When Lientje, owing to a concussion, is bedridden – she fell on her way to dance training – a new tenant brings her a bunch of hand-picked flowers. She is charmed by this tall, blond boy with his blue eyes and cautious smile. His name is Eberhard Rebling, and he is a German musicologist and concert pianist who fled National Socialism and his militarist father in his homeland.

Eberhard in turn is fascinated by this petite dark woman with her sharp tongue. On paper, they could not be more different, and yet they fall deeply in love. They quickly become a pair in music too: as soon as Lien is back on her feet, she teaches dance and performs, accompanied by Eberhard on the piano.

They become friends with other students visiting the house and for nights on end they discuss the ominous political climate in neighbouring countries. Among their friends are Gerrit Kastein, a young doctor, oboist Haakon Stotijn, his wife Mieke and Bob Brandes, economics student, son of a famous family of architects from The Hague.

In the summer of 1938, when Lien is starring in a revue and has temporarily rented a room on Leidseplein in Amsterdam, her younger sister, Janny, often comes by after work to share a meal. One evening when Janny visits Lien, she meets Bob Brandes, who teasingly challenges her political views. Bob is on the board of the Social Democratic Fraternity and works in Amsterdam as an intern at communist publishing house Pegasus. He enrages Janny to the extent that she starts throwing pillows at the height of the discussion to silence this know-all. But when a few weeks later Lien gives her the keys to her room in The Hague, she soon starts using them to see more of Bob. 'This place is like a left-wing brothel,' one of the other tenants mutters as yet another relationship in the house is sealed.

Mrs Brandes, Bob's mother, gets wind of the affair and calls that nice pianist who once gave a concert in their front parlour, Eberhard Rebling, to see if he would have a word with his friend Bob – that girl from a dubious merchant milieu is absolutely below her son. Eberhard listens smilingly, calms Mrs Brandes and assures her the Brilleslijper family has some fine daughters indeed. In January 1939, Bob takes Janny out to the cinema in The Hague, accompanies her home afterwards, and never leaves again.

Bob's parents refuse to give their consent to the intended marriage. They think both Janny's social background and her Jewish descent are too much of a risk in times like these. Though saddened by their attitude, Janny follows the example of her headstrong parents: in September 1939, almost twenty-three years old, she marries Bob, twenty-six years old, from her parental home in Amsterdam. Without father and mother Brandes, but in the presence of Bob's sisters, including Aleid, with whom Janny gets along well. Joseph butters sandwiches for everyone, Fietje has returned from hospital and Janny, radiant, her round belly impossible to ignore, is the centre of attention. Bob, mischievously, has placed an announcement of their marriage in the newspaper in The Hague and as a result, his parents are flooded with congratulations from their distinguished circle of acquaintances.

A month after the wedding, on 10 October 1939, Robert Brandes is born. Janny, Bob and the baby move into two rooms on Bazarlaan in The Hague with a landlady, Miss Tonnie de Bruin, who solicits on Prinsenstraat – an open secret to everyone.

The young couple is over the moon but needs to put food on the table too. Before she got pregnant, Janny worked behind a knitting machine in a factory. She was given a small maternity allowance, but this is shrinking fast. Bob quits his studies and enters the civil service; Janny stays at home to look after little Robbie.

The family quickly expands: in winter 1939, their first man in hiding moves in. Alexander de Leeuw is an eminent lawyer from Amsterdam, board member of the Dutch Communist Party, CPN, and director of Pegasus Publishers, where he met Bob. De Leeuw is known for his surly demeanour but also for his fierce battle against fascism and widely read publications. As a well-known communist and CPN lawyer, he has become a target in an increasingly hostile Amsterdam.

Many years of austerity policy by the Colijn government have not helped the country overcome the economical crisis. On the contrary: there is hardly any recovery and the persistent scarcity causes tensions to rise. At the same time, hundreds of thousands of Jews and socialists try to escape Germany and countries further east, fleeing the orgy of violence unleashed in the Kristallnacht in November 1938, when Jews were lynched in the streets. The Dutch government, for fear of insulting Germany, has shut the borders for refugees, who are marked 'undesirable elements'. Besides, reasoned Colijn, a mass influx of Jewish refugees would only aggravate the existing anti-Semitism in the country.

'To be avoided is anything conducive to permanent settlement in our already densely populated country, seeing as a further invasion of foreign elements would be damaging to the preservation of the character of the Dutch tribe. The Government is of the opinion that our confined territory should in principle remain reserved for our own population,' the Dutch government wrote in 1938.

The Dutch soil, too, proves fertile for a scapegoat and public displays of hatred increase. In the winter of 1939, various cinemas in Amsterdam show *Olympia*, Leni Riefenstahl's documentary, commissioned by Adolf Hitler, on the 1936 Berlin Olympics – a long, drawn-out idealization of athletic Aryan bodies. The film attracts young and unruly DNP (Dutch Nazi Party) members, and fights erupt in the city between groups of Fascists and young leftist and Jewish men.

When Alexander de Leeuw even stops feeling safe in his favourite pub, Café Reynders on Leidseplein, he starts looking for a place to hide. In Janny and Bob's upstairs flat in The Hague, he sleeps in the attic and quietly washes himself in the room of newly born baby Robbie. Janny is struck by his introversion and awkwardness. When, one morning, Lientje pays a surprise visit and finds De Leeuw breakfasting in Janny's living room, they stare at each other in shock. De Leeuw mutters something, grabs his stuff and, head down, rushes past Lien to the attic. She raises her eyebrows enquiringly towards her sister, but Janny ostentatiously presses her lips and shrugs her shoulders, as if she has never seen the man before.

When, on 10 May 1940 at 3.55 a.m., German armoured trains cross the Dutch border and Luftwaffe squadrons enter the airspace, it comes as no surprise to Janny. It is the day when the illusion of Dutch neutrality is shattered. The day when Queen Wilhelmina issues the following proclamation:

Although our country has, with utmost con-
scientiousness, maintained strict neutrality all
these months, and had no other intention than to
maintain this neutrality firmly and in all its consequences, German troops without any warning
made a sudden attack upon our territory last night.
This happened despite the solemn promise that the
neutrality of our country would be respected so
long as we maintained it ourselves.

The first few days Janny and Bob still hope the Brits
will drive the Germans out, but nothing happens. From
their small house on Bazarlaan, they can almost touch
the royal stables of Noordeinde Palace, so when, on 13
May, they see a convoy of expensive cars leave, it really
hits home: the Netherlands are occupied.

That night, when Robbie is asleep, Janny and Bob
discuss the situation. They know the stories of refugees
from the east, the traumas of those who fought in Spain.
They are aware of the hostility in their country in the
run-up to this moment. And yet they are determined:
they shall resist fascism. Although they are not naive
about possible consequences, they cannot possibly imagine what lies ahead.

A few days later, when Janny is taking Robbie for a

walk in his pram and suddenly the air raid siren goes off, she runs through the streets of The Hague searching for help. Ominous blaring fills the airspace, circles around her, low and heavy at first, to then shoot up – again and again, as fear ties a knot in her stomach and paving stones shoot by beneath her feet. She spots a familiar façade, rings the doorbell at acquaintances of the Brandes family and, gasping for breath, asks them for shelter. Ashamed, but resolute, they show Janny and her baby the door.

# 2

# The Brown Plague

The first one they lose, after the capitulation, is Anita, a cheerful young woman who lives with them on Bankastraat.

On 14 May 1940, Lien, Eberhard and their friends are by the window in their front room, silently staring at the black plumes of smoke above Rotterdam in the distance – a minor mistake by the Germans, who failed to call back their airplanes when the Dutch capitulated.

Suddenly, they hear someone moaning on the first floor. Lien hurries up the stairs with Eberhard following, and they find Anita on her bed, white as chalk, limp, a glass tube by her side.

The girl had fled Germany because of increasingly violent manifestations of anti-Semitism, and she had once told Lien about the dose of arsenic her father, a

Jewish doctor, had given her when they said goodbye. Although the story, again, confirmed the gravity of the situation in Germany, they had also thought the gesture somewhat dramatic. Until now. 'Rather dead than in Nazi hands,' Anita's father had emphasized.

In the rest of the Netherlands, many agree; after the capitulation is announced on the news, hundreds of people take their own lives.

And yet, public life fairly quickly resumes its course; people go to work, shops are open and newspapers published. Janny and Lien regularly visit their parents and younger brother in Amsterdam, and there, too, everything looks deceptively normal. Inspired by the commune in The Hague, Bob's sister Aleid starts something similar in Amsterdam: a community house on Nieuwe Herengracht, close to the botanical gardens, filled with many of the sisters' mutual friends. It isn't until they visit Aleid, and find hardly any of their friends there, that they realize some already have one foot in the resistance: they stay here and there, and only come home occasionally to collect some things.

Janny and Lien learn about the lists now circulating with names of volunteers in the Spanish Civil War, leftist youth, social democrats, communists and other anti-Fascists who the Germans are keeping an eye on. To draw them up, they depend heavily on input from the fifth column: citizens sympathizing with fascism, keen to contribute and share long-cherished information – varying from Dutch entrepreneurs exposing their 'red' customers, to German maids telling on the families whose dirty laundry they took care of for years. Janny worries that she, Bob and their friends might already be registered somewhere, and discusses the lists with her husband. But he simply shrugs: 'If we are, we will find out eventually.'

And so begins the waiting.

**On 29 May 1940,** Reich Commissioner Arthur Seyss-Inquart gives his first speech as the highest official of the occupying forces, at the Hall of Knights in Dutch parliament. The Austrian lawyer with slick hair and small round spectacles emphasizes the Dutch people have nothing to fear from the Germans:

> We have not come here to oppress and destroy a national character and to deprive a country of its freedom [. . .] This time it was not about national character nor money nor freedom. The goods of this land were never under threat. This time the question was whether the Dutch would be abused as a stepping stone for an attack against the faith, the freedom and the lives of the German people

[. . .] Those are the words I have to say to the Dutch people today, as I take over the highest governmental authority of the Netherlands. We have come with force of arms reluctantly; we want to be protectors and promoters to then remain friends; all of this, though, in the light of the higher duty, we, Europeans, have, because we have to build a new Europe, where national honour and collective labour are the guiding principles.

The entire country sighs with relief. Things will be different here than they are in the eastern occupied countries: the Germans will at least show respect for this civilized Western country. Hitler has always been clear that he considers the Slavic people as rubbish that needs to be removed from his backyard, where he wants to create Lebensraum, and he hopes his Germanic brothers in the West will help him to achieve this goal. The Netherlands has not interfered with the German oppression policy and is offered mild treatment in return – or so the Dutch people hope. Even the German soldiers turn out not to be that bad: in bright summer weather you can see them out and about on the streets, and on Scheveningen beach, strangely enough, they enjoy their hot chocolate with whipped cream.

In the commune on Bankastraat there's a sense of

optimism too: surely one of the Allied superpowers will quickly defeat Hitler, the question is merely if it will take one year or two. Either way, there will be very few consequences for Jewish people in the Netherlands; they are fully integrated into society and the rest of the country will not allow anything to happen to them.

When Lien, bright and breezy, drops by her sister's house for coffee, Janny does not agree with her positive story. She is remarkably absent and curt.

'You should stop coming here this often.'

She says it even before offering her sister anything to drink. Lien thinks of the strange men she keeps seeing in the small apartment, the illegal newspapers, the secret meetings. Surely Janny trusts her own sister?

'Is it Eberhard?'

Lien can barely say it. She narrows her eyes, tilts her head and looks at her younger sister.

Lien knows Janny does not see shades of grey in this occupation – she believes each new day with the Germans inside the country borders is one too many. And Eberhard is a German.

'What makes you think *that*? I trust Eberhard like I trust my own family.'

Janny presses Lien against her chest and sighs. Then she holds her sister, her arms outstretched, looking her straight in the eye.

'This is a dangerous place, Lientje. You have no idea what those Krauts are capable of. Trust me: the less often you're here, the better. For both of us.'

Shortly after this conversation, Lien is outside the dance studio, waiting for the next class, when a strange man approaches. She is startled when he starts speaking to her, but then recognizes his voice. He's one of her Eastern-Jewish students; he has shaven his long beard and corkscrew curls, and is unrecognizable with his smooth and pale face and new clothes. He hardly dares to look at Lien. With great difficulty she manages a smile and cheerfully starts the lesson, but the rest of the afternoon her stomach is tight and her limbs feel so heavy she can barely lift them.

**One night** in October Bob returns home from work with a form. It is an Aryan declaration, on which all civil servants in the Netherlands are obliged to fill in whether they or their family are Jewish.

As soon as they have put Robbie to bed, they sit down together and carefully read the declaration:

*The undersigned:* . . .
*occupation:* . . .
*position:* . . .
*born on* . . . *at* . . .

*living in . . .*
*declare, that to the best of his/her knowledge*
*neither he himself/she herself, nor his/her wife/*
*husband/fiancé(e), nor one of his/(her)/their*
*parents or grandparents has ever been part of the*
*Jewish community of faith.*

*It is known to the undersigned, that he/she,*
*should the above declaration prove false, is*
*subject to summary dismissal.*

*. . . , 1940.*
*(signature)*

They let their eyes rest on the paper at the last sentence. Then they look at each other. It has begun. Bob says nothing, makes a wry face, lifts the paper by a corner, opens the lid of the round iron stove and slowly lowers the form into the fire.

'What are you doing?' Janny asks.

'I am not filling in any declarations and neither are you. I want nothing to do with this, and we'll see what happens when we get there.'

**One month** after Bob has lit the fire with his Aryan declaration, everyone in the civil service who is known to be Jewish is fired. Among them is the father of their friend Tilly, President of the Supreme Court, Lodewijk Visser. Not one of his colleagues objects.

Janny and Bob are as yet unaware what the tightly organised registration of Jews is the prelude to, and they don't fret about the declaration. Much more interesting are the encouraging signs of resistance around them. They hear about dozens of pupils at Vossius, a prominent grammar school in Amsterdam, going on strike and about the civil disobedience by Professor Rudolph Cleveringa of Leiden University. Students illegally distribute thousands of copies of Cleveringa's speech throughout the Netherlands. Janny and Lien, too, get a copy. Cleveringa, like Bob, is part of the very small group of civil servants in the country who decide not to sign the Aryan declaration – in his case in solidarity with two Jewish colleagues, professors Meijers and David, who have just been fired. Everyone refusing to fill in the form, however, is in danger of losing his job too. Cleveringa is not a man of impulsive bravura – he is very aware of the potential consequences but determined to take a clear stand nonetheless.

On 26 November 1940, Cleveringa goes to Leiden University in the morning, supposedly to take over the lecture his colleague Meijers would give. In front of his unsuspecting students he delivers a protest speech, which is still regarded as one of the best speeches ever held in the Netherlands. In his address, Cleveringa, as a tribute to his master Meijers, discusses the diversity of his work and thus brings Dutch law to life. He examines the foundations of various areas of law and Meijers' merits throughout his impressive career, and then makes an appeal to the reason, the conscience and the sense of justice of his young audience:

Meijers is this Dutchman, this noble and true son of our people, this *mensch*, this father to his students, this scholar whom the foreigner presently ruling over us with hostility 'removes from his office'!

I said I would not speak about my feelings; I shall keep that promise, close as those feelings are to streaming, like hot boiling lava, through all the cracks that sometimes seem as if they might burst open in my head and heart.

But in the faculty, that according to its objective, is devoted to observing justice, *this* may not be left unspoken: in accordance with Dutch tradition, the constitution states that every Dutch person may serve his country in any way and can be appointed to any position or dignity, enjoying equal civil and citizens' rights, regardless of his religion.

After Cleveringa has said his final word, there is a burst of applause and several students start to sing the national anthem, soon followed by the rest of the hall. The feeling of solidarity swirls through the streets of Leiden, but is brutally crushed the next day with the arrest of Cleveringa, who will spend the rest of the war in the House of Detention in Scheveningen as punishment for his resistance. Leiden University is closed.

Janny and Lien discuss the action with their friend Tilly, to hearten her and emphasize the courage of her father, Lodewijk Visser, who is President of the Dutch Supreme Court. They admire how determined he is, even after being fired by the Nazis and their collaborators at justice, and abandoned by his fellow judges. When asked about his dismissal, he persists it is not valid; the queen has appointed him and only she is authorized to discharge him from his office – everything else is unlawful. Lodewijk Visser does not leave it at that and keeps actively offering resistance against the Germans. He is a contributor to the underground newspaper *Het Parool* and will become Chairman of the Jewish Coordination Committee, a national, autonomous organization, founded by two Jewish religious societies.

To Lien, people like Lodewijk Visser set a benchmark for resistance; an attitude that will surely get the masses moving against the occupying forces – who might have thought the Dutch would offer them free play but are facing a nasty surprise. Janny, however, is neither counting on the Germans for mercy, nor on the Dutch people for salvation. So when in January 1941, a few months after the mandatory Aryan declaration for civil servants, *all* Jews in the Netherlands are compelled to register, she does not report. As one of few people among her acquaintances, she refuses to have the black capital J for Jew stamped in her identity card. The only thing she will later regret is that she didn't urge everyone else around her to do the same. That she didn't tell Lien, who makes no fuss about this bureaucracy, reports and gets a J stamped in her identity card, just like 160,820 other Jews in the Netherlands. A small administrative action that will prove to be most helpful for the deportation system that soon starts running, facilitated by the efficiency and professionalism the Germans so praise the Dutch for.

In Amsterdam alone, some 70,000 thousand Jews are registered – 10 per cent of all the inhabitants of the city. At the *Zentralstelle für Jüdische Auswanderung*, the Central Office for Jewish Emigration on Adama van Scheltemaplein, later in the war, a few simple card-index boxes suffice to keep track of those who have been taken away and those who still need to go. When each train leaves, a copy of the list of passengers is sent to the *Zentralstelle*, where an accountant then transfers the card corresponding to each passenger's name from one box to the other. One card per transported man, woman or child until the box with Jews registered in Amsterdam is almost empty and the box with the deported full.

# 3
# Strike! Strike! Strike!

It is a freezing-cold winter, the first since the German invasion, and, led by Anton Mussert, the DNP paramilitary squads known as the 'blackshirts' are becoming bolder. The DNP is hitching a ride on the German forces' wagon; before foreign occupation the party had very little say in the Dutch political landscape. Despite a fanatical campaign presenting Mussert as the saviour from the Bolshevist threat ('Mussert or Moscow?'), the Dutch Nazis got less than 4 per cent of the votes at the national elections of 1937.

The boldness of the Dutch Nazis, protected by Hitler's strong arm, becomes increasingly tangible in daily life. The party organizes targeted provocations in predominantly Jewish neighbourhoods and among the people in the Amsterdam Jewish Quarter, in the city centre, the atmosphere is tense.

The Germans have issued new directives for the Dutch police, instructing them to better protect Dutch Nazis in confrontations with Jews and rebellious civilians. Furthermore, arresting blackshirts is no longer allowed.

Janny is often in Amsterdam. She sees the tight faces, hears the whispering in the alleys, feels how the tension in and around the city centre rises. Everyone seems to be in a constant hurry and those without a reason to be out stay in.

Café owners who have not put up a 'no Jews allowed' sign yet are visited by groups of blackshirts – and treated anything but kindly. All the windows of Café Restaurant De Kroon on Rembrandtplein have been smashed and in other cafés the squads destroy every piece of furniture. German soldiers support them as Dutch policemen helplessly stand by.

'This is bound to go wrong, Bob,' Janny says to her husband at home in The Hague. 'Ordinary people don't put up with this, either. There have been fights with Dutch Nazis – one of them even died.'

She is talking about Hendrik Koot, a committed blackshirt who died in hospital on Tuesday, 11 February after a brutal fight in the Jewish Quarter. Koot is the martyr the Fascists need to take the next step.

That same night, the Jewish Corner, the heart of the Jewish Quarter, where 25,000 people live, is hermetically sealed. The bridges are raised and barbed-wire fencing is set up to block the entrance, with *Grüne Polizei* (Green Police), Nazi police officers, standing on guard in front of it.

A day later the occupying forces demand the formation of a Jewish Council: a central body, acting on behalf of the Jewish, for the Germans to communicate with – quickly turning into a body to use for carrying out their orders.

Lodewijk Visser, frontman of the Jewish Coordination Committee, instantly objects to the Council and the policy of its chairmen, Abraham Asscher and David Cohen. Asscher and Cohen believe they can negotiate, on behalf of the Jewish community, with the Germans and perhaps even exert positive influence, but Visser believes their attitude is too cooperative. He refuses, on behalf of the Jewish Coordination Committee, to communicate with the Germans and only speaks to the Dutch government.

Later that year the Germans will order the Jewish Coordination Committee to cease its activities and name the Jewish Council as the only national representative of the Jewish Community.

Following the death of Koot, the Nazi propaganda machine goes full speed ahead. DNP weekly *Volk en Vaderland*, People and Country, says:

Juda has thrown off the mask! [. . .] Sergeant Hendrik Evert Koot is killed. Killed? No, trampled down with sadistic delight! Crushed under the ponderous feet of a nomadic people – whose blood is different from ours. This eastern slaughtering method is typically Jewish. [. . .] Let it be said to the criminals that this is the last, the very last time, that one of us was killed by Jews.

In the following week articles in a similar tone appear in various Dutch newspapers. They mention the many bite wounds Koot apparently had, worse even: that a Jew bit through his throat. Within days, Koot's death has assumed mythical proportions, and Joseph and Fietje Brilleslijper have to stand by helplessly while the Jewish Quarter is fenced off from the rest of Amsterdam. Everywhere, around their home too, signs are put up saying: *Judenviertel*/*Joodsche Wijk*.

But it is not over yet. On 19 February, there is a fight around ice-cream parlour Koco between *Grüne Polizei* and a defence squad of regular customers who have, for some time, been protecting the owners, Alfred Kohn and Ernst Cahn, two German–Jewish refugees. On this occasion the Germans are sprayed with a specially prepared bottle of ammonia. Owners and customers are arrested and the incident is reported directly to Heinrich Himmler, leader of the *Schutzstaffel*, the SS.

With the first fight on Friday, 9 February following Koot's death and the gas incident at Koco, the Germans now have enough excuse for launching a large offensive against the Jews – without anticipating much opposition from Dutch citizens. There is only one thing left to do: instruct the Jewish Council to disarm its community. The brand-new chairmen of the Council, diamond dealer Asscher and professor of ancient history Cohen, call on the Jewish population to surrender all arms before Friday, 21 February 1941. 'If this call is not obeyed, strict government measures will inevitably follow.'

That weekend the Dutch are introduced to a phenomenon they will soon become familiar with: raids. People are dragged from their homes, men who look Jewish are pulled from their bicycles and women who interfere are violently pushed aside.

During these first raids, on 22 and 23 February 1941, a total of 427 Jewish men between twenty and thirty-five years old are arrested; a great many around the synagogues on Jonas Daniël Meijerplein in Amsterdam, a small triangle between Waterlooplein and the canal. The Dutch police had not been informed and many non-Jewish civilians, visiting the Sunday market, witness the action. The Jewish men are rounded up, forced to squat on the ground with their hands up or behind their head. Their faces are white as chalk, their pupils dilated. They are guarded by soldiers kicking them into place with their boots, while other soldiers usher new arrivals towards the square, beating them with the butts of their rifles. Trucks pull up, a group is rushed in, the driver accelerates and they are gone. Move over, arms up, shouting, a smack. They are Jewish men in work clothes, men in their Sunday best, one man in a tailcoat. Bystanders are watching, glued to the spot; others run home. When the last truck has left the Jewish Quarter that Sunday night, the silence is deafening.

Among the men who are arrested are friends of Janny and Lien. Most of the deported end up in Mauthausen labour camp, a concentration camp in Austria where granite is extracted. Again it is Lodewijk Visser who appeals, more than once, to the secretaries general – the same secretaries general who had turned their backs on him when he was dismissed – to stand up for the fate of the Jewish men who are arrested and transported. Visser has heard that prisoners in the labour camp die en masse as a result of working in the quarry, owing to hunger, disease or torture, and he believes the Dutch government should intervene. But again, no one listens.

In the meantime, the Germans are so annoyed with Visser that they threaten to send him to a concentration camp if he doesn't keep quiet. They need not have worried. In early 1942, Lodewijk Visser dies of a brain haemorrhage. None of his former colleagues on the Supreme Court are present at his funeral.

The entire group of men deported from the Netherlands during the weekend of 22 and 23 February 1941 dies within a few months – with the exception of two 'lucky ones', who are sent on to Buchenwald concentration camp and survive.

Ernst Cahn of the Koco ice-cream parlour is shot by a firing squad in the dunes near The Hague in March, which makes him the first civilian in the Second World War to be killed this way. His partner, Alfred Kohn, does not return from Auschwitz.

**Then something** extraordinary happens. One day after the raids, late at night, the banned Communist Party distributes leaflets through the entire city. In black typewritten letters and with many exclamation marks there's an elaborate call, on just one sheet of paper, for strike and solidarity with the Jews:

> Organize the protest strike in all companies!!!
> Fight against terror as one!!!
> Demand immediate release of the arrested Jews!!!
> (. . .)
> Keep Jewish children away from Nazi violence, take them into your families!!!
> BE AWARE OF THE ENORMOUS POWER OF YOUR UNITED ACTION!!!
> This is many times greater than the German military occupation!
>
> STRIKE!!! STRIKE!!! STRIKE!!!

A few hours before, in the early evening of 24 February, some hundred members of the Communist Party, mostly civil servants, gathered for an open-air meeting on Noordermarkt near Amsterdam Centraal Station, at the top of the Prinsengracht. They turned up on the square from all directions, braving the cold in thick coats, hats pulled over their ears. A cloud of people's breath mingled with cigarette smoke floats above the men at the foot of the church as the initiators give a glowing speech.

An earlier strike, when Dutch metalworkers were sent to Germany, had been called off, but the CPN leaders expect a broader base for action after the recent chain of anti-Semitic violence. Everyone here at Noordermarkt, the party leaders emphasize, must not only obey the call to action themselves, but also encourage others to participate, in a collective protest against the German treatment and deportation of the Amsterdam Jews – *their* Amsterdam Jews.

The fury about what happened on Jonas Daniël Meijerplein – the severe ill treatment of the Jewish men – has stirred something up and many people that night are in favour of organizing a massive protest. At the end of the meeting piles of leaflets are handed out. People disperse and return to their own part of town to further spread the word.

The following morning the February strike breaks out: a large-scale, organized and open protest against the persecution of the Jews. A crucial first act is the strike of the Amsterdam tram drivers; people waiting at the stops wonder why trams don't show and are unable to get to work. It has a domino effect; the news quickly spreads through the city.

For many the start of the strike is nerve-wracking, an unnatural act of disobedience – but in each company it only takes one person to set the process in motion. A boy at the hat factory extinguishes the large stove with a bucket of water; without steam to make hats, the entire production comes to a standstill and workers leave the building en masse. A young seamstress has prepared her plan with her husband; in the sewing studio on the first floor she waits by the window for him to signal from the street below that the strike has begun. She then turns nervously to the room full of women, clears her throat, and calls on them to put down their work and strike against the occupying forces and their criminal treatment of Jews. To her surprise, all the other seamstresses rise and follow her outside.

Once the first workers, without permission, leave their place and appear on the street, their coats on and their hats pulled over their ears, the floodgates are open. Everywhere in the city people gather outside in the wintry cold; men and women, clerks and road workers. At first they are hesitant and huddled together, but as more houses and factories empty and their numbers increase, they stand up straight with their shoulders back, awaiting an inevitable reaction.

The Germans are completely taken by surprise by the resis-tance and on the second day the strike spreads to other parts of the country: the north, Utrecht and, cautiously, also The Hague. The sense of solidarity is overwhelming. The tension, prevailing everywhere after recent violent events, makes way for hope and bravery.

But not for long.

Already on the first day of the strike, the gathering on Noordermarkt is roughly broken up by Green Police and people feel their fear return.

On the second day a large police force is mobilized, as are the SS, the German blackshirts, older brothers of the Dutch Nazi squads. A state of emergency is declared and the strikers' resis-tance broken with brute force.

In The Hague, Lien and Janny follow everything, excited at first but soon concerned. Police cars are racing, sirens wailing, and people are told through speakers to stay indoors and immediately resume their work. It is obvious: the Fascists are panicking. A strike like this has not occurred in any of the occupied territories before.

In Amsterdam, alleys fill up with battalions, hastily turned out to drive the civilians back inside. While work shoes crowded the streets on the first day of the strike, they are thick with police boots the next. At least nine people are killed, dozens seriously injured, and hundreds of men are arrested. The participating cities are fined by the Germans – Amsterdam alone must pay 15 million guilders – and Mayor Willem de

Vlugt is replaced by a pro-German: Edward Voûte. And, finally, the recently installed Jewish Council has to urge all employees to resume their work.

When Janny and Lien learn about the bloody end of the strike from their communist friends, they disagree on the effect of recent developments. For the first time since the raids, Lien is confident about their chances again; the two-day strike in Amsterdam has shown that you can resist even the worst terror. But Janny, as always, will not have any of this; she predicts the actions will backfire for the Jews. 'The Jewish Council is now trying to calm the Jews down,' she tells her sister, 'and that is exactly what the Krauts like to see.'

Immediately after the war, a commemoration of the strikes is organized and on the first occasion, in 1946, Queen Wilhelmina announces that, inspired by the February strikes, the motto 'Valiant, Resolute, Merciful' will be added to the coat of arms of Amsterdam. Despite, or perhaps thanks to, the non-recurrent nature of this organized protest against the persecution of the Jews, the legitimate credit for starting it will be disputed for decades to follow. The leading part of the CPN is either denied or kept quiet; in the first years after the war, the myth is peddled that people spontaneously took to the streets, infuriated by Nazi policy. During the Cold War, party members were, for many years, excluded from the official commemoration of the strike.

To this day, the connection between the CPN and the famous action is not widely known. A symbol of justice has, strangely enough, itself become a symbol of injustice.

On Jonas Daniël Meijerplein in Amsterdam, the place where the victims of the first raid were lined up and squatted in the cold for hours, a sculpture commemorates the strike: *De Dokwerker*, the dock-worker – a heavy, indomitable man with rolled-up sleeves, his chin up but his hands helplessly empty.

# 4

# Children of the War

As the February strike takes place, Janny is literally on top of the enemy. The flat on Bazarlaan is above the printer where a Dutch Nazi magazine is made and as fast as the fascist propaganda rolls off the press downstairs, she and Bob stencil illegal resistance papers on a monstrously large machine one floor up. Like an accomplished printer, Janny copies her first underground newspaper, *Het Signaal*, The Signal – a nod to the Wehrmacht propaganda magazine *Signal* appearing fortnightly in twenty languages with a circulation of 2.5 million copies. Janny is not quite there yet, but she bravely prints on, Robbie sleeping by her side.

To expand her activities, Janny rents a space about half a mile away in The Hague, where she sets up a proper underground press. Fear and mutual distrust are growing day by day: after the February strike, all intermediaries and contacts with Amsterdam were arrested, and more and more often, Janny has to deal with perfect strangers. It makes her nervous. Every eye contact, note without a sender, meeting on the corner of a street to exchange information – she never knows who she's facing. Are they moles, naive adventurers who can put her at risk? Or people like her who have devoted themselves to the good cause after very careful consideration? With each new face suspiciously peering up from beneath a hat, she wonders if that person can be trusted. Thankfully, both parties receive code words to quickly make clear what purpose their encounter has.

There is a good reason for the increasing paranoia: the stories about labour camps at home and abroad, where arrested Jewish men are taken, become more and more persistent. But the rumours of people dying there are blamed on the harsh conditions: the cold, disease or hard work. Jews are now banned from visiting cinemas, cafés or markets, and in Amsterdam they have to state exactly how many houses and shops they own, where their children attend school, which tram or bus routes they take and which cultural organisations they visit. Travelling is almost impossible for them.

The next goal of the occupying forces is to round up

as many Jews as possible, first from Amsterdam, then from all over the Netherlands, at one central location. The Jewish Quarter, cut off from the rest of the city, seems ideal, but the blockade doesn't last; there are too many Jews in Amsterdam to fit in that small area and at least 6,000 non-Jewish Amsterdammers live behind the drawbridges. Forcing them to leave is not that easy. Also, they want to keep receiving guests and go to work elsewhere in the city. The barriers are removed, but the signs stay: *Judenviertel/Joodsche Wijk.*

Jews are not allowed to move house any more. With everyone stuck in their place, mapping out the entire community can begin.

One night in December 1941, Lien has given a dance performance. As she packs her bags she discusses the current situation with her close friend Ida Rosenheimer, who played the piano during the show. Lien is optimistic and she cannot imagine the occupied countries will allow Hitler to press further ahead with his plans – the logistics of transporting tens of thousands of people alone seem almost impossible to her – but Ida is far more downcast. Her family told her that Jews in Poland and Czechoslovakia are rounded up in ghettos and that anyone offering the least resistance is moved to newly built concentration camps. Ida finds her friend naive and tries to warn her: for twenty years Hitler has been saying he wants to destroy the Jews. He has already started in the east and there is no doubt they shall see the same thing happening in the Netherlands.

Lien's younger sister does not need this warning; Janny is rapidly expanding her underground activities. Bob works at the Central Food Supply, which will prove to be of great value later, and Janny, in addition to printing and distributing underground resistance newspapers, is also involved in other ways to save people's lives. If necessary, their little home provides shelter for people in danger – political refugees and members of the resistance who have already caught the attention of the Germans.

Soon, the first communists knock on their door. Among them is Kees Schalker, former member of the Lower House. He is one of the leaders of the illegal CPN and is on a German list. Dressed as an old man, with a hat and a grey beard, he tries to transform himself, but like Alexander de Leeuw, who hid with them previously, Schalker will not live to see the end of the war.

All Robbie knows is that sometimes there are friends who stay for a while, and when Lien visits her sister and yet another stranger is reading the newspaper in the tiny kitchen, she no longer asks any questions.

Forging and stealing identity cards has become a

matter of urgency too. False documents are of vital importance for those who seek shelter – when they are stopped on the street, during a raid or when they travel, they must be able to identify themselves as not Jewish, or prove they are officially resident at the hiding address they pretend is theirs. The call earlier that year for Jews to report for additional registration has been very successful: over 160,000 Jews in the country have registered – people with a large J stamped on the left page of their identity card, next to their passport photo. Only a few – like Janny – have no J there.

The identity card has thus become a powerful instrument, a small piece of paper which, in crucial moments, can make the difference between life and death. A forged card could help a Jewish man, woman or child get through inspection, travel to family and friends, find safety at a hiding place. The personal details on the right page of the identity card are often forged too; from a distinctly Jewish name to a Dutch-sounding one, from Simon Wallach to Hendrik Akkerman.

In addition to the forged identity cards, a second important market develops: the trade in coupons and rationing cards. Because of the occupation, international trade is almost entirely at a standstill, with shortages of goods and provisions as a result. Every household needs a registered distribution card to record exactly which distribution coupons have been issued. On the left side of the card various categories are listed – provisions, shoes, birth, illness, fuel, miscellaneous – with boxes behind them to cross what and how much has been distributed.

Although the card seems a simple administrative matter, this, too, is an important weapon. The First Registered Distribution Card, introduced at the start of the war, is followed in 1943, as the deportations are well under way, by a Second Registered Distribution Card, only available to 'ordinary' Dutch people. This excludes all the people in hiding or with a forged identity card. Numerous families with people hiding in their homes – sometimes just one person, sometimes an entire family – lay down the condition that those people don't eat from their distribution card but arrange their own card and coupons. An effective way to continue starving people who have not yet reported for transport, or to flush them out of their hiding place.

And so distribution cards and coupons, too, are stolen and circulated on a wide scale by members of the resistance. Janny has an entire network of permanent, reliable contacts with whom she arranges this.

She travels back and forth between The Hague, Amsterdam and Utrecht, with papers hidden in her bra or underneath her skirt.

The fights with the blackshirt squads as well as the first raids have made clear that both the DNP and the occupying forces have stopped showing mercy. But it still takes time for Janny to realize how dangerous it is, what she and Bob do.

The hunt for communists is on. People working underground for the CPN are arrested and disappear without trial. The next target is the Dutch volunteers who fought against the Fascists in the Spanish Civil War. Among these former 'Spain Fighters' are many friends of the Brilleslijper sisters. Most of them are again or, rather, still active underground – there is good reason the Spanish Civil War was called a dress rehearsal for the Second World War. Former Spain Fighters contribute to illegal newspapers such as *Het Parool*, *Vrij Nederland* and *De Waarheid* and form new resistance groups together.

Janny is in each of the Fascist enemy categories and three times at risk: she is Jewish, communist and was, although stationed in the Netherlands, also involved in the Spanish Civil War.

In May 1941, it is announced that all registered

former Spain Fighters will be interned in Germany. From that moment onwards, they shall be considered stateless criminals. They will be transported from all over Europe to Dachau concentration camp, where special barracks are set up: the *Interbrigadistenblock*.

Janny learns this news from her friends and it begins to dawn on her what consequences her actions might have. It doesn't stop her from continuing her work; helping Jews and other people in need becomes more and more urgent and she expands her network as much as she can, with people she trusts. To remove the J for 'Jew' from identity cards she travels, for instance, to Hans Verwer in Amsterdam. Hans is a ballet dancer and a close friend of Lientje – they danced with Lili Green together until the war started. The fine motor skills and gracefulness that made her such a good dancer come in useful during the war; Hans and her husband are top forgers.

Useful contacts come via Janny's parental home too; although her father often expresses his concern about her work. Above Joseph and Fietje on Nieuwe Achtergracht live their friends Leo and Loes Fuks. Leo has a large network of Jewish intellectuals and puts Janny in touch with people she needs for her underground work. She has, for instance, a contact at city hall, who prints out papers from the municipal register for her, and another who supplies her with real identity cards with authentic stamps. Janny trades them for false ones, which are then used for newborns.

In the summer of 1941, preparations for rounding up and mapping all Dutch Jews are in full swing. As well as being registered, their freedom of movement is limited and they are no longer allowed to visit markets, swimming pools or beaches. Companies have been taken, radios have been confiscated.

Civil servants in Amsterdam, where more than 80,000 Jews live, have been ordered to make a 'dot map' – a map of Amsterdam, where dots, accurate to within a few feet, show where Jews live and how many; each dot representing ten Jewish inhabi-tants. At a single glance it is now clear how much work there is to do: some areas are swarming with dots, others show a calmer pattern.

Little by little and with no significant opposition from the Dutch government, an entire population is deprived of its rights and dignity, isolated from the rest of society and charted in great detail.

And yet, for most, life goes on. Imagining a better future after the war, without Nazi terror, is what keeps many people going and among the sisters' acquaint-ances, several couples are even expecting a baby.

To their sorrow, Lien and Eberhard are not married – the Nuremberg Laws of 1935 determined that Jews were no longer allowed to marry people of German blood. Lien is still madly in love and is consumed by the question whether or not to start a family. Janny and Bob, despite all their underground activities, are very happy with their little Robbie, as are Haakon and Mieke Stotijn with their baby, René. Haakon, son of internationally renowned oboist and conductor Jaap Stotijn, first worked for a radio symphony orchestra in Hilversum but is offered a position as solo oboist at the Royal Concertgebouw Orchestra in Amsterdam. He proudly accepts this excellent job and the family moves to 26 Johannes Verhulststraat, right behind the Concertgebouw – an address that will become of great importance to the sisters.

And so, many people are building a life, assuming the occupation will not last much longer. When Lien visits friends in Amsterdam, her last lingering doubt disappears as soon as she holds their newborn baby in her arms.

Shortly after, both sisters are expecting: Lien her first and Janny her second child.

Sometimes Eberhard and Lien joke about his German father and how horrified he would be if he could see his son now. This proud Prussian officer from the imperial army, who hated all music except military marches, fathered a son who grew up to become everything he detested: Marxist, pianist, promoted musicologist, unmarried, living with a Jewish woman – pregnant even – in an artist commune in the Netherlands.

Eberhard had loathed his father's militaristic nature from a young age: the stories about the great German Empire, the romanticizing of the First World War, when his father was stationed in Belgium, the rousing music that came with that. Eberhard will never forget how his father tried beating obedience and *his* preferences into his son with a stick.

Once, during a night with his old regimental comrades, his father had asked him to play. Each year on the Emperor's birthday the men hired a room to celebrate the happy event with three cheers, speeches and the exchanging of glorious memories of that good old war. It was for one of those imperial celebrations that his father Rebling had asked sixteen-year-old Eberhard to play something nice on his piano and the teenager was looking forward to performing Beethoven's 'Waldstein' sonata, a piece he had been practising for a long time. Father Rebling and his friends passionately stamped and clapped along with the music. Then his father asked if Eberhard, after that sonata honky-tonk, would now play a decent military march. With a red face, Eberhard dared to refuse, despite his father's insistence. As an excuse, he argued that he had been instructed by his teacher only to play what he had studied properly.

Eberhard was fortunate enough to be taken under the wing of conductor Otto Klemperer and he developed into a gifted pianist. Klemperer introduced him to the world of Stravinsky, Hindemith, Wagner and Beethoven. Eberhard studied History of Music, German and Philosophy in Berlin, and was increasingly drawn to communist ideas. In 1935, at age twenty-four, Eberhard obtains his doctorate on the sociological foundations for the change of musical style in Germany around the mid-eighteenth century'. During that period, he is already working for the Communist Party, and the current climate in his country *and* family is increasingly suffocating him.

With the NSDAP seizing power two years before, the Weimar Republic had come to an end and Adolf Hitler had assumed dictatorial powers to set his plans for the German Reich in motion. Eberhard's older brother, Dietrich, who, in their father's eyes, at least *did* grow into an honourable son, joins the National Socialists and Eberhard makes a decision: as soon as he has paid off his student loans, he will leave the country that has set a course he doesn't want to be part of and the family only too glad to ride on Hitler's tanker.

A year later, in 1936, Eberhard leaves his homeland and arrives, with his typewriter and few pennies, in The Hague, where he meets his great love, Lientje.

The rest is history.

# 5
# The House Search

Janny and Bob's upstairs flat in The Hague is a hot-bed of underground activities. They accommodate state enemies: hunted Jews, resistance people, members of the illegal Communist Party. First the moody lawyer, Alexander de Leeuw, then the politician, Kees Schalker, and sometimes their friend Frits Reuter stays for a while, as well. Frits, too, is a prominent communist and one of the initiators of the February strike. With him, Janny runs the underground press. She keeps printing and distributing pamphlets, leaflets and underground magazines. With Robbie in the pram, her big belly in front, she walks her rounds through The Hague. Sometimes she's alone, other times she has someone on the lookout as she sticks stencils on pillars and posts.

She not only keeps the keys to the underground press at her home, but she also hides the entire Communist Party archive there. Gerrit Kastein, now a communist resistance fighter, placed it with Janny immediately after the occupation. So much activity from one address is too good to last and indeed, that summer, it goes wrong.

Germans have intercepted pamphlets with anti-Fascist texts in The Hague. Someone is arrested who, probably not voluntarily, gives the names of Janny and Bob. Then he, or she, gives away the address of the apartment where Janny, panting with the heat, her ankles swollen, counts the last weeks before giving birth to her second child.

It is Sunday, 17 August 1941, a sultry summer's day, when a group of men bursts into the house and storms up the stairs with a lot of noise. They are agents of the SD, the German State Intelligence Service, accompanied by a handful of Dutch police officers. Janny happens to arrive with Robbie and a pram full of baby stuff; she had gone to the Home Nursing Service and collected a bedpan, a rubber sheet and bed blocks. There is no time to turn around. Thankfully, Bob is at the office. Some of the men who are still downstairs stop her.

'Does Bob Brandes live here?' one of them barks.

'He used to live here, yes, but he moved away a long time ago.' Janny says the first thing that comes to mind.

She feels intimidated by the men and little Robbie clings to her, crying. A Dutch policeman leans towards her, his nose almost touching her face.

'You are Bob Brandes' wife.'

Janny is too afraid to speak and silently holds up the key, like a shield. If they had asked nicely, they would not have had to kick in the door.

The men guide Janny and Robbie upstairs, and sit her down on a chair in the tiny kitchen. Other policemen are already searching the house: they pull open cupboards, rummage through clothes, plunder bookshelves. Janny starts to panic. In great haste she tries to come up with a plan to prevent them from finding all the illegal things – it seems impossible with so many men within very few square feet. She grabs her belly, shouts that she's heavily pregnant and asks what they want from her. When no one responds, she says her baby is coming. Not far-fetched in itself – with just a few weeks to go her belly is round as a ball. The men are alarmed; a birth is the last thing they need and when Janny begs for permission to call a doctor, one of the SD agents gives in.

With Robbie by the hand, she rushes across the

street to the grocery shop where there's a telephone. Janny calls her friend Joop Moes, the doctor at Vol- harding hospital. Joop helped to deliver Lientje's baby one week before. She immediately understands the situation and jumps on her bicycle. Janny takes Robbie back home, manages to steal the keys to the printer, lies down in the bedroom and waits, keys clutched in one hand, Robbie's hand in the other. As she hears the men turning everything upside down with brute force, she prays they will not find the archive: it is hidden in the tiny kitchen in several pans and a bucket.

The weather is warm and the air is heavy between the walls of the flat. Janny listens to how the men keep going into the kitchen for water. Every time someone turns on the tap to fill his glass, she thinks of the entire CPN archive, just a few inches above his head. If they find it, that is the end of her. She presses Robbie closer and listens with bated breath how the glass is emptied with large gulps. Each time she is sure *this* is when the policeman spots the shelves above him. But each time again, the glass is slammed back on the worktop and the man continues his search.

Then Joop arrives. She hurries up the stairs to the bedroom and throws out the German agents. 'Gentle- men, the lady needs an internal examination. Would you be so kind as to leave immediately?'

While Janny takes off her trousers, just for show, she slips Joop the keys to the printer. Janny's partner Frits Reuter is staying at Joop's, near the beach; the keys are safe with him.

Joop leaves again, but not before writing out a prescription. She makes sure she is overheard when she gives Janny instructions: 'This is a prescription for sedatives, which you must collect from the pharmacy instantly, or else the baby is in danger.'

It is almost five. At five o'clock Bob will leave his office.

Janny grabs Robbie and flies out of the door. The pharmacy is opposite Bob's work and she must catch him before he walks into the arms of the policemen.

One of them follows her.

The pharmacy is at a little square – Bob's office is on the other side. Janny is walking around the square, leading Robbie by the hand and with the man right behind her, when suddenly it starts pouring with rain. Within a minute, the summery shower gives the dull cobbles a dark shine.

Janny dives into a doorway and waits until the policeman rushes past in the rain. A door opens across the street and Janny sees Bob leave his office. He stares at his wife and child in the doorway, a surprised look on his face. He walks around the square, straight past the policeman, without either of them realizing who the other person is, and gives Janny and Rob a kiss.

'What are you two doing here?' he asks. Then he notices how upset she is. 'What on earth is going on?'

'You must get the hell out of here. Now!' says Janny.

Bob turns around and jumps on a passing tram without looking back. From behind the wagon the policeman appears. He had been looking for her on the square.

'You were on your way to the pharmacy, madam?'

'Yes, sir, I was just taking shelter.'

Janny collects the medicine and she and Robbie return to the house to which Bob will never come back again.

The agents turn almost every item in the house upside down; they even chase Janny out of bed to cut open her mattress. Most books from their collection are taken, almost all of them Bob's, but also a book Janny had loved as a child. One of her friends, a bookbinder, had bound it in beautiful red leather for her – enough reason for the Germans to be suspicious.

The books are gone, all the kitchen cupboards emptied, but no one has looked in the pans on the shelves. As dusk falls and not a single thing in the house is where it was, except for the party archive, the men leave.

The tension makes Robbie cry terribly; he howls and screams until he develops a fever and Janny worriedly puts him to bed. Then the bell rings. Downstairs in the dark, a boy is at the door. Conspiratorially, he says he has heard what happened.

'Give me the keys,' he whispers.

Janny answers that she does not know what he is talking about.

'I have to contact our go-between; can you give me the address?'

'No,' says Janny, 'I can't. Meet me at Noordeinde tomorrow, in front of the Willem the Third statue.' And she slams the door shut.

With her heavy belly she runs up the stairs, wraps up Robbie, who is almost too tired to walk and glows like an electric heater, puts him on the back of her bicycle and rides to Joop's place.

There, gasping for breath, she consults Frits Reuter. What to do? It is obvious they are in trouble; someone has given them away. Bob's name is on a list and probably theirs are too. How much do they know? Who was that boy at the door? Do they know about the printer or are they just randomly searching?

They have not found anything incriminating Janny in the flat and Bob, as far as she knows, has got away safely. She and Frits decide that Janny will go to Noordeinde the next day. He will stand by at a distance to see if they are good people or not.

After a restless night, both for little Rob and Janny, she leaves for Noordeinde in the morning, exhausted and tense. She can tell as soon as she approaches and remembers what she promised Frits: 'When there are Krauts, give me a sign, so I can get the hell out of there.' Janny signals. She is stopped and plays ignorant. She keeps silent, even when they put pressure on her and Robbie starts to cry. The Germans have come upon her address because one of their contacts has talked, so Janny has set one firm intention: keep your mouth shut, always.

The Germans let her go but make it clear that they are watching her.

From that moment, Bob goes into hiding with Haakon and Mieke at Johannes Verhulststraat, Amsterdam. Janny stays behind in the flat in The Hague with little Robbie and a big belly. She burns all the valuable papers in the stove.

Soon after, Liselotte is born.

# 6

# Axis of Resistance

Janny had been an active member of the resistance from the very start of the war. All the while, Lien, Eberhard by her side, was still focused on the arts. She was a welcome guest at the Keizersgracht artists' commune in Amsterdam. But as the occupation wears on, the demand for dance performances weakens and, besides, Lien is expecting.

Then Mik van Gilse enlists her help: people in hiding are in urgent need of forged identity cards. Thanks to her itinerant existence, Lien knows a lot of people in different cities. Mik suggests she visit as many friends as possible and persuade them to report their identity card as lost. They can apply for a new one at their local council, while the 'lost' identity cards enter the underground circuit.

And so in 1941, Lien's underground work begins. First, she goes to the young sculptor who does the masks for her shows. He hesitates at her request, but then his father enters, asking what they are talking about. When Lien explains, the old man bursts out laughing.

'Are you saying you haven't lost your ID yet, son? How embarrassing! Hand it to her right now. There. Off you go then, apply for a new one at city hall. They can't very well refuse you, can they?'

He winks at Lien, and from that moment her business is up and running. Lien is quick on the uptake; she may not be as experienced as Janny, but they share the principle requirements for this work: they fear no one and both realize that these are desperate times.

Lien's career as a dancer is on the back-burner, but her agility serves a more important purpose than ever. Quite often, for example, she will go and swim a few lengths in the public pool, ignoring the 'No Jews Allowed' signs. Afterwards, she squeezes herself into other people's changing cubicles via the floor, her big belly in a bathing suit touching the slippery tiles, to steal identity cards from various pockets. When she grows too big to slide underneath, she scrambles over the top. The walls are so thin that she fears one day they will give way under the load.

First, she takes all the identity cards she can lay her hands on. It becomes harder when she has to find very specific documents, such as one for a fifty-five-year-old woman with black hair. A number of Jews has already been caught with forged papers, so the resistance must deliver better and more detailed work. The Dutch identity card is one of the most difficult documents in Europe to forge; it contains both a passport photo and a fingerprint, and, to prevent forgery, the cards are linked to a central register as well. The ink is hard to counterfeit; with a chemical reaction it is fairly easy to trace changes on the paper, and once you remove the photo from the document, an invisible seal on the back, carrying the fingerprint, is broken.

Lien consults Mik, who has already come up with a solution. Their graphic designer has developed an ingenious technique to separate the passport photo from the identity card while leaving the back and the fingerprint intact. The new paper-thin photo is stuck on the card and the seal then repaired. The team has skilfully forged hundreds of identity cards already. Although the fingerprints don't match, the document is safe enough for random street checks.

One day Mik gives Lien forged identity cards to take to the food office at Laan van Meerdervoort in The Hague. He tells her she will find an ally from the resistance there. Mik describes him in great detail. 'Remember: only when it's *him*, because he works for us. If it's someone else there, you turn around instantly.'

The man will give her rationing cards for the following month to distribute in the underground circuit. The rationing cards in turn can be traded for coupons.

That first time Lien walks to the small office, her heart is beating fast. Once inside, she recognizes the man and hands him the false documents. When he looks up at her, she briefly fears it will all go wrong. But the man doesn't bat an eyelid and hands Lien the cards. She will remember this moment for the rest of her life. Two people who don't know the other person but simply have to trust them. Two people acting casually despite the risk they are taking by helping others – who are at even greater risk.

In the first months of her pregnancy Lien still does some shows and gives classes alongside her underground work. In Amsterdam, she performs at music and cabaret nights for Jewish audiences. She is onstage with Jewish artists who are no longer allowed to work. It's a prominent group with many well-known actors and cabaret artists who fled Germany, such as Max Ehrlich and Otto Wallburg. Max Hansen, the Danish tenor, is part of it too. In 1932, he wrote a satirical homoerotic song about Hitler: '*War'n Sie schon mal in mich verliebt?*' (Have you been in love with me yet?), invoking the eternal wrath of the Nazis. Another member of the group is Dutch cabaret artist Henriëtte Davids, known by her stage name Heintje Davids from both the musical and the film *De Jantjes*.

Lien is widely admired for her rendition of Yiddish songs and people know her from all the great revues she starred in. She loves performing with such a prominent company; it upsets her greatly when her pregnancy becomes too advanced for her to keep doing the shows. 'Finally, we have this gifted young artist,' Max Ehrlich teases her, 'and then she decides to have a baby!'

Lien withdraws from the company, a disappointment that will soon prove to be tragically good luck. The entire group, with the exception of Heintje Davids and Max Hansen, is rounded up and sent to Westerbork transit camp. They all end up in Auschwitz; not one of them returns.

Contractions start on 8 August 1941. Eberhard is away, performing somewhere with an orchestra. Lien sways her big belly over the crossbar of his bicycle and peddles to Volharding hospital. Her friend, Joop Moes, delivers the baby and when Eberhard calls for an update during the interval of his concert, Joop proudly tells him he has just become a father.

On 12 August 1941, Eberhard writes to a friend in New York:

> It's a daughter, Kathinka Anita, 7 pounds 8 ounces, dark hair, light eyebrows, dark blue eyes, her mother's nose and her father's mouth. Thankfully, all went well. Lien is spoilt by all our famous and wealthy students – flowers, fruit and chocolate truffles (really very good ones!).

It is the last letter he will write to his friend: postal traffic overseas stops first. When on 7 December the Japanese attack Pearl Harbor, and the United States become directly involved in the war, any other connections to the rest of the world are broken too.

Janny is glad she and Lien had a daughter at the same time; they are a great comfort to each other. First, she worried about Lien's new underground activities, but now Janny is grateful to be working with her sister. Bob is still in Amsterdam, hiding with Haakon and Mieke Stotijn, so she operates the underground press on her own from their upstairs flat, toddler Robbie by the hand and baby Liselotte on the hip. Janny now keeps part of the underground newspapers at Lien's place, in the body of Eberhard's Bechstein grand piano – which both sisters find amusing. The owner of the eminent grand piano brand, Helene Bechstein, is a well-known friend and sponsor of Hitler, whom she regards as a son and affectionately calls 'mein Wölfchen'. If only the lady knew how her instruments were treated.

Janny is proud of Lien crossing the entire city with newly born Kathinka in the pram, the mattress underneath the baby bulging with piles of the illegal magazines her sister prints: Signaal, De Waarheid, De Vrije Katheder. Lien prefers to meet at the child health clinic, where she meets with a friend and her baby. They talk about the development of the children, pick the little ones up from their prams, exchanging their thick woollen blankets, filled with packs of stencils and magazines to be distributed later. After the examination, the babies are put back on the smuggled goods and each of the women goes her own way.

But the work is not without risk; they are starting to lose more and more friends. Lien's friend from the child health clinic is arrested too; she and her baby are transported and do not survive Auschwitz.

Although Janny is on her own now, fortunately she sees a lot of her family. Father Brilleslijper and brother Japie often visit and then spend the day with Lien, Eberhard and little Kathinka in Janny's flat on Bazarlaan. Her brother Jaap is the apple of her eye. He's five years younger than Janny and as dexterous as a Swiss clockmaker. When Fietje gave birth to Janny, the midwife called that she saw the head of a little boy. When she fished out a girl, after all, Joseph, who was convinced he would have a son, was so upset he gave the woman a smack on the head. Of course he was soon blissfully happy with his daughter.

Japie looks a lot like his sisters. High cheekbones, full lips and black bushy eyebrows; it's no surprise many people think Jaap and the girls are from the Dutch East Indies. But where his sisters have a round face, Jaap's is elongated – and with his round metal glasses he looks just like an inventor. The boy has his father's imagination and his mother's work ethic. For as long as they can remember, he invents and designs the strangest creations, and actually puts them together with his own hands.

According to Janny, Japie is the inventor of the very first bicycle radio. He spent weeks in his room until one day he had built a real radio. The thing creaked and crackled, but there were indeed voices. They sounded scrambled and nasal but intelligible, and when he got hold of England they all had to come and listen. *Daventry calling!* From a plank, a few caps and a crystal, Japie fabricated the radio that he then mounted on the front of his bicycle. The contact was on the handlebars, the aerial was a thin copper wire and the power was supplied by a dynamo. And so he cycled to school, singing along to the music from his handlebars.

While his older sisters have homes and children of their own, Jaap, at twenty years old, still lives with his parents in Amsterdam. There was no money for him to finish his secondary education; it was during the crisis and Father had been off work for some time because his sight had got so bad. Jaap had started an evening course in business correspondence, but at the end of August 1941 all Jewish students were expelled from school.

Several years before, Jaap had set up a bicycle parking business opposite his parental home to make some extra money. Entirely in the spirit of his sisters, he now begins an underground distribution centre there. With the parking as a cover-up, he accepts post, packages or messages from the resistance and distributes them throughout the country.

While the Jews become more and more isolated and the rest of the population withdraws further and further, turning a blind eye, the underground network of the extended Brilleslijper family reaches an ever-larger part of the Netherlands. At the risk of their own lives, they solder an axis of resistance between Amsterdam and The Hague.

# 7

# The Starvation Cure

As it was, it was neither the Jewish sisters, nor the German deserter, who was forced into hiding first, but the Dutchman. It almost makes them laugh, but they do realize either one of them can be next.

Their worry is justified when Eberhard is conscripted for military service. He and Lien have barely spent a fortnight with their daughter, Kathinka, when a letter arrives, summoning him to report at the German army office in The Hague four weeks later. If he passes the medical examination this autumn, Eberhard will have to join the Wehrmacht in January 1942.

That evening, the young parents want to talk about the letter and what to do next. They ask Jolle Huckriede, the clarinettist in the room next door, to help get Kathinka to sleep. Jolle is happy to play for the little one; it's in his own interest that she stops crying. Everyone in the house is over the moon with the arrival of new life, but the girl has inherited her mother's temperament. Only once before has Kathinka been quiet for a few consecutive hours; this was when Lientje, before breastfeeding the baby, emptied a bottle of sparkling wine to celebrate her birth.

As soon as Kathinka is asleep, Jolle leaves and Eberhard and Lientje start discussing the options. Does he have to go into hiding? But where? Or should he just report and see if he passes the examination? Perhaps if he fails, he can just come home. They cannot work it out and for the first time in a long while their positive spirit fails them. When Eberhard goes to the front, it could be the end of him – which perhaps would be justifiable if he were fighting his own battle. Not the enemy's one.

'Go see Rhijn,' Lien finally says, 'he'll know what to do.'

Rhijn is dear friend Rhijnvis Feith, whom they know through Janny and Bob. A son of the wealthy Feith family and a neurologist in The Hague, he has been a pivotal figure in the Dutch resistance from the very beginning. A man marked for life by polio – stooped, hunchbacked, an enormous head on his narrow shoulders – but mostly known for his flawless moral compass.

Rhijn is also the one who, with Gerrit Kastein, set up the Solidarity Fund to collect money for underground purposes and redistribute it where needed. It makes sense for Lien to send Eberhard to him: he helps many in need. His practice serves as a contact address for people working in the resistance, simply registered as 'patient', and he had also been a great help to Janny when Bob had to go into hiding some weeks before.

The morning after Janny's nerve-wracking house search, Rhijn walked all the way to Bazarlaan from his practice, carrying a cup of ground coffee in one hand and a pack of cigarettes in the other. He climbed the stairs to her floor and said to the heavily pregnant Janny: 'So. Here I am. Now, you make us some fresh coffee and then we'll discuss how to go about this.'

As Rhijn smoked and Janny slurped the hot coffee, he asked her directly how she would pay the bills with Bob gone, a child by her side and a baby on its way. She was unable to answer. She hadn't even thought about it yet, but if Bob didn't show up at work, they would obviously not receive his salary, either.

'How much did he make, this Bob of yours?' Rhijn asked.

Janny did not know exactly, but she told him how much money, more or less, they had to spend. Rhijn wanted to know the number of their account and whether she herself had access to it. Then he left.

A few days later, Janny got paid Bob's entire salary into her account, not from Bob's office but from a certain P.G. Jonker – pseudonym for Rhijnvis Feith Esq. Until Bob earned money again, she received the equivalent of his salary from Rhijn, who came by her house each morning, drank a cup of coffee, smoked exactly two cigarettes, left for his practice and got to work.

**In the** autumn of 1941, Eberhard goes to see Rhijn. It is of vital importance he is declared unfit. Rhijn comes straight to the point.

'How much do you weigh now?'

'Ten and a half stone, more or less, at five foot nine.'

'That will be a starvation cure then. I want you to drop to seven stone nine, eight stone two at most, so you will cut such a sorry figure that no one wants you any more. Now, we just have to think up a disease for you.'

'I remember my older brother had a kidney problem, so he failed his Wehrmacht medical examination at the time.'

'All right,' says Rhijn, 'I'll give you a rhubarb medicine ten days before the examination, so your urine will show you had an early kidney infection. I have to warn you: it's disgusting stuff – but you'll survive.'

Eberhard instantly agrees on the plan and Rhijn prescribes a strict diet; he tells Eberhard how to transform from a fit, handsome young man into a pathetic bag of bones in the shortest possible time.

'What you'll do is this: you work till three in the morning, then you drink several cups of strong coffee, sleep for one or two hours, no more, then you get on your bicycle and peddle through the city as fast as you can for five or, better yet, ten miles. You come see me twice a week for a check-up. From now on you are my patient.'

Eberhard starts training immediately. The early rising is hardest; at five in the morning, when the house is still quiet, he drags his hungry body outside to cycle through The Hague. His stomach rumbling, his legs soft as chewing gum, he races across the cobbles like a competitive cyclist then returns to Lien and Kathinka, still warm in bed, at dawn. He is exhausted and sweaty, he sees stars and almost collapses, but he keeps focusing on his goal: not to be sent to the Wehrmacht, away from his wife and newly born daughter.

As Eberhard rapidly loses weight, reports trickle in of Hitler's offensive in the Soviet Union. There, German troops have started the largest military action in history: Operation Barbarossa. Hitler's ultimate goal lies in the east, where there is enough Lebensraum to realize his plans for the German people. In *Mein Kampf*, he had already voiced his contempt for the Slavic people, the *Untermenschen*, and their reprehensible ideology, Communism.

On 22 June 1941, without prior declaration of war, the Wehrmacht had invaded the Soviet Union with four million men, 600,000 horses and 2,000 aircraft. Eberhard, and therefore Lientje, had been optimistic from the first day of the Dutch occupation onwards; this war would not last long. But with the opening of the Eastern Front and reports that the *Blitzkrieg* had taken the Soviets by surprise, the first cracks in their positive outlook begin to show.

A few weeks later, on a dismal autumn day, a shadow of the former Eberhard reports at the committee in The Hague. A vast space has formed between his upper legs, his skin is painfully tight around his bones and he permanently seems to suck in his cheeks. Yellowish bags underneath his eyes and a glistening layer of sweat on his forehead make him look sickly. A line of well-fed men in tight uniforms eyes him disapprovingly as he strips down to his underpants. Eberhard is measured and weighed.

'Eight stone!' a voice shouts.

'Not much, something wrong with you, or what?'
another says.

'Yes, I'm short-sighted,' Eberhard answers.

'Irrelevant!'

'I have bandy legs and can't walk very far.'

'No infantry then, but we need people at the anti-
aircraft guns too.'

Eberhard begins to doubt. He has been feeling
wretched for days but drew courage from the shocked
responses of his housemates to his appearance. He had
hoped this plan would succeed if only he would persist.
As the men look on unaffectedly, it starts to dawn on
him that anything with a beating heart passes; they
simply need cannon fodder.

'I've had three serious ear infections as a child, so—'
Eberhard tries.

'You're a musician, so nothing wrong with your
hearing, right?'

'And I've had severe kidney infections at least twice.'
His protests sound weaker; he understands all his ef-
forts have been in vain.

'*Beding kriegsverwendungsfähig*! Conditionally
fit for war!' a uniform growls at the man filling in the
forms.

'We shall be in touch.'

They turn away from him; the examination is over.

The men before and after him are declared fit and called up on the spot. Eberhard has been tossed a sliver of hope: conditionally 'fit for war'. His fate hangs by a thread. They shall have to wait again.

The following weeks, Eberhard eats anything Lien serves him to gain some weight. While he checks the letterbox at least ten times a day, they discuss the possible scenarios for when the call arrives. Should he put on the hateful uniform and fight for the enemy, hoping one day he will return to Lien and Kathinka alive? Or shall he go underground, like so many people they have helped? Perhaps they could all have seen this coming, but it is still a tough decision to make: if Eberhard is conscripted, he shall go into hiding.

On 6 December 1941, the letter arrives that will officially make Eberhard a deserter. Public enemy number one. Hitler has always been clear about treason or *fahnenflucht*: at the front one might die, as a deserter one must. He has to report on 15 January 1942 at a regiment in Wolfenbüttel in Germany, where he has been assigned to the NSDAP for office work. A one-way train ticket has been enclosed. He holds it in his hand, knowing he will not go, certainly after the latest reports about the Eastern Front.

Through the resistance he has heard about the *Blitz-krieg*: the blazing stroke of lightning that would force the Soviets to their knees has morphed into a slow, ice-cold funeral march. After a series of German triumphs in the first months, the war machine is faltering. The infantry cannot keep up with the armoured divisions, supplies lag behind and Hitler's strategic decisions are beyond comprehension. Millions of men rush forwards across steppes and tundra, and the merciless Russian winter is yet to come.

On the day when Eberhard receives his call, 29 degrees below zero are measured in Moscow. In the first phase of Operation Barbarossa, the Soviets lost almost 800,000 men, but in early December, they strike back viciously. German soldiers lose limbs, eyelids, hair, noses and ears to the frost – but are forced to carry on. The zombie army marches further, leaving a trail of scarecrows behind on the Russian steppe. Some Red Army soldiers, hit hard by the 'blond monsters' of the Nazi troops themselves, make a game out of putting up the dead in the snow; bodies are left in the most bizarre positions, like macabre sculptures in a war dance.

The Soviet territory is vast and the Russian supply of soldiers makes Hitler's men pale into insignificance; the Red Army is a living cushion and the Germans punch until they go numb. Stalin has six million men at his disposal and another fourteen million active reserves – cannon fodder slowly colouring the snow red.

**In January 1942,** Janny has not seen Bob for six months – and he still has not met his daughter, Liselotte. He is still hiding with Haakon and Mieke Stotijn in Amsterdam and Janny misses him terribly.

Her sister-in-law Aleid comes up with a plan so they can briefly spend some time together. She has married into a prominent family with a large network in the province of North Holland; her Jewish father-in-law, Jaap Hemelrijk, had been a headmaster in Alkmaar and councillor in Bergen until he was fired as a result of the German measures. Janny looks up to him and affectionately calls him 'Grandpa Hemelrijk'. Despite his suffering owing to the oppressive regulations, he exudes a certain invincibility that inspires Janny with her own activities.

Aleid and Jan Hemelrijk live in Bergen; she will ask her husband and her father-in-law if they, or someone else in the family, know of a holiday cottage in the neighbourhood, where Janny, Bob and the little ones can secretly spend a few days together. It works out differently.

Janny learns from her sister that Eberhard is conscripted, after all, and she tries to comfort her. Lien is terrified the Germans will come and get Eberhard, or that he might be arrested as a deserter when he refuses to report – they both know what that would mean. Janny has a plan but wants to run it by their dear friend Rhijn first. She thinks it would be wise for Eberhard to go to Bergen first; Janny will find another opportunity to see Bob – this is more important.

Rhijn agrees with her, but time is running short; Eberhard has to report in Wolfenbüttel on 15 January and the freedom of movement in the Netherlands is increasingly restricted. Jews have not been allowed to move for quite some time now and the Germans are preparing a forced relocation, referred to with the strategic euphemism 'evacuation' – a word quickly adopted by the Dutch population and media. This 'evacuation' implies that Jews from all villages and cities in the Netherlands must leave home and hearth and move to Amsterdam – leaving all of their belongings behind. The plan is to concentrate everyone in one of the four Jewish areas: Transvaalbuurt, Rivierenbuurt, the Jewish Quarter and Asterdorp.

Rhijn and Janny agree that she will contact Jan Hemelrijk and ask him for help, and that, for security reasons, they will not tell Lientje anything. Gestapo interrogation methods are notorious and what Lien doesn't know, cannot be beaten out of her, either.

And so it goes: Janny speaks to Jan and they decide it is safest for Eberhard to go into hiding at Jan and Aleid's own place, at Karel de Grotelaan, Bergen. No one, except Janny and Rhijn, will know.

Eberhard is preparing for his imminent departure, supposedly to report to the regiment in Wolfenbüttel; even his housemates are not allowed to know about the actual plans. He says goodbye to his piano students, packs his music books in a chest and gives them to Jolle in the adjoining room to look after. Finally, he writes to his parents saying they might not hear from him for a while but need not worry.

After packing just the strictly necessary, Eberhard fills the rest of his suitcase with books; he hopes reading and studying will make the isolation and loneliness awaiting him less bleak.

They celebrate New Year's Eve together in Amsterdam, their spirits low, at the home of Father and Mother Brilleslijper and their little brother Jaap. Among each other they dare to voice their wishes for the year ahead. With a nod to a prayer, they hold hands around the table, allaying their fears with a curse and a spell. Father Brilleslijper leads: 'We wish for the Soviet Union to gain important victories, and for England and America to decide to open a second front in Western Europe. Furthermore, we wish the Fascists a speedy downfall and Hitler personally dead.' At that last sentence, Fietje raises an eyebrow, but she cannot deny feeling the same. 'And finally, may we ourselves have enough strength to endure this war until the final victory, and may we fight our sadness with optimistic dreams for the future.'

They raise their glasses and see in the New Year with a bittersweet toast.

**On 14 January 1942,** Eberhard sticks his supposed new address in Wolfbüttel on the community board next to the telephone in the hall, clearly visible for everyone. He kisses Lien and his little Kathinka goodbye and takes the train to Amsterdam. At the exact same moment an anonymous young resistance worker crosses the Dutch border with Eberhard's train ticket, as is arranged by Rhijn and Jan Hemelrijk, making it seem as if Eberhard did indeed travel to Wolfbuttel.

In Amsterdam, Eberhard has his head shaven in the Jewish Quarter – who knows when he might get a decent haircut again – and late afternoon he arrives at a hostel for artists on the Prinsengracht, an address Rhijn had given him. Eberhard will stay the night there before travelling thirty miles north to Bergen the next morning. But whether it's his freshly shaven head or the heavy suitcase, one way or another, the landlady suspects he is about to go into hiding and before Eberhard has made himself comfortable, she sends him back into the cold. Eberhard had seen his Jewish wife get snubbed more and more often, but he himself had always been treated with respect. From now on he is a pariah too.

In the twilight, he walks down the Prinsengracht to Centraal Station, where he joins the busy commuter traffic as inconspicuously as he can. He travels to Alkmaar by train, gets on the steam tram to Bergen and, following the instructions Rhijn provided, walks to the house of Jan and Aleid Hemelrijk. Rhijn has also given him a forged identity card. The man in the photo is about the same age, also a pianist by profession, and his name has a Dutch ring to it. When Eberhard, enclosed by the dark but right on time for dinner, arrives at Jan and Aleid's home in Bergen, he is Jean-Jacques Bos.

# 8

# The Imprisonment

Spring 1942. A watery sun reflects off the clinkers of Nieuwe Achtergracht in the centre of Amsterdam. When Jaap leaves his parental home in the morning, to walk to his bicycle parking operation, he is not aware he finds himself in the heart of the Jewish Quarter, at a moment in time when this is inadvisable.

The occupation, the raids, the fact he and his friends are no longer welcome anywhere in the city – it's all far away at this moment. The light is beautiful and the world, briefly, is how it used to be.

At his one shoulder is the back of Carré Theatre, at the other the street where his bicycle parking is located. He loves Weesperstraat, with its bustle, all the shops, all the people and tram 8 tinkling in between. He knows everyone around here.

Across the street from the delicatessen they used to own was the workshop of Uncle Meijer Waterman, the cigar maker. His family ran a cigar shop in the large premises on the corner, Weesperstraat 74. Jaap always enjoyed watching Meijer skilfully roll the cigars – a precise bit of work. Next to Waterman was a shop with second-hand goods and next to them was Werker, the coppersmith. His family shared the building with two other households: above them lived the Elzas family and down below the Korper family. Not only did old Grandmother Korper run a greengrocer's shop in the basement, but two boys and a girl with beautiful reddish-brown curls, pale skin and freckles also lived in that flat. There must have been parents too. From the early morning, the basement stairs were filled with crates of vegetables and large potato bins, but they never saw any of the family members step over those crates to enter or leave the house.

Across from Korper lived Cripple John, a man with one wooden leg who was nonetheless quick on his feet. He sold songs for a cent or less – but he sang them first and afterwards no one was willing to pay any more. And then there was the man on the cart, who Father always called 'the spineless brickadier'. His wife pulled him, weak as a kitten, through the streets on a hand-cart, with him shouting at the top of his voice: 'Unlucky bricklayer, broken spine! Worked from the age of twelve till twenty-six, fell off the roof and no one cared!' A heartbreaking sight, even when you'd seen it a hundred times. His wife then passed the hat around and would shove her husband, handcart and all, into Hovingh's pub. The tavern was on the corner of Weesperstraat, opposite Uncle Meijer Waterman – a beautiful place with a wooden façade. Late in the evening, neighbours would see the spineless brickadier go home, slurring, the swaying cart pushed by his drunken wife and chased by a handful of screaming children.

As Jaap pulls the front door shut behind him and is about to cross the street to his bicycle parking, a local police officer walks towards him. He's from the office on Jonas Daniël Meijerplein; Jaap has known him his entire life.

Jaap wants to greet the officer, but the man looks straight ahead. In passing, he hisses something at Jaap.

'They've got Henk. Get the hell out of here.'

For a few seconds, Jaap freezes. Pinned to the cobbles, he tries to process what he has just heard. Henk is his partner. Together, they run the bicycle parking and coordinate all the underground contacts. Then he braces himself, buttons up his coat and heads in a straight line for the tram towards Centraal Station, where he takes the train to The Hague. A few hours later he knocks at Janny's door on Bazarlaan. Without a word, she pulls him off the street and takes him upstairs.

The next morning, they learn that the Germans, in reprisal for missing their catch, have dragged their sick and half-blind father out of his house and put him in a cell.

They thought they had been so cautious with their ingenious network of contacts, code words, warning systems to protect themselves and their underground activities. But they had not seen this coming. Jaap and Janny, against their Brilleslijper nature, are at a loss. The thought of their father imprisoned is unbearable.

But Janny quickly gathers herself and decides who in her network is the right person to handle this immediately. She contacts Benno Stokvis, a well-known Amsterdam lawyer. She knows he has good German contacts; Stokvis has his own ways and means and has successfully mediated for arrested Jews before.

Janny implores him to do whatever it takes to get her father out of the cell as a matter of urgency. Stokvis succeeds, with money and sweet-talk, and after a few days the cell doors open for Joseph Brilleslijper, who cannot embrace Fietje tightly enough. Janny, in the meantime, has come to Amsterdam, too – Jaap stays behind in The Hague, with little Rob and Liselotte.

In the privacy of the small home on Nieuwe Achtergracht, Janny thanks the lawyer for his services and discusses her concerns with him. The Germans were already after Bob. These past few weeks they have repeatedly called at Lien's house asking where Eberhard has gone, and now they are chasing brother Jaap, as well; the noose is slowly tightening. It is a miracle the sisters themselves have not been caught yet.

Stokvis shares his advice with her.

'Get out of here. Take your parents, close the door behind you and don't come back again. It's going to get worse than you and I can imagine.'

Janny does not doubt the gravity of his words for a second. Admitting no argument, she orders her mother to pack only the strictly necessary, grabs her father by the arm and takes them with her to The Hague, where Jaap and the little ones are waiting for them at home, on Bazarlaan.

Father, Mother and Jaap stay with Janny. None of the three will ever return to their beloved Amsterdam again.

**While the** family regroups as best as they can, the Nazis prepare for the next phase of their population policy. Most registered Jews in the Netherlands are concentrated in and around Amsterdam, and Reich

Commissioner Arthur Seyss-Inquart almost has the system for the intended deportations in place. Groups of unemployed and foreign Jews are already transported to Westerbork, the camp built in 1938 for accommodating refugees from neighbouring countries. But the Germans now have a different purpose in mind: Westerbork will start serving as a transit point to concentration camps.

At the Polish town of Os´wie͜cim, some 700 miles east of Westerbork, a camp was built on a former army barracks in 1940 to handle the enormous influx of Polish prisoners. Os´wie͜cim, in German, is quickly corrupted to Auschwitz. On the grounds of this camp, between 15,000 and 20,000 people can be held captive in stone barracks. It isn't enough. Hitler orders the construction of a new, much larger camp, and in March 1941, a few miles away from basecamp Auschwitz I, a plain of 432 hectares is reclaimed for building Auschwitz II, also known as Auschwitz-Birkenau. As the war proceeds, another forty sub-camps will be built around Auschwitz, where prisoners are set to hard labour, ranging from factory work to toiling in the fields.

A next step towards the 'Final Solution' is the secret Wannsee Conference on 20 January 1942. In Villa Marlier, a country estate at the Wannsee, south-west of

Berlin, fifteen top Nazi people gather. They are invited by SS-*Obergruppenführer* Reinhard Heydrich for a meeting that will take little more than two hours. The discussions are summarized in fifteen pages of notes, part of which is an inventory detailing the size of the Jewish community per country. The number below the line is 11 million; the Netherlands is listed with 160,800 people.

During the meeting, various solutions pass – from confinement to mass sterilization. How the big clear-out of eleven million Jews will eventually be organized is recorded literally:

> As part of the practical implementation of the Final Solution, Europe shall be combed out from the west to the east. The national territory, including Bohemia and Moravia, goes first, if only for reasons of the housing problem and other socio-political necessities. The evacuated Jews will first be gathered, train by train, in so-called transit ghettos, and transported further east from there.

The Germans commission Dutch National Rail, the NS, to construct a railway to the grounds of Westerbork, so trains can both stop in the camp and depart from it, making logistics a lot easier.

The mayor of Beilen, the neighbouring village, briefly protests against the construction of these tracks through his farmland, because of 'potential destruction of the natural beauty', but the Germans dismiss his objection. It is, after all, a temporary construction, they write in a response, '*das wieder entfernt wird sobald das Lager seinen Zweck erfüllt hat*' – which shall be demolished as soon as the camp has fulfilled its purpose.

With about a hundred prisoners, the NS build a branch from Hooghalen station to Westerbork concentration camp. This extension will not make the journey much faster: at Hooghalen station the cattle wagons with thousands of people often have to wait a long time before getting on the main track – goods carriages with supplies for the Germans are given priority. Local residents and civil servants speak of howling and wailing coming from between the planks of the wagons, from babies and the sick and the disabled to women giving birth. The NS charge the occupying forces for the cost of constructing the railway, setting up a timetable to the German border and ultimately for each transportation of Jews to the concentration camps in the east. The Germans pay with money stolen from the Jews.

In the meantime, experiments are conducted in the

base camp, Auschwitz I, with poison gas Zyklon B. In one of the crematoriums 1,000 prisoners, mainly prisoners of war from the Soviet Union, and prisoners who are seriously ill, are used as guinea pigs. The poison, in the form of small marbles, is scattered straight into the space, which is then hermetically sealed. As soon as the marbles are exposed to open air, they dissolve and a deadly gas is released: hydrogen cyanide, or hydrocyanic acid. It takes hours before all the prisoners are dead.

In 1941 and 1942, more experiments follow – mostly on people from Polish ghettos and more prisoners of war from the Soviet Union – until the right amount of poisonous gas is determined. When trains from all over Europe start running in 1942, the step towards a large-scale, mechanized approach is only a small one. For this purpose, the second, much-larger, site next to Auschwitz is approved; at Birkenau village a small city for about 100,000 people will be built. Ultimately, this is where the mass destruction of Jews, the 'Final Solution to the Jewish problem', will take place.

The intention shows in every aspect of the design of the camp. There are no facilities with running water and no decent, washable floors – making the risk of disease enormous. Instead of one person per cage, as is custom in German prison camps, four becomes the norm, which brings the total capacity of the camp to 129,456 people. Four large gas chambers and crematoria are built next to Auschwitz-Birkenau, where the death toll of Treblinka and Belzec, two other extermination camps, will soon be exceeded.

# 9

# On the Run

The majestic lime trees on Lange Voorhout are blossoming and throughout the city roadsides are dotted with crocuses. Janny, for the first time in her life, doesn't care, doesn't feel relief at the arrival of spring.

The first two years of the occupation were the setting up of a trap. Little by little, the Germans have isolated all Jews from the rest of the population. Step by step, discrimination, suppression, and the theft of property and dignity have increased. Some walked into the trap believing all would end well. Some were lured in by their leaders, such as the Jewish Council. Most were kicked into the nets by squads or the police.

One or two had a lucky escape; a stroke of luck, stubbornness – often a combination of the two. People who weren't registered as Jews, who got their forged papers on time, who went into hiding on time. People who gathered a network of other stubborn lucky ones, who became self-sufficient and didn't need help from anyone who might prove to be a collaborator or a coward. And now they have to save as many people from the trap as they can.

In Amsterdam the oppression of their former Jewish neigbours has, Janny knows, become increasingly public and aggressive. The Jewish Council, led by Asscher and Cohen, has supplied lists of unemployed Jews to the Germans. These men were subsequently arrested and sent to labour camps. The Council now has a department in The Hague, too, on the corner of Noordeinde, where the royal palace is located, and they have sub-offices in the rest of the city. To further complicate things, Frits Reuter moves back in with Janny. His host was caught and Frits urgently needed temporary shelter.

The imprisonment of her sick father is lingering between them, heavy and undiscussed, in a house that is already tiny. Although they got their father back, Janny is more aware than ever that she is playing with fire. The Germans are after her brother, her husband and her brother-in-law, and her own underground activities are only increasing; the need to ask for help rises by the day, by the hour. In many Jewish families blind faith, credulity or hope for protection by Dutch dignitaries has turned into panic. Those who first, whether or not by order of the Jewish Council, had a J registered in their identity card understand now that this is likely to mean their 'evacuation'.

And so it happens that desperate people call at Janny's house, shouting across the street: 'Is this where Mrs Brandes lives? Please could you remove the J from our ID?' Father Brilleslijper is getting nervous and when, in broad daylight, another distraught woman bangs on the door, calling her name, he forbids Janny to go downstairs. Fietje tries to quiet her granddaughter, Liselotte – the girl seems unable to stop crying since she was born in September – and Jaap distracts Robbie. While the thumping at the front door gets on everyone's nerves and Janny would like to run down and slap the woman in the face, Father takes his daughter aside in the hallway.

'You are driving us all to our death, Janny. This has got to stop!'

His whispers sound like a storm in a wind turbine, louder almost than the shouting of the woman downstairs. Janny stares at her father and suddenly remembers the night her parents saw *The Merchant of Venice* in Carré Theatre. They came back in high spirits and for months her father whistled, hummed and sang all the songs – or what passed for them. It all seems such a long time ago.

While the woman on the street below is still calling her name, Janny realizes they have to leave this place. Now.

Again, her brother-in-law, Jan Hemelrijk, offers the solution; he and his father find an empty home in Bergen for the Brilleslijper family. The house is called Het Aafje and lies hidden in the forest, away from the village centre, towards the coast. Even better news is that Bob will join the family again. Officially, the DNP have him registered as a communist in the province of South Holland, but two years of underground work has taught them that the administrative systems are not interconnected; there is no structural exchange of information between regions. They are willing to take the risk; the authorities in North Holland probably don't know his name. Besides, Bob is not Jewish and has no J in his identity card; if he were arrested in Bergen, there is little chance of local Nazis thinking him suspicious and taking him away.

Janny arranges an official permit for moving to Bergen with her children; she will have to hide the rest of the family in the removal van. The resistance has found Frits Reuter a new hiding place.

On the day of the move, Janny is on the street, ready to leave. Her belongings are in the removal van, Liselotte and Robbie are sat in the front, and she is just closing the back, where her parents and Jaap are hiding, when she sees her neighbour opposite approach. Janny dislikes her; she always sees the woman peeping over the half curtains of her living room and suspects she has German sympathies.

'Are you moving?' the woman asks without greeting her.

'As you can see,' says Janny.

'I already said to myself: all those Jews in there. That can never last.'

Janny's cheeks begin to glow. She arranges her scarf and gets behind the wheel, implying that the conversation is over.

'Are you moving to a larger house?'

Janny hears the woman but slams the door shut, starts the engine and steps on the accelerator a few times. The woman jumps aside, onto the pavement, and Janny drives up onto the road. Beside her, Robbie cries out with joy; she absent-mindedly strokes his head as she sees the silhouette of the woman become smaller in the mirror. Her heartbeat drowns out the rattle of the moving van and does not calm until they have reached the house in Bergen. For the first time in months she can embrace Bob and introduce him to his daughter, Liselotte.

**For Lien,** too, The Hague is becoming too dangerous; she is widely known from her dance and singing performances, and many of her students live in and around the city. With her striking appearance it's hard not to notice her and, on top of that, she has a J in her identity card; it still infuriates Janny that her sister let that happen.

Germans keep calling at the house at the strangest hours asking where Eberhard has gone. Thankfully, everyone consistently refers to the address he left on the notice board. And yet, Lien is not at ease. She wants to leave The Hague with Kathinka before anyone arrests her to find out where Eberhard went, and before the registered Jews in The Hague are up for 'evacuation'.

Friend Jolle Huckriede, the clarinettist next door whom Eberhard had given his box of precious objects to look after, comes up with an idea. His brother Jan is going steady with Violette Cornelius, a young photographer, also active in the resistance. Violette's mother lives along the Prinsengracht in Amsterdam and is willing to offer Lien shelter. She even agrees not only to have mother and daughter move in, but to let Eberhard join them too.

Eberhard has spent the winter at Jan and Aleid's, who lovingly took care of him. But all those months he had to hide in his room, lonely and frustrated about his powerlessness. Apart from Lien's letters, sent to him by Rhijn, he had no connection to the outside world. Oddly, the one thing that cheered him up was the terrible frost. That winter was exceptionally cold in the Netherlands, with temperatures far below zero degrees. It was impossible to keep warm and for months the entire country complained about the cold. But Eberhard was pleased. Via the radio, he and Jan followed reports on German troops in the Soviet Union, crashing against the wall of wintry cold Hitler had not equipped them for. Every day Eberhard spent in his room with Jan and Aleid was a day he was not at the Wehrmacht.

It was obvious to Jan Hemelrijk that his friend felt awkward as their underground guest – his presence put the family at risk – and he managed to find Eberhard a little house all to himself, still in Bergen. So these days, Eberhard spends the day in the vacant studio of a sculptor friend and sleeps in a summer cottage on Breelaan, within walking distance from the studio. This way they spread the risks for the fugitive Eberhard and if there is any danger, he can get away via the forest.

Eberhard can stay in the summer cottage until 1

May and will soon have to look for something else. That in itself makes hiding in Amsterdam with Lien a great idea. Their friend, journalist Mik van Gilse, takes care of everything for them: he contacts Mrs Cornelius, keeps Eberhard posted on when he can join his family in Amsterdam, and lets Lien know when she and Kathinka can move out of The Hague.

And so, in May, the time has finally come; Lien, Eberhard and Kathinka are reunited in the canal house of Mrs Cornelius. They immediately feel at home; the household is very similar to their place in The Hague, full of creative and politically involved people. There are always visitors and Eberhard relishes the conversations he so missed in the forests of Bergen. Although the bustling Amsterdam life from before the war is smothered in terror, underneath the surface a parallel city has come into being. A city with routes and passages the Germans are unaware of, secret cafés in dark cellars, people playing cards in the lofts of canal houses, concerts starting after curfew when night lights are switched off.

At first, Lien and Eberhard love being part of this community again, but they soon realize this life is no longer for them. Ordinary Amsterdammers, no matter how much the occupation has influenced their lives, still have some freedom of movement. But Lien has a

J in her identity card and still does underground work for Mik – she regularly travels up and down to The Hague – and Eberhard is a wanted German deserter. Although he has grown a moustache and goes by the name of Jean-Jacques Bos, that is no guarantee. The house is too busy; there are people visiting who are strangers to them and they cannot tell whether they are trustworthy or traitors. The streets are not safe, either: they are swarming with police officers, squads, Nazis. Eberhard barely dares to leave the house and Lien has had a narrow escape from the Germans twice.

The first time was in The Hague, where another resistance worker would give her new distribution cards. Lien wanted to drop by her former home on Bankastraat, collect some final belongings, but was clever enough to call the house from a friend's place first, just to make sure the coast was clear.

'Hello, madam,' her friend Ankie answered formally as soon as she heard Lien's voice, 'you are mistaken, I'm afraid. We are supposed to meet tomorrow, not today. Bye now!' And she hung up.

Lien immediately understood what was going on. There had been a German, or a Dutch Nazi, right there next to Ankie, looking for Eberhard, and perhaps also for her. She stood with the receiver in her trembling hand and felt the physical proximity of the enemy.

Lien sat on a chair at her friend's place, trying to pull herself together. Hours passed without her daring to leave. She remembered what she told Ankie and her friend Jolle before leaving with Kathinka: 'Why don't you use the Bechstein grand piano while we're away? If we don't survive the war, you can keep it.' She had said it half-jokingly, but the scenario suddenly no longer seemed improbable.

Her friend called the house again later, and this time too, Ankie answered. She confirmed there had indeed been a house search. Everyone had insisted Eberhard had taken the train to Germany and they did not know where Lien lived now – but the whole situation had upset them terribly.

Unsteady on her legs, Lien travels back to Amsterdam that evening, where the incident keeps her from sleeping, for several nights on end.

A second time she narrowly escapes the Germans is when she walks into a police blockade at Amsterdam Centraal Station after midnight. This time, too, she is returning from The Hague with forged papers for Mik, but it is late – too late. She should have been back on Prinsengracht on time, not only because curfew begins at midnight, but also because Kathinka should already have been fed.

She is waiting for hours at the station in The Hague,

but the train is not coming; the only train finally passing says 'for relations of the German Wehrmacht only'. Lien imagines Eberhard pacing up and down with the crying baby and other people in the house entering their room to see what is going on – so she climbs in.

The train seems to drive with syrup in the wheels. The platform clock at a station it passes shows it is past midnight; if she gets through at Centraal Station, she will likely be stopped on the street later. Lien closes her eyes and searches her acting experience for a way to get herself out of this situation.

When she opens her eyes again, she stares straight into the face of a soldier. He is a few seats away – large, heavy and does not come across as very bright. The boy keeps staring at her and while his comrades are busy talking among each other, she winks at him. When she gets off at Amsterdam Centraal Station, he follows her.

'Can I walk up with you?' the soldier asks.

Lien smiles shyly and nods.

'All right, but it is past the curfew; I don't know how to get home.'

'Don't worry,' the soldier responds as he grabs her elbow.

Together they approach the checkpoint, where between the Dutch officers two SS men are posted, scanning the platform. The soldier walks straight towards them and Lien too holds her chin up. The SS men salute the soldier. He salutes back and says: 'This lady is coming with me.'

And they are past the gate. Lien is too frightened to breathe or swallow and presses her bag tightly against her chest, the forged documents almost burning through the leather. Trams no longer run and, without a word, she walks out of the faint circle of light on the station square, into the city immersed in darkness. The boy can hardly keep up with her – she hears him cursing as he trips over a paving stone. Lien is breathing so fast now, she fears the soldier will hear her panting. The street is dead quiet. The music, the lights, the drunkards, the working girls, the nightlife public and the dots of tourists blocking the roads – all gone. Amsterdam is deserted.

Lien walks faster and faster, ignoring the questions of the man following in her wake. Only when they reach Westermarkt does she check her step and look at him apologetically.

'I live near here. My mother must be worried sick about me being so late. Thank you.'

And before the astonished boy can say a word, she dashes off, onto Rozengracht, where she dives into a doorway to see if he has followed her. When after a few minutes she still doesn't hear any footsteps, she braces herself and runs onto Prinsengracht, straight to their hiding place.

As soon as the door sways open, she is welcomed by a screaming Kathinka and a desperate Eberhard, who was already assuming he would never see his love again.

'Have you completely lost your mind?' Mik is pacing up and down in front of the long windows, pressing his index finger against his forehead like an arrow. The sun rises above the houses on the other side of the canal, reflecting inside off the water; a shadow silhouette of Mik is swimming laps on the wooden floor.

Lien hears the tram pull up in Leidsestraat around the corner. She does not dare look Mik in the eye. Never has she seen him this furious. She came over to deliver the documents and told him about the disaster she escaped last night. After she had fed Kathinka in the middle of the night, the girl slept like a log. But she and Eberhard lay wide awake in silence until the singing of blackbirds announced the break of dawn.

'Rebekka Brilleslijper, with a fat J next to it. What madness!'

Mik now stands in front of her, his hands on his sides; Lien feels his eyes burning in her crown. She never told him she had registered as Jewish, so when this morning he asked her, because of the latest incident, what identity card she had, he nearly exploded. Just as Janny had done before.

'Listen. You are walking home in one straight line now, and you stay there until we've taken care of this. All right?'

As Lien hears the heavy door slam behind her and she walks down the stone steps to the canal, she suddenly realizes her life, the lives of her friends and family, at this moment in time, all depend on a string of remarkable friendships.

A few days later she receives her new identity card. Lien stares at it for a while, then she walks to the mirror and pins up her dark, heavy locks in a bun, like a woman from the East Indies. From now on, Kathinka's mother is called Antje Sillevis, born in Surabaya in Indonesia (then part of the Dutch East Indies). The time to leave the city has come.

# 10

# The First Train

Jan Hemelrijk succeeds in finding a place in Bergen for Lien, Eberhard and Kathinka too – close to Janny and the rest of the family. As they prepare to leave Amsterdam, other Jewish families keep arriving. Trains packed with people from all over the country who were chased out of their homes and villages and will be crammed into designated areas. Amsterdam slowly transforms into a ghetto: a city where Jews are gathered, isolated from the rest of the Dutch population, fully prepared for the next logistical step in the 'Final Solution'. The Municipal Housing Service raises rental prices of the houses Jewish families must move into. On top of that, they ask for a deposit of ten guilders per home – which, in most cases, was never returned.

And then the *Zentralstelle für Jüdische Auswan-*

*derung*, the Central Office for Jewish Emigration in Amsterdam, where the index cards of those to be deported are kept, is given a new task. The registrars will have to put in a huge amount of overtime.

Reich Commissioner Seyss-Inquart was initially summoned to supply 15,000 Jews in the year 1942. This target for the Netherlands was greeted with indifference; it could be met by deporting the foreign Jews alone. Seyss-Inquart was not expecting any fuss among the Dutch about this. But the Nazi heads have learned France will never reach their assigned 100,000 deportations that year and in great haste they decide the deficit must be compensated elsewhere. With one stroke of the pen, the annual quota for the Netherlands is raised from 15,000 to 40,000 people. On 15 July 1942, the first 4,000 Jews shall have to report at Amsterdam Centraal Station.

The mayor of Amsterdam immediately orders the civil servants at the register to draw up a list with names of Dutch Jews. The initial thorough registration of 160,000 Dutch Jews and the notorious dotted map facilitate this process.

On an administrative and organizational level, supplying 40,000 Jews will not cause anyone to lose any sleep, but both the occupying forces and the DNP expect an uproar among the people now that Jewish neighbours, former colleagues and friends suddenly have to pack their belongings in such large numbers. The *Zentralstelle* thinks it wise to call in the Jewish Council as an ally, so all will go smoothly and without too much panic.

On Friday evening of 26 June, during Sabbath, the head of the *Zentralstelle*, Ferdinand aus der Fünten, summons one of the chairmen of the Jewish Council, David Cohen. He tells him that at very short notice the first Jews will be deployed for forced labour under police surveillance in Germany. Cohen writes in his memoirs that this announcement frightens him terribly, that he protests and threatens to resign, but is assured by Aus der Fünten that most Jews will be allowed to stay in the Netherlands and that working conditions in Germany will be decent.

Either the Jewish Council assists in drawing up the lists – and decides who shall be exempted from deportation, such as themselves, their families and friends – or Aus der Fünten will do it himself, without regard to person. The Jewish Council opts for cooperation. They will have to supply 800 names per day.

From 5 July 1942 onwards, the first calls arrive in the post:

CALL!

For potential participation in the expansion of
police supervised employment in Germany, you
are called to proceed to transit camp Westerbork,
Hooghalen station, for personal and medical
examination. To that end you must be present on
[date] at [time] at assembly point [station].

Panic breaks out. People want to go into hiding or
they fit out their baggage with secret compartments,
sewed-in pockets with money and photos. They try to
find out who else in their circle of friends or family has
been called up, and why, or why not.

Cohen, Asscher and Aus der Fünten gather once
more, because the chairs of the Council have heard
that in time all Jews *will* be deported. Aus der Fünten
reassures them; it is indeed the ultimate goal, but he
promises that the Jewish Council and its staff need
not worry about deportation. Cohen and Asscher can
tell their people that correspondence with the labour
camps will be possible.

The Council immediately hires more staff, who are
all exempt from deportation by the Germans.

Mik informs Janny, and she in turn tells her husband, father, mother and brother what she knows. All

registered Jews in Amsterdam have been summoned to report and they will be sent to labour camps, she says. Her family falls silent. What does this mean? Is it cause for concern? So many unimaginable things have already happened. Whatever frame of reference they had is gone.

Joseph tries a matter-of-fact approach; in itself it is no surprise the Germans need manpower, certainly with the war spreading over a larger area and even America getting involved. And it seems the call is only for Jewish men between the ages of sixteen and forty. Fietje agrees; of course, extra hands are required to keep the war apparatus going, both in the factories and on the fields. It is probably nothing to worry about. But Janny looks intently at her little brother Jaap, her eyes narrowed. He is twenty-two years old and would have been a perfect target had he still been in Amsterdam. She crushes their wishful thinking with one remark: 'Everyone who is called up now ends up in a concentration camp and never returns again.'

The call has indeed set all alarm bells ringing within the Jewish community in Amsterdam. People want to go into hiding en masse. The Germans notice their next step in the secret 'Final Solution' is likely to go wrong and they plan a raid, exactly one day before all designated Jews have to report. On Tuesday 14 July, within a few hours, between 700 and 800 Jewish people are arrested at random. They have to march to Adama van Scheltemaplein and Euterpestraat, Amsterstam-Zuid, in a long procession.

There, the *Sicherheitsdienst* (the Intelligence Agency of the SS) and the *Zentralstalle* have taken up quarters in a former secondary school for girls. The school has become a place where resistance people are tortured and the deportation system is finalized. In the gym, and other parts of the building, Jews await their deportation. The notorious *Hausraterfassungsstelle* (Office for the Registration of Household Effects), partly led by Willem Henneicke, is based on Adama van Scheltemaplein too. This group of twenty, sometimes thirty civil servants – the Henneicke Column – is charged with creating accurate inventory lists of expropriated Jewish homes. They also trace undeclared Jewish goods and have everything removed to depots of the Liro looting bank. Lippmann, Rosenthal & Co was a Jewish bank, expropriated by the occupying forces. Already at the start of the war it was deployed as a 'reliable organization' for the Jews to hand in their belongings. Part of the home contents subsequently goes to German families, but the profit will mostly be used to fund the 'Final Solution'.

With the arrest of well over 700 Jews – including children, women and babies, and elderly people – the occupying forces have the hostages they need to get the Jewish Council back to work. Asscher and Cohen are given a choice: either they call upon their community to report obediently for the labour camps, or this group will be sent to a concentration camp, probably Mauthausen. The Council immediately issues an extra edition of *Het Joodsche Weekblad* (The *Jewish Weekly*):

EXTRA EDITION
Amsterdam, 14 juli 1942

De Sicherheitspolizei informs us of the following:
About 700 Jews have been arrested in Amsterdam today.
If the 4000 designated Jews do not leave for the labour camps in Germany this week, the 700 who have been arrested will be transported to a concentration camp in Germany.

The chairmen of the Jewish Council for
Amsterdam,
A. Asscher
Prof. Dr. D. Cohen

The next day 962 Jews report to Amsterdam Centraal Station and the first train from Westerbork to Auschwitz-Birkenau leaves. The train carries 1,137 people, including a group of orphans. Almost all passengers are killed upon arrival.

Up until 13 September 1944, another ninety-six trains will depart from Westerbork, filled with 107,000 people – 5,000 of them return alive. All across Western Europe trains run to remove 'unwanted elements' from society – with varying degrees of success. In Belgium, 30 per cent of the community will be deported to concentration camps, in France 25 per cent. The Netherlands will transport 76 per cent of its Jewish community within twenty-six months.

# 11

# *Bergen aan Zee*

On 16 July 1942, one day after the first train has left Westerbork for Auschwitz, Eberhard and Lien walk down the Prinsengracht towards Centraal Station, Kathinka in the pram, a small suitcase in their hands. They get on the train and watch as the city slowly disappears into the distance. The gates of Amsterdam are closing and their escape to Bergen is just in time.

There, Jan Hemelrijk is waiting for them on the platform. With his face serious, his blond hair neatly combed back, he looks older than twenty-five. He has arranged for Lien and her young family to stay in the empty home of some acquaintances until 1 September. Then they can move into the summer cottage, where Eberhard spent part of last winter. Between Breelaan, where the cottage is, and Buerweg, where Janny and the rest of the family live, is just over a mile of wooded area. All on the western outskirts of Bergen, towards the coast. Concealed by nature, they can walk to the others anytime.

And so, in the summer of 1942, the Brilleslijper family is reunited, partners and children alike. But the circumstances are grim and the mood is far from cheerful. Their little houses are fine and the surroundings of Bergen beautiful, but within two years the places they called home, the people who live there, have changed beyond recognition. It is all the sisters and the rest of the family can talk about.

After the first call to report at Westerbork, after the raid – which Lien, Eberhard and Kathinka narrowly escaped – there is a sudden rush for *Sperres*. The occupying forces have provided the Jewish Council with 17,500 of these provisional exemptions. Among the Jewish community in Amsterdam, a feverish struggle to secure one breaks out. There is fighting and desperate pleas at the doors of the Jewish Council at 58 Nieuwe Keizersgracht. People try, at the very last minute, to marry someone who *has* been exempted and others beg the Jewish Council for a job. In addition to a group of prominent Jews, deemed important to the community by the Council, their own employees and family are the first to receive a *Sperre*. No less than 17,000 people are 'employed'. It will eventually give them a year of respite.

Meanwhile, Janny's resistance work continues – even from Bergen. She works for the PBC, the Identity Card Centre, co-founded by their friend Mik van Gilse, and spends a lot of time travelling to forge and distribute the documents. She must often try to find identity cards with specific birth dates for Jews who are about the same age. Janny mostly works in tandem with her friend Trees Lemaire; she will deliver her stolen cards to Trees, who then passes them on to the next person in the underground network.

**The night** before Kathinka's first birthday, Lien and Eberhard sit in silence together and read *The Jewish Weekly*. Eberhard has gone up and down to Amsterdam for some treats to celebrate; in the local shops in Bergen sweet things cannot be found any more. He dropped by and saw Mrs Cornelius at Prinsengracht, who told him about a new raid among the Jewish community, just the day before. She gave him the latest extra edition of *The Jewish Weekly*, dated 6 August 1942. With the magazine pressed between his shirt and his trousers, he took the train back to Bergen.

## THE JEWISH WEEKLY
Extra edition

Any and all Jews not immediately responding to
the call addressed to them for the expansion of
employment in Germany, will be arrested and
taken to Mauthausen concentration camp. This or
another punishment will not be imposed on those
Jews still reporting before Saturday, 9 August 1942
at five o'clock, or those who declare to be willing
to participate in the expansion of employment.

Any and all Jews not wearing a Star of David, will
be taken to Mauthausen concentration camp.

Any and all Jews changing the city or house they
live in without permission of the authorities –
even if this is only temporary – will be taken to
Mauthausen concentration camp.

It is quiet for a moment as both of them digest the
message. Actually this is positive, Lien concludes pensively, pointing at the first point of order; the Germans
implicitly admit that many Jews have not reported and
that people go into hiding as soon as they receive the
call. Eberhard raises his eyebrows, pointing at point

two. That allows for an encouraging interpretation too; the fact that they threaten with deportation means the Star of David is sabotaged. But how long will this stubbornness last? By now everyone in the Netherlands knows that you don't spend more than six months in Mauthausen. Many new, and much larger, concentration camps have been built in Poland, from which no one returns.

They agree these are false rays of hope; the Jewish Council is simply calling for absolute obedience to the Fascists.

Eberhard's finger rests on point three; this is about Lien, about the entire Brilleslijper family. They have evaded the authorities *and* their whereabouts are unknown. Eberhard folds the magazine and Lien walks towards the kitchen. There is nothing left to discuss; there is no way back.

**In September 1942,** two months after the first train left Westerbork for Auschwitz and the Jewish Council issued their call, Jan Hemelrijk asks Eberhard to accompany a child to its hiding place. Eberhard has done this before; among themselves and with a touch of irony they call him 'the merchant of children'.

The last gullibility prevailing among the Jewish has been wiped out by recent developments and people go to great lengths to save their children from the hands of the Nazis. With or without parents, brothers and sisters, with or without explanation, with acquaintances or perfect strangers: throughout the Netherlands children are hidden like Easter eggs. Sometimes they are old enough to understand what is happening and sometimes there is a chance to say goodbye, but there are also families where father and mother are suddenly put on the train and the children are left behind at home in despair.

A nursemaid in Groningen remembers the instructions her boss, a Jewish woman with seven children, gave her: 'When they come and get us, I will put the baby in the back of the closet, underneath a pile of blankets. Keep an eye on our house and look for the child if you think we have been taken away!'

And so it happens; parents and six children are deported, and the nurse finds the baby in the back of the closet, hidden under layers of wool but alive. She wraps him up warm, straps him onto the back of her bicycle and, against the wind, peddles the long road towards the north, to the sea. There, she gives the child to fishermen on a cutter, who take it across to Norway, where an unknown Norwegian couple lovingly take it in and raise it. The only things they know about the baby are the first and second name the nursemaid gave them.

Decades later, just before she died, the former nurse reads the name she never forgot in a newspaper and contacts the man to tell him about his parents. She can also finally hand him the albums with photos capturing his entire murdered family, which she took from the house at the time and kept for him ever since.

The assignment Jan Hemelrijk has for Eberhard is less complicated but no less dangerous. It concerns sixteen-year-old Herbert Spijer, a Jewish boy who lives with his parents in Amsterdam. With the deportations and raids in the city, the family fear for the life of their son. They want him to go into hiding before it is too late.

With a moustache and a hat as poor disguise, Eberhard travels to Amsterdam by train and takes the anxious teenager back to their home in Bergen to hide with them for the time being. It is a miracle it goes well. The checks at Centraal Station have increased considerably since the calls started and Eberhard sees 'mutes', in civilian clothes, everywhere. They stare expressionlessly at the narrow stairs with the crowds coming down from the platforms, making their way towards the central hall and, from there, outside. Eberhard suspects the mutes always position themselves right underneath the stairs to take in the stream of passengers properly. Anytime he accompanies children, he makes sure they walk right behind him, hidden behind his tall figure, which is perhaps no longer as impressive after the failed starvation cure but still good enough.

In November, Eberhard goes on a new mission for the Spijer family. Their seventeen-year-old daughter, Elleke, is hiding somewhere in Amsterdam and has to be moved to Velsen. After Eberhard has brought the girl safely to her new address, it appears that his tram from Alkmaar to Bergen is no longer running. Eberhard does not know the way, just roughly the direction, and he walks into the darkness with the curfew breathing down his neck. To reach the summer cottage he must, at some point, take a road running between a pond and a soldier's camp; there is no other route. It is already well past ten; no one is allowed outside, certainly not a German deserter. He steals through the bushes like a spy and finally arrives safely back with Lien, who is waiting for him, crying. She had almost resigned herself to the fact he had been taken by the Gestapo.

It almost goes wrong on a few more occasions, when Eberhard is stopped at Amsterdam Centraal Station. As soon as the train doors open, he walks along in the stream; out of the train, onto the platform, down the stairs, head low, don't do anything suspicious, don't hide yourself, but don't draw attention, either.

'*Ausweis, bitte!*' ('Identity card, please!')

In the few seconds that follow, everything seems to happen excruciatingly slowly; reaching for the pocket, showing the paper, eagle eyes scanning from top to bottom, looking at him, then back to the paper, his attempts to swallow, his heartbeat banging inside his ears, heavy and drawn-out, like a steam locomotive heading for a concrete wall in slow motion, he sees it happening, cannot avert the crash.

'*In Ordnung!*' ('All right!')

The sudden relief, the syrupy blood slowly flowing again, walk on, take off almost, melt into the masses, until his heart is back in its place.

Even at an advanced age, Eberhard cannot descend the stairs at Amsterdam Centraal Station without an acute terror taking his breath away. It takes a few minutes at the station square, sheltered by the city, to recover before he can continue on his way.

# 12

# Mushroom Steak

Each time Janny hears loud explosions blowing over from the sea, she runs outside, pricking up her ears, hoping it is finally happening. Hoping that here, on the land, the Allies have opened the second front Stalin spoke about on the radio. Hitler's troops, as has become clear, cannot be beaten with a counter offensive from the sea and the sky – to stand a chance, the Allies must create a front on the European mainland.

Operation Barbarossa came with brute force and, in the first instance, great speed. But towards the end of 1941, Hitler had lost 750,000 men and the morale of the German troops was lower than the wintry temperatures. In December, Minister of Propaganda Goebbels gives a patriotic speech on the German radio, in which he calls on the people to send the army warm gear.

'The homeland must not have one quiet hour as long as there is a single soldier left at the front, who is not as yet equipped to withstand the rigor of winter cold.'

Although the Germans themselves have been suffering under rations for two years, the call yields over seventy-six million warm items of clothing – but the war has lost its lightning speed. First, Moscow unexpectedly holds out until January 1942. Then, after a long and reasonably successful new German offensive in spring 1942, follows the infamous Battle of Stalingrad, from August 1942 to February 1943. This bloody battle symbolizes the culmination of the duel between Adolf Hitler and Joseph Stalin, both sacrificing millions of people.

But Janny has no idea what is happening at the Eastern Front. She is not aware that Hitler's Lebensraum plans don't make the leap from drawing board to territory that easily. All she knows is that the Allies still haven't landed and daily life in Bergen is becoming increasingly hard.

Given the circumstances, Robbie is doing reasonably well, but Liselotte still cries all the time and Janny doesn't know what is wrong with her. Kathinka is not doing well, either – she is listless. There is a dysentery epidemic, and Janny and Lien are very concerned about the little ones. Rumour has it the outbreak occurred in the soldiers' camp down the road and the bowel disease spreads to the nearby families, where it mainly affects children.

Kathinka falls ill. The little girl runs empty until all the baby fat has gone and her ribs press against her skin. When nothing but blood comes out of her, Lien is close to despair, but Jan and Aleid Hemelrijk arrange for a doctor friend to come and examine Kathinka. He prescribes medication and a diet of rice with cinnamon. Jan makes sure they get everything and for over a week they sit by her bed, anxiously praying she gets something down. The family next door, Catholic with eleven children, loses two of them. Just as Lien and Eberhard are about to lose hope, Kathinka begins to eat and recuperate, and when she even takes some bites of normal children's food, her parents, for the first time, dare to smile again.

The winter of 1942 is a severe one. Food is scarce and where that was problematic at mild temperatures, with nature in bloom and animals looking after themselves, it now causes major problems. The sisters find chanterelles in the forest and, thankfully, fried and seasoned, the mushrooms are a huge success with the children. To be on the safe side, they preserve baskets full of chanterelles and keep them in jars. Janny has also heard that a reddish bracket fungus is very nutritious and those final weeks of the year they mainly live off various mushrooms. Thankfully, they can laugh about it.

'What are you having for dinner tonight?' Bob asks Eberhard when he drops by.

'Mushroom steak. And you?'

'Mushroom steak.'

In December, the temperature drops further below zero; the freefall will end at a record of minus 27.4 degrees Celsius in the following weeks. The frost creeps into the walls and it becomes impossible to heat their homes. Jaap Brilleslijper asks Jan Hemelrijk to bring him a saw and an axe, and he fills his days with cutting trees, chopping logs and lugging wood to both of his sisters, who let the stoves glow day and night.

Janny and Eberhard regularly travel up and down to Amsterdam for their resistance work and there they learn new raids have taken place – the largest so far. In October the SD, helped by the Dutch police, has arrested around 15,000 Jews in Amsterdam and in the rest of the North Holland province. In November, they do the same with some hundred Jews at various places in the east of the country.

All detainees are transported to Westerbork, where panic and chaos arise upon the arrival of so many. Not only because the barracks become overcrowded, but also because of the presence of numerous women, children and elderly people; the remains of belief in 'labour camps' quickly evaporate.

A streamlined deportation can only succeed with peace and order, and the right camp commander plays a crucial part in creating those. Two previous camp commanders of Westerbork, Erich Deppner and Josef Dischner, were sadistic, unpredictable men who only caused panic with their behaviour. Prisoners reasoned: if this is how we are treated in Westerbork, a former refugee camp, what on earth is awaiting us where we go next? A new camp director has to bring calm, so the Dutch quota for deportation can be met.

In October 1942, SS-*Obersturmführer* Albert Konrad Gemmeker is appointed, a man with the symmetrical features of a film star and the aura of a principal. He comes from Beekvliet hostage camp in the village of Sint-Michielsgestel in Brabant, where the Dutch intelligentsia are kept as living security; no hair on their heads will be touched as long as the Dutch people obey.

With velvet gloves, Gemmeker re-establishes the order in Westerbork. He moves into the beautiful commander's house at the camp entrance, a stately wooden villa with pointed roof and a rectangular conservatory extension. Gemmeker lives there as if he is a proper mayor and Westerbork his city, letting himself be served by Jewish staff. He organizes the daily activities in the camp, making things as normal as possible, with work, a lot of sports, and cabaret and music performances in the evenings. There is a laundry, a sewing studio and a large garden with crops to make the inhabitants self-sufficient.

Just as orderly as Gemmeker manages daily life, he draws up the deportation lists. The numbers are determined per week in Berlin and passed on to The Hague, from where Gemmeker receives his orders. During a weekly meeting the transport lists are drawn up, with Gemmeker largely relying on the Jewish administrative staff.

During the first months, trains leave on Monday and Friday. From 1943, it is every Tuesday. People are told who needs to pack their bags per barrack, some with and some without their family members – the question no one dares to ask is which is worse. Everything happens in a despondent but organized atmosphere, right up to pressing together the passengers when carriages are overcrowded. Heads are counted and the amount is chalked on the outside with large numbers. Then, doors are hermetically shut and the train departs.

Gemmeker thus runs a smooth deportation system which, much to the delight of Berlin, allows him to put the 40,000 Jews on the train from the Netherlands to Poland by the end of 1942. He celebrates with a festive meal.

Janny and Lien realize how blessed they are to be together while most families in the country have been torn apart – if not deported already. Via the resistance they have sufficient access to coupons and Janny does not think of stopping her activities. She is not reckless or naive but simply sees no other option; when the times call for it, you have to fight.

For the children they try to let days pass as they normally would. They even celebrate the feast of Saint Nicholas at Janny and Bob's place at Buerweg. For a moment, everything seems like it was before the war. Which, they suddenly realize, is only two and a half years ago.

That night, everyone is relaxed and embraces the rituals of the magical feast, for the sake of the children. Liselotte and Kathinka are too young to understand, but when Jan Hemelrijk, dressed as Saint Nicholas, takes Robbie on his lap and speaks to him in a deep voice, the boy stares back, his eyes wide, not stirring a finger.

'Lost your tongue, have you, young man?' Saint Nicholas grumbles.

'No, Uncle Jan,' the child stammers, making the entire family laugh.

Robbie doesn't understand what is happening and is about to burst into tears.

'The Secret Service should sign him up,' Jan Hemelrijk mutters from behind his fake beard as he hands the child to Janny.

When they say goodbye late in the evening, the rain comes pouring down. The heavens are silvery grey with a dark rim, but in the distance a starry sky is glowing, predicting a dry night. Lien and Eberhard leave for their cottage, Kathinka warm inside her father's rain coat, and Jan and Aleid walk along with them to their own house at Lindenlaan. As they wave to Saint Nicholas, Bob loses his precious bag of tobacco in the pouring rain. In an exuberant mood, he and Janny look for it until wisps of hair stick to their cheeks and their knees shine through the fabric of their wet trousers – in vain.

Days later, Janny finds the pouch underneath the shrubs. The tobacco is drenched and half perished, but that doesn't stop Bob from smoking it. These days even imaginary pleasure is welcome.

# 13

# The Jansen Sisters

It does not come as a surprise that they have to leave, but the news hits them hard nonetheless. On 1 February 1943, German soldiers will evacuate the entire coastline from Den Helder to Hook of Holland, from door to door, for the construction of the Atlantic Wall.

Hitler has ordered this defence line along the coast of Northwest Europe to prevent an invasion of Allied forces – the invasion Janny so hopes for. A line or rather, a chain of obstacles and fortifications, covering no less than 3,000 miles, from the north of Norway to the South of France. Thousands of bunkers will be built in the Dutch dunes, as well as anti-tank obstacles, such as high concrete walls, sand bags and deep trenches. They need extra paths and roads to ammunition depots, anti-aircraft defences and minefields. All villages up to six miles inland must be empty by 1 February 1943. This announcement is bad enough for regular residents of the coastal areas, but for people in hiding it means they are trapped.

Slowly, the final days of 1942 pass. Janny tries to hide her worries from her parents and the children, but the unrest is not just brewing indoors. Around them, people begin to move. 'Normal' people, officially permitted to relocate, not people like them: Jews on the run, German deserters for whom death awaits. As the moving vans and cars, loaded up to the roof, leave Bergen, a new stream of soldiers marches into the village each day. The men in the wooden barracks of the encampment nearby and the noise they produce keep Janny awake at night. She lies in bed with her eyes wide open, her hand in Bob's, staring at the ceiling. Above their heads English aircrafts fly across the dark dunes and open fire on the camp in Bergen, whereupon German soldiers come running outside to shoot back.

One night they shoot an English aircraft from the sky. It lands on the wooden barracks, burning, and sets everything ablaze. As if by a miracle, Robbie and Liselotte don't wake up, but Janny, Bob, Jaap, Fietje and Joseph all gather at the window in the front room, which is lit by the sea of flames as if it were a glorious summer's day. Petrified, narrowing their eyes against the bright light, they stand behind the curtain. Bob and Janny exchange glances: the soldiers are closer to Lien and Eberhard, and to Jan and Aleid.

The next day they learn that, thankfully, they are all unharmed, but it is clear: each day here is one too many. They must find new homes.

The sisters gather for emergency talks with Bob and Eberhard. Who do they know? Who do they trust? Jan and Aleid have to relocate too; they cannot move in with them. Should they split up and give the children to strangers? The latter is unthinkable and the idea is immediately dismissed. But then what? They are a large group and they want to, have to, stay together in order to survive this. It is impossible to stay in Bergen, returning to The Hague is no option and Amsterdam is hermetically shut. Moreover, they know with great certainty: if you get into Amsterdam, your only way out is to go to Westerbork.

In the end, they decide that Janny and Eberhard will each set off on their own into the country, on the off-chance of finding remote places and vacant houses. It is a shaky plan, but it is all they have.

Jan Hemelrijk, who is constantly looking for hiding places, has told them there are hardly any families left in urban areas willing to take people in – too much risk, too little space, too many Nazis on the lookout, both German and Dutch, and the Dutch police are also eager to accept tips about where Jews might be hiding. The reluctance of non-Jewish Dutch to dissociate from their Jewish fellow citizens has, in two years of occupation, mostly turned into acceptance of their fate.

Friends in the resistance tell them Amsterdam is crawling with traitors without a uniform. Ordinary civilians betraying their neighbours, former colleagues, even their very own family. Nazi bank Lippmann, Rosenthal & Co is thriving. With the number of deported Jews increasing, more and more houses become vacant and the Henneicke Column always appear like a shot to make an inventory of the home contents. The *Hausraterfassung* squad becomes increasingly important. The men travel the entire country, drawing up lists in houses people were forced to leave – sometimes sheets are still warm, teacups still on the table; sometimes the residents themselves are still there when the gentlemen neatly perform their administrative tasks. Then, they must witness how a blueprint is made of their daily lives; meticulously, as befits a true civil servant, and in quadruplicate. One copy of the inventory goes to the head office, the *Zentralstelle*, one travels along with the goods, one stays with the Column member as proof of his work and the final copy is handed to the family itself. A receipt as a last reminder of their normal existence before they close the door behind them.

Remote areas then, that is where they need to focus. With his Aryan appearance, false identity card and flawless Dutch, Eberhard still dares to travel and Janny will combine her trips to Amsterdam for the resistance with combing out the neighbouring villages. They decide that the wooded area east of Amsterdam is most promising, so each morning Eberhard takes the train to Hilversum to explore from there.

One day he travels to Hollandsche Rading, a tiny village surrounded by nature. Via the station, he walks down the high street and rings at each door. With his handsome, tall presence, blond hair, light eyes and eloquence, people speak to him with slight suspicion but without any problems.

'Do you, by any chance, let out rooms?' he keeps asking, followed by: 'Or would you happen to know a vacant summer cottage nearby?'

Nothing. Door after door, street after street, until at the other side of the village he finds only trees.

It is December – the temperature has dropped below zero. He tries to warm his numb fingers and rejects the desperate action crossing his mind in a flash – to

camp in the forest in tents with the entire family . . .
And yet, he is drawn to the woods – perhaps there is a
hunter's cabin, an empty little home? He thinks of the
family in Bergen, steels himself and dives between the
tree trunks.

A long walk through the forest of Baarn follows;
Eberhard encounters nothing or no one. After a few
hours of brisk walking, frozen and about to lose courage, he suddenly notices a clear sandy path. He is already beyond hoping it will lead to a house, but perhaps
it will lead to a station.

It's getting dark. Although he fears the disappointed
faces at home, he cannot stay away for ever. Then
something glistens between the trees – a building,
white walls, long windows closed up with blinds, and
as he comes closer an enormous villa emerges. Further
down are some smaller houses and for the first time
that afternoon Eberhard feels his blood begin to flow.
He walks to a house with the lights on and rings the
doorbell. The door swings open and a man looks at
him, annoyed.

'Good evening, sir. I noticed that large building over
there in the woods,' – Eberhard nods towards the villa –
'and I was wondering, because it looks so uninhabited,
whether any rooms are being let out or—'

'Out of the question!'

Even before he has finished speaking, the man slams the door shut in his face.

Empty-handed, Eberhard goes back to Bergen, where the others are waiting for him behind the dark window. They don't ask; Eberhard's face speaks volumes. Jaap stokes the fire and while Eberhard warms himself, he recounts his experiences, including the unpleasant encounter with the man chasing away his last remaining hope.

For a moment, Lien and Jaap look at each other pityingly. Then they burst out laughing.

'Are you out of your minds?' Eberhard stares at his beloved. 'It's not funny, is it?'

'You know what that large building was?' says Lien.

Even Herbert, the Jewish boy staying with them, is now chuckling. Eberhard is struggling to shrug his shoulders.

'The royal palace, Soestdijk!'

It would take years before Eberhard could see the joke.

**Over Christmas** their mood is far from cheerful; the holidays are a reminder of the new year and the evacuation approaching, and there is still no solution in sight. They all gather at Janny and Bob's; even their good friend Frits Reuter and his girlfriend Cor Snel risk the journey so they can come and stay. As a leader of the illegal Communist Party in Amsterdam, Frits has a lot of news to share. His reports, however, do not improve the atmosphere.

On 13 December, the DNP organized a huge celebration at The Concertgebouw in Amsterdam, in honour of its eleventh anniversary. In an overcrowded hall, decorated with waving flags, banners and swastikas, Reich commissioner Seyss-Inquart declared that Hitler recognized Anton Mussert, founder of the DNP, as 'Leader of the Dutch People'. Underneath a row of outstretched arms, Mussert accepted his position.

They listen stoically and eat. Janny and Lien have baked doughnut balls and made a rice table. Late in the evening, the larger party waves goodbye to Lien, Eberhard – a sleeping Kathinka over his shoulder – and Herbert, who leave for their house at the other side of the woods. They kiss each other goodnight and everyone goes to bed, hoping that night will bring the miracle they need.

And the miracle happens. Just as Janny and Eberhard want to stop their random expeditions in the wintry cold in order to prepare for a forced split of the family, Jan Hemelrijk arrives with news.

'I've got something. Just below Amsterdam, in the

woods of Naarden. A detached house, only used in summer by two rich ladies. It should be big enough for all of you. This is the ladies' address.'

After a restless night, Bob and Eberhard, dressed in their best suits, leave for Amsterdam at dawn, all tense, holding out the note with the address like a divining rod. The Jansen sisters live on Minervalaan, a fashionable street with stately mansions. With the fate of their loved ones, their children, the entire Brilleslijper family resting in their hands, they ring the doorbell.

As they try to come across as reliable and charming as possible, Bob and Eberhard disclose their precarious situation – or at least: its safe version. No one can be trusted these days, not even seemingly good people. So Bob and Eberhard are two perfectly normal, non-Jewish, Dutch young men living in Bergen with their families who have to leave at very short notice because of the Atlantic Wall. They conclude their story with the pressing question: can they please rent the summer cottage in Naarden until the end of the war?

The ladies are visibly impressed by these nice young gentlemen. They agree and tell them to come back in two days to sign the lease. Bob and Eberhard quickly return home to the family, who await the verdict at Janny's. It appears that they are saved, but the thought of being separated from the children has been heavy on their hearts for weeks and no one is able to respond enthusiastically to the good news.

They have a place but no official permit to move to Naarden. The only person who could still try to request one is Bob. The rest of the party is Jewish, or, in Eberhard's case, a deserter. Before he went into hiding, Bob worked at the National Office for Food Supply, and there Janny sees their only option.

She instantly travels to The Hague to speak to the right people. With gentle charm but a look that will not take 'no' for an answer, she arranges for Bob to be allowed back at the Food Supply, this time stationed further north. His new office is in Weesp, a village between Amsterdam and Naarden. During her mission there is no mention of Bob's status as 'wanted resistance worker', so Janny's suspicion that he is only registered as such in the province of South Holland seems justified. In any case, they will just have to take the risk; there is no other option.

With the required documents in the bag tightly pressed to her chest, she begins her journey back north. It is Friday, late afternoon, and she braves the crowd of commuters rushing towards the weekend. Only men are left, perhaps a few disorientated women. Those who have no need to travel, don't – certainly not at this late hour. Those who have no business with someone else are not looking for contact.

Janny makes herself small and stares outside. As dusk falls, the meadows behind the window fade and the reflection of her face slowly appears. Her straight hair, tucked behind her ears, protruding cheekbones like tent poles holding up her tightly stretched skin, her dark eyes. The responsibility for all those people depending on her rarely feels heavy, but now she is suddenly overwhelmed. The powerlessness of recent weeks, the imminent threat of being separated from the children, or worse, all of them being arrested . . . and then what?

Her shoulders feel heavy and tense and when she breathes out, it seems as if she tumbles through the seat, through the floor, towards the ground underneath the carriage. Then a stabbing pain in her lower abdomen, behind the bag with their lifeline. She doubles over and peers around to see if anyone is noticing her. The seats next to and opposite her are empty; the gentlemen sit together further down – thank goodness.

She exhales softly. Another stab, fiercer this time. She stifles a cry and begins to feign a cough, folding her upper body over the bag. As she coughs, a grip tightens around her belly, squeezes her empty, squeezes the life out of her until she can no longer breathe. One of the men further down looks up briefly. Janny tries to make herself even smaller in the corner against the window.

Then a warm flow spreads between her legs, pleasant in the coldness of the compartment. The pain is gone and she feels faint. Her feet sway loosely above the linoleum at the rhythm of the switches. The flow turns cold and her thighs feel dirty and sticky. She sits up a little, turns her wet woollen skirt two quarters to the front and stares at the dark stain on her lap. She covers the stain with her leather bag and rests her head against the window, which now only shows a black wall. Some pinpricks of light here and there in the distance. Her breath steams up the glass while warm tears run down from her cheeks and fall apart on her hands.

With great effort, she manages a smile when she comes home, waves the papers Bob eagerly takes care of and retreats to the bedroom to change her clothes. Everyone is relieved they have the permit. She tells no one about the miscarriage.

On 30 January 1943, two days before the coast around Bergen will be evacuated, the men return to Amsterdam and Eberhard, by his false name J.-J. Bos, signs a lease with Ms C.M. Jansen, for renting the villa The High Nest, Driftweg 2 in Naarden. The rent is 112 guilders and 50 cents per month for the furnished house – and the promise to be careful with the furniture and not use the fine china.

'You might want to register as new occupants with the mayor of Naarden,' one of the sisters remarks casually, 'or he might claim the house for the Germans.'

Bob and Eberhard thank them for the tip and exchange a quick glance – that would be a complete disaster. They want to go, now, pick up the family and leave the village before the evacuations start, but the sisters are all too glad to have the young men visiting and keep lingering in the hall of the fashionable house on Minervalaan.

'Tell me,' says the other sister, placing her hand on Eberhard's forearm, 'you don't sound like you're from The Hague at all. Where are you from originally?'

He has been asked that question before.

'You know,' Eberhard answers with a conspiratorial voice, 'I grew up in Limburg, in the south. I fear you'll be able to hear that in my accent for as long as I live.'

All four of them laugh and say goodbye warmly.

The last hurdle. The mayor of Naarden. The Nazi mayor of Naarden, Marinus van Leeuwen. While Bob rushes to Bergen to prepare for moving the two households, Eberhard gets on the train to Naarden-Bussum. From there he race-walks to Naarden, enters the fort

via the bridge and heads in one straight line to the town
hall on Markstraat, opposite the Great Church.

The town hall is a beautiful building, consisting of
a pair of houses, side by side, like two brothers. One is
larger than the other but in an identical style, with ser-
rated gables and an open tower with a bell and a weather
vane at the rear. In the largest, the house on the left, is
a stately, arched front door, which Eberhard enters, his
mouth dry and his limbs all stiff. Inside, a friendly lady
leads him to the room of the mayor, who is working
behind his massive desk, flanked by portraits of Adolf
Hitler and Anton Mussert. When Eberhard enters, he
pushes back his chair, stands up and greets him with an
outstretched arm.

*'Heil Hitler!'*

Eberhard thinks of Lien and Kathinka, screws up
his courage and, for the first time in his life, answers
the Nazi salute. He shows his papers. The official lease,
the work permit Janny arranged for Bob and a medical
certificate from the doctor in Bergen, declaring that
'Kathinka Anita Bos, in order to recover from severe
dysentery, must move to higher areas in the municipality of Naarden'.

Van Leeuwen leafs through the stack, straight-faced,
while Eberhard tries to keep his hands still. His fingers

keep moving across his palms, as if he wants to rub the seconds ahead. Then the mayor rises.

'Identity card?'

Eberhard presents the identity cards of Jean-Jacques Bos, Antje Bos née Sillevis, and Kathinka Anita Bos.

Behind his back the bells begin to ring. In their echo, Eberhard breathes out. He thinks back on the failed examination after his starvation cure, his flight to Bergen, to Jan and Aleid, then to Amsterdam and back to Bergen again. This cannot fail. If this goes wrong, it is over. For all of them.

'Agreed.'

Van Leeuwen presses the required stamp on the municipal papers, puts his signature underneath and, ten minutes later, Eberhard is back outside. He looks up at the Great Church of Naarden and nods briefly. To whom or what he does not know.

# Part Two
# The High Nest

'The house at Driftweg was called The High Nest.
It was a very large house with grounds and
    woodland stretching out to the water.
And there, with our people in hiding, we had all the
    adventures a person can possibly experience.'

Janny Brandes-Brilleslijper

# 1
# A Villa in the Woods

A safe place to wait out the war was all they had asked for. How much longer this war would last, no one dared to say. And also: not to be separated from the rest of the family – especially the children, like so many of their friends and acquaintances had been forced to. Any shelter would have been fine, be it a barn or an empty warehouse. They had expected anything. But not this.

It is dark when they approach their destination. Naarden village is five, perhaps ten minutes behind them; they have been driving through the heath, followed by woodlands, for some time when, according to the directions, they are almost there. They have been dead quiet the entire journey, tired, worn out by tension, afraid to be stopped along the way. The paved way turns into a sandy path with deep cart tracks – the forest is closing in on them. If they drive any further, their rickety removal van might get stuck.

Bob turns off the ignition and as the headlights dim and the sound of humming of the engine blows away between the trees, a thin calm descends upon them. Clouds of breath in the cabin, Bob is the first to move.

'Come on. It has got to be here somewhere.'

Janny helps her mother climb out of the van and takes Liselotte in her arms. Outside, the rain hurts their tired cheeks. Trees are creaking in the wind above their heads while the sound of their own footsteps is muffled by heaps of leaves along the path, which they follow onto what seems like a dead end – a tall black wall. The forest.

Janny glances at Bob, who is holding Robbie's hand. The little one is too tired to cry. He shrugs his shoulders and they move on. Jaap has given Fietje his arm and holds his mother tight. She is shivering with cold. The rest of the party is still on their way – Eberhard with Father, Lientje with Kathinka. It is too dangerous to travel together.

When they reach the edge of the forest, they discover a path square to theirs. It emerges from an open patch of heath to their right and disappears between the trees to their left. Bob gives a nod and they dive into the forest. As soon as Janny finds herself between the black trunks, her shoulders relax – a weight is lifted. She feels at home here.

On the right side of the narrow path, an enormous shadow looms. Around them branches groan, trees sway to the rhythm of the wind, but the house just stands there, solid and unperturbed, not the least bit impressed.

The rain has stopped and a weak moon pushes itself through the clouds above the open fields behind them. They hold still on the path and look at the house. Janny's eyes glide up along the heavy façade to a white sign between the windows of the ground floor and the first. The black letters read: The High Nest.

The house, a robust cube with a thatched roof, is built in the middle of a vast nature reserve between the villages of Huizen and Naarden. It is obvious this home does not think much of civilization; ignoring all rules of bourgeois architecture, it looks at nature instead. The High Nest has its back turned towards the road and the path that took them here; the entrance to the central hall as well as the kitchen door is at the back. Anyone visiting must follow the narrow path, then go past the house towards the back – which is in fact the front – to ring the doorbell. All the while, the occupants can keep a close eye on the visitor from one of the many windows. These windows are all around the house, spread evenly between the first two floors – their white panes enclosed by claret-coloured shutters.

The front door opens onto a spacious hall, giving entry to three rooms. Straight ahead, overlooking the path, are the living and dining room, on the left side of the hall is a kitchen, on the right an extra room and then a toilet. There is even a telephone downstairs. They giggle as they press the receiver to their ears – to their surprise, the phone is actually connected.

There are four bedrooms and a bathroom on the first floor. Above those, underneath the thatched roof, an attic covers the entire length of the house. Both sides of the roof have man-sized, semi-circular windows, like those in the tower of a church, offering a spectacular view of the surrounding woods and heath, and of the miniature version of The High Nest in the garden; a large shed with a thatched roof and identical paned windows.

Three chimneys rise up from the villa like pillars, making the building seem indestructible. It is the perfect place to hide.

**That night,** for the first time in months, Janny sleeps like a baby. No firing above their heads, no noise from the village, no fear of soldiers starting evacuations early, no more worrying where to go. There is nothing but the silence weighing her body down and she sleeps until the winter sun has found its way back to the house. Beside her, the bed is cold. Bob has already taken the children downstairs, so she would not wake.

Last night, in the dark, they had quietly collected their stuff from the van and brought it to the house. After putting the children to bed, they had sat in the living room, anxiously waiting for Lien and Kathinka, and then for Eberhard and Father. When everyone had arrived safely, they had all gone to bed, too tired to talk, too cautious to turn on the light. She has not seen the interior of the house yet. Janny presses herself up on her elbows and takes a look around. The space is bathed in light. The large windows on either side of the attic are merely covered with thin cotton curtains. An ingenious beam construction supports the top of the roof, several feet above her head. In the corner she sees a porcelain sink, a mirror and a cupboard with towels. Broad planks cover the entire floor length.

She swings her legs across the edge of the bed and walks towards the window. Cautiously, she pushes the cotton aside and looks out. No one. She opens the curtains in one go, stands in front of the window audaciously. Trees everywhere, trees as far as her eyes can see. Not one house, not one street, not one person. She breaks into a smile. Voices drift into the room via the staircase and she rushes downstairs, to the children.

Everyone is already busy. Jaap immediately dived into the shed, where he found enough material and tools to start his own studio. Mother is cleaning the windowsills and has set the kitchen door wide open; an ice-cold current of air dispels the mouldy smell of wood and damp – the house had been empty since the end of summer.

Janny gives Fietje a kiss, puts on her coat, walks outside and is transfixed. In front of her is a lawn as large as a park, with tall shrubs, birch hedges, stately trees, voluminous rhododendrons and circular flower beds. She looks around, astonished.

Seats of wood and worn iron are scattered about, some green with moss and half overgrown, others clean, used relatively recently. She discovers bird boxes hanging in various trees above her head, an empty run further down.

The garden at her feet slopes down. She had not realized the house was on a hill and snorts at her own slow mind; The *High* Nest. The villa is enclosed by wild heathland and woods. In the middle of the lawn is a gazebo, square with a pointed roof and large windows all around. Lien is standing there with the three children all wrapped up in hats and scarves. Janny waves and walks towards them. Robbie has already spotted her, an ear-to-ear smile appears on his face. Janny presses her lips on his forehead, caresses Liselotte and Kathinka on the head, and steps beside her older sister, their shoulders touching.

'Gosh,' Janny says.

With their backs towards the gazebo they stare at The High Nest, elevated above its surroundings by the earth.

'Good, isn't it?' says Lien.

Janny can only nod. Their situation is too precarious to be cheerful, but they could not have been luckier than this. With her chin, Lien points at a place behind the villa.

'The next house is a few hundred feet from here.'

Janny scans the surroundings but cannot see any roofs or other signs of human presence. Lien turns around, gesturing towards the back of the garden with her hand.

'When you keep walking that way, you get to the sea.'

Janny raises her eyebrows, tilts her head.

'The sea?'

'Or whatever is it called, Ijsselmeer or something. Water, in any case.'

They snigger.

Janny thinks back on their journey the night before and tries to orientate herself.

'So, Huizen is over there . . .' She points to the left of the house – rugged heath with dots of trees. 'And Naarden is over there . . .' She gestures to the right – trees as far as her eyes can see. Right at that moment, Jaap's head pops out of the shed, his glasses on the tip of his nose, a dazed expression on his face. The sisters laugh.

'Hey!'

Janny quickly covers her mouth with her hand, but Lien says reassuringly, 'No one can hear you here.'

In Bergen there were neighbours, passers-by, soldiers quartered near them; there was always a reason to urge others to be quiet, to get the children inside as soon as one of them started crying.

Japie comes running towards them, a heap of stuff pressed against his chest.

'Look what I found!'

He opens his arms to show them his treasure. A claw hammer, trays with nails, a cigar box, rope, tarpaulin, electrical cables with split ends, a receiver with curled wire – but no phone. In Janny's perception it is junk, but she knows not to say that out loud. Her brother's eyes are glistening.

'The whole shed is full of stuff – you must come and see it! I'm going to start with a radio and then I'll make something for the kids, all right?' And off he goes, his trousers slipping down from his skinny bottom as he runs.

The sisters discuss what needs to happen in the following days. Janny has a few errands for Mik and won't be around in the daytime. Bob will start working in Weesp immediately, so it is up to Lien and Eberhard to explore the area and do the shopping for everyone.

While talking, they circle around the children like shepherds around their flock, watch them play in the forest, their cheeks all rosy. The house disappears from sight as they leave the lawn, wandering deeper into the forest garden until all they can see are the claret-coloured shutters, glistening through the trees.

Robbie dives into a heap of leaves and throws two handfuls on his sister's head. Liselotte screams with laughter. Kathinka takes the shortcut, diving head down into a heap before Lien quickly pulls her out.

That afternoon the little ones are drowsy and tired from playing outside, and for the first time in months all three of them fall asleep like a log without whining. After Janny has put the children to bed, she checks in on her father. She finds him in the living room, stoking the fire to dispel the icy cold his wife let in when she was cleaning earlier that day. His fragility strikes her. He looks so different from the round, loud merchant he was in Amsterdam. The Germans took more than his freedom when they kept him imprisoned for ten days. On top of that came the journey to The High Nest, which was hard, too hard, really – his resilience has run out. She takes the log Joseph is holding and has him sit in the comfortable chair at one of the large side windows, where the view of the forest is magical.

**Before the** rest of the family came to The High Nest, Eberhard had made a few trips to Naarden on his own and moved part of their belongings. The first time he also brought Herbert, whom he transferred to one of their contacts. The boy would go to a new hiding place, closer to his parents.

Each time Eberhard approaches Amsterdam Centraal Station with his heaps of luggage, he is sweating with fear. But the influx of evacuees from coastal areas has become enormous – he can always blend into the crowds. It is a mass migration; men and women scurrying across the platforms in a daze with their children, grandparents, pets and furniture, some with a clear destination in mind, others without the prospect of an alternative address.

The steps are overcrowded, the main hall bursting

at the seams with swarms of people, branching off towards the station square. This is perfect for Eberhard, who, with his bags and suitcases, does not attract any attention. After changing for Naarden-Bussum station, it is about a three-mile walk to The High Nest – mostly through the heath.

He had seen the piano the very first time he entered the villa, but there had been no opportunity to tell Lientje about it. Too much going on. He travels back to Naarden-Bussum station, empty-handed, on to Amsterdam, Alkmaar, the steam tram to Bergen. His last trip as a workhorse.

When he arrives in Bergen, he finds the summer cottage empty and dark. There is a smell of bleach, the curtains are drawn. It is as if they have never lived there. Lien has left with Kathinka, Eberhard's detailed instructions impressed on her mind.

He locks up, puts the key in the letter box of the main house and walks to Janny's bungalow at the other side of the deer park. There, a similar scene awaits. The home is spotless, chairs around the dining table all pushed in, not a crumb on the carpet. No trace of the little children who have been roaming around here for months.

In a dark corner of the living room, Joseph is waiting in an armchair.

'Come,' Eberhard says, offering his father-in-law his arm. For a moment Joseph seems to have no intention to move. He has not left the cottage since they came here to hide. Eberhard takes his upper arm and helps him to get up, cross the threshold to their next shelter.

On the train to Amsterdam, Joseph's discomfort becomes more and more visible. His breathing is heavy and he keeps looking around. Without seeing much, really; his last eye surgery failed and, despite his jam-jar glasses, he cannot tell the difference between a soldier and a coalman. It makes Eberhard nervous, but he cannot reassure the old man without giving both of them away.

As the train enters Amsterdam Centraal Station, night falls over the canals. The crowds have dissolved; the platforms are mostly deserted. Eberhard thinks of the mutes underneath the stairs and prays Father will hold his own. On the platform, Joseph briefly hesitates before the familiar arrival sign of his beloved city; Eberhard believes he might wiggle free to walk home, down the canal towards Weesperstraat, turn left, through the front door, straight to his own comfortable chair. He can find the way with his eyes closed. Eberhard tightens his grip around Father's upper arm, but there is no need. Joseph turns around and follows him in silence to the next train.

The last part is the hardest. When they walk out of Naarden-Bussum station, they are welcomed by a rain shower. No cloudburst, but the type of steady rain you hardly notice until suddenly your coat has become heavy and is sticking to your skin. Both of them are exhausted and Joseph is taking small, unsteady steps. But Eberhard is in no hurry – this is their last journey. All that matters is arriving, even if it takes them all night.

At first they pass well-lit living rooms, people on sofas, people walking to the kitchen, unaware of being watched. Carefree people. As they leave the town centre of Naarden, houses thin out and the lights appear at larger intervals. The street is dead quiet, only the soft thrumming of raindrops on asphalt follows them, washes their footsteps away. Joseph's spectacles have steamed up and water is running from his forehead, over the glass, onto his cheeks, but his gaze is fixed on the ground as he lets his son-in-law guide him.

After walking in silence, arms linked, for over thirty minutes, a rhythmic squeaking closes in on them. They hold still. Eberhard feels a shiver run through the old body beside him. He cannot tell if it is cold or fear.

Eberhard peers into the night, wondering if he should pull Joseph into the shrubs. Then he recognizes the sounds of steadily moving pedals grating a mudguard, of bicycle tyres hissing softly on the wet road surface. A bent silhouette passes, six feet away, without noticing them in the dark. They continue on their way with relief.

Eberhard does not know how long it took them, but when they finally arrive at The High Nest, he can tell from their tight faces how worried they must have been. They were all sat waiting in the living room with the curtains closed. The flickering candle illuminates the deep lines around Fietje's mouth. She gratefully takes her husband from Eberhard and gently dries his face with a towel.

Eberhard will later confess to Lien it was one of the most anxious nights of his life. But they made it. All ten of them.

**And so** begins, in February 1943, the extraordinary Brilleslijper enterprise at The High Nest – host family, hiding place, underground centre.

Since July 1942, trains to Westerbork and beyond have been running without a pause and, everywhere in the country, Jews are looking for places to hide. In this third year of occupation, aggression stops at nothing and Nazi ideology is practised even without German pressure. As a young Dutch police officer says: 'It's no proper Sunday unless we beat a couple of Jews to a pulp.'

Still, there are many non-Jewish Dutch who help others. But the relationship is always skewed. People in hiding are very aware that they eat from the supplies of their host family and they live in a space not intended for them. Children in hiding, added to an unknown family, sense they must not be difficult; the mercy of the host or hostess is a lifeline which, at any given moment, can be cut.

Janny and Bob have officially moved to Naarden with their two children, but the rest of the party is illegal and wanted. Joseph and Fietje for being Jewish and because they should have reported in Amsterdam. Jaap because he is Jewish and worked for the resistance from his bicycle parking operation. Eberhard because he is a German deserter, guilty of racial disgrace by fathering a child with a Jewish woman. Lien because she is Jewish and connected to the disappearance of Eberhard. It is Janny's good fortune she is not registered as Jewish – and she married her husband before the law forbade her to.

Perfect administration and well-oiled logistics ensure that deportations from the Netherlands run smoothly. Nonetheless, the Germans become aware that large numbers of Jews are missing. About 25,000 people have disappeared; they have not reported and their present whereabouts are unknown.

In March 1943, one month after the Brilleslijper family moved into The High Nest, the authorities call in the Henneicke Column, the men travelling the Netherlands from their Amsterdam office, to inventory the properties of deported Jews. Their new job is in line with their previous activities but brings in a lot more money – they will be hunting for Jews in hiding, at a premium of seven guilders and fifty cents per head.

# 2

# The Free Artist

Before long, the resistance spreads the news about a safe and well-hidden place, close to Amsterdam, run by two Jewish sisters. They have only just moved into The High Nest when Janny starts bringing in more people in distress. Trees Lemaire, her friend and colleague at the PBC, asks her to take in an acquaintance: Jetty Druijff, with her fiancé Simon van Kreveld, son of a well-known paediatrician. Pauline van den Berg arrives via Haakon and Mieke Stotijn. With her red hair, steel-blue eyes and Rotterdam accent, it is hard not to notice her. She goes by the name of Aagje Honing and moves in as 'the maid'. Bram and Loes Teixeira de Mattos, two elderly friends of Bob and Janny, come to The High Nest from The Hague with their daughter Rita and son-in-law Willi Jaeger.

And so, in the course of February 1943, the household is made up of a core group of seventeen people already. Those are joined by a steady stream of visitors seeking shelter for a short while; a few days, weeks, months. Joseph urges his daughter to be cautious, but Janny doesn't give an inch and Joseph doesn't really want to stop her, either; desperate times call for desperate measures. It has become increasingly difficult to find somewhere to hide; people are frightened. Janny is frightened too, but she never refuses anyone access to The High Nest, even when, at times, twenty to twenty-five people are staying in the house.

Most of them are from the artistic scene, via Lien and Eberhard, and from the resistance, via Bob and Janny. The house is located in the heart of the Netherlands and as such a perfect stopover. Sometimes Jan and Aleid Hemelrijk bring guests, and their former Amsterdam neighbours, Leo and Loes Fuks, seek shelter at The High Nest too.

Leo is a specialist in the Yiddish language, which he starts teaching Lien. Before the occupation, both of them were members of Sch.-Anski, the Eastern Jewish cultural society promoting Yiddish literature, art and drama. Leo was their secretary and Lien studied the songs she would later specialize in. Until the war came,

Lien performed throughout the Netherlands as a solo singer, with Eberhard as her regular accompanist. Her stage name, Lin Jaldati, was from the lyrics to a Hebrew song: '*Jalda Jaldati, Jaffa Jaffati*', 'Girl, my girl, Beauty, my beauty'. During the occupation, performances became few and far between, and those last months in Bergen went by without any music at all. Eberhard did not have a piano at his disposal; Lien was not in the mood for singing or dancing. It would have been too dangerous at that.

But The High Nest is like a fortress: outside it seems heavy and robust, but inside there is light and space – and for the first time in a long while, the residents feel free to live, to move. Slowly they speak out loud, laugh again. Eberhard claims the piano in the front room and spends hours on end practising complex scores, his back bent. Lien picks up her repertoire and others indulge in playing music too; Simon on the drums they found in the shed and Pauline, or Red Puck as they call her, practises the violin in the gazebo.

At the height of the war, The High Nest must have produced more noise than all the summer holidays of the Jansen sisters combined. Sometimes Janny, after running errands for the resistance all day, walks home through the forest and is welcomed by a cacophony of sounds even before she can see the house – it is as if the trees and the animals sing for her, accompanied by the drumming sound of the earth beneath her.

Providing for at least twenty people is not easy. Bob's part is crucial here; he brings in the money. He leaves the villa early each morning and rides to the Food Supply Office in Weesp. On his bicycle – a privilege very few Dutch people still have; the bikes belonging to Jewish people were claimed last year and these days non-Jewish civilians are often forced to give their bicycle to German soldiers too. Everything on wheels is precious: prams, wheelbarrows, home-made cargo bikes and unicycles. To save their bikes from being commandeered, people give them wooden wheels or put a small scooter wheel at the front – the Germans turn their nose up at those strange creations. But the mayor of Naarden gives Bob a special permit stating his bicycle is 'required in the exercise of his duty as civil servant at the Agricultural Crisis Organisation'. The bike is invaluable and saves an incredible amount of time when they, as soon as Bob has returned from work in the afternoon, ride to the surrounding villages to buy bottles of milk and heavy sacks of rice and wheat for everyone.

Bob's boss is the local office manager of the Food

Commissioner for North Holland, but he is a member of the DNP, so not someone Bob can take into his confidence. Instead, Bob steals coupons and waybills on a daily basis – official documents with all the stamps required for food and transport. Checks are strict; you cannot get anywhere without papers these days. Bob and Janny pass most of the documents on to Mik van Gilse or Frits Reuter, who further distribute them.

Bob receives a salary of 150 guilders per month from the North Holland Government Office – by no means enough to cover the rent and food for everyone. Some of the guests bring in a little money, but the Brilleslijper family desperately needs more to feed all those mouths. When Mik next visits The High Nest, he has a solution from the most unlikely place – connecting the Nest directly to the largest brewer in the Netherlands.

**Mik looks** forward to his trips to Naarden. The forest, the house filled with friends he can trust, like a commune of resistance in wartime. The peace and quiet do him good. Soothe him. He is only twenty-six years old and has known nothing but stress and danger. When he gets on the train at Amsterdam Centraal Station, having passed the checks unscathed, he slumps down in a compartment, which seems emptier each month, and his narrow shoulders slowly begin to relax. He is a precocious twenty-something with too many responsibilities – not unlike his dear friend Janny.

At a young age, Mik travelled to Spain to report on the Spanish Civil War, while his brother Janrik joined the CPN. 'Never underestimate the opponent and always remain on your guard,' has always been their motto. Their current resistance is met with approval, and it seems more and more people are joining in. Another success is his underground society of artists with its own magazine called *The Free Artist*.

Mik had started *The Free Artist* with his father Jan van Gilse, composer, and his friend Gerrit van der Veen, sculptor, to mobi-lize resistance against the *Kulturkammer* (the Reich's Chamber of Culture). Many people joined them – prominent writers, painters, musicians, journalists – and a few wealthy folks, well-disposed towards their cause, donated money. Artists refusing to register at the *Kulturkammer* lose their income, so the financial support is more than welcome.

But his activities are starting to attract too much attention; there is not only *The Free Artist* and the PBC, but also resistance group CS-6, in which he thinks up sabotage acts with his friend Gerrit Kastein. The *Sicherheitspolizei* has been close on their heels for some time, but so far they have always managed to outsmart them. The High Nest is the only place where Mik can catch his breath.

Today, Mik has brought the latest edition of *The Free Artist* for the Brilleslijper family; tucked underneath his waistband, the paper rustles at each move. They have made a couple of thousand copies, a fantastic print run, which go hand to hand. The magazine is not for keeping – it must reach as many readers as possible. On the cover they have printed: THIS COPY IS NOT JUST FOR YOU – PASS IT ON. *The Free Artist* has grown into a proper underground publication, supported, completed and read by influential artists and wealthy benefactors. The thought briefly fills Mik with optimism and pride, but those feelings are smothered when he remembers the dangerous plan he is devising with Gerrit van der Veen and a few other resistance friends.

At 36 Plantage Kerklaan, next to the entrance of the zoo, Artis, is the Amsterdam register. This is where the records of some 70,000 Jews are kept; the administrative driving force behind the Nazi trains. The PBC tries to supply as many Jews as possible with forged identity cards, but it is not enough. Carrying identification papers became compulsory in 1940, the identity card was introduced in 1941, and since then, Jews are cornered by the administrative capacities of Dutch civil servants. Gerrit figured that one action would solve all of their problems: blowing up the register. Without – this is of paramount importance – any casualties. It is a complex job. At night, all possible tactics cross Mik's mind, but he has not as yet found the perfect strategy.

At Naarden-Bussum station he gets off, ignores the tram stop and begins the long walk to The High Nest. It is cold but he is glowing with effort and enjoys being in nature. Heavy buds in all the trees announce the arrival of spring.

After a warm welcome by Lien, Jaap, Joseph and Fietje – Janny and Bob are out working – Mik and Eberhard leave the hustle and bustle of the house, taking a random forest path towards the water. Eberhard can tell Mik is excited about something and, as soon as they find themselves in the shelter of the trees, he drops the chit-chat and puts his arm around his friend.

'Spill the beans. What do you want to tell me?'

'That obvious?'

Mik smiles, looks around as if squirrels might overhear them, lowers his voice.

'Listen. *The Free Artist* is a success. It has actually become a broad underground organization, with a large following among artists as well as wealthy folks who want to do something but don't know how.'

Eberhard nods.

'We have a great new backer. You will never guess who it is.'

They walk on and Eberhard raises his eyebrows, curious about the name.

'The king of all brewers. Heineken.'

Mik glances sideways to see his friend's expression. Eberhard stops and turns toward him.

'Are you serious?'

'Yes,' says Mik. 'Dirk Stikker, their general manager, has promised us one million guilders. One million!'

They both draw a deep breath, impressed by the intangible number, then walk on, climbing a small hill, the last barrier between the forest and the water. They are panting, their shoes slipping away in the loose sand.

'Well,' Mik mumbles, placing his feet in Eberhard's large steps, 'of course he's making a good deal of money out of those beer-sodden Krauts.'

They stand side by side on the top, catching their breath. At the foot of the hill, behind a strip of sand and a fringe of reeds, lies the Lake IJsselmeer. It is cold, but calm. The water is motionless and grey, the sky crisp and clear, no clouds, no rays of light.

Mik breaks the silence.

'From now on you and Lien, as underground artists,

will receive a monthly allowance from *The Free Artist*, so you can make ends meet.'

Eberhard's skinny face breaks into a smile. He had shared with Mik how embarrassed he felt to see everyone bringing in something to keep the oversized household at the Nest going. Bob earns money for his family, most guests contribute something – it's only him, Lien, Jaap, Joseph and Fietje who are cut off from any flow of money. This amount is not just for Eberhard and Lien, it is for the entire Brilleslijper family – there's no need for Mik to tell him that.

'That's settled, then.'

Mik runs down the hill, his arms wide like the wings of a bird. Eberhard follows him. They turn onto the path on the right, which leads them along the water towards Huizen.

Before he leaves, Mik gives Eberhard the address of a contact in Laren, where he can collect the money each month.

'He will also give you stolen coupons to use for the family,' Mik whispers when they embrace each other, 'but don't tell anyone, all right?'

# 3
# Neighbours

One day Janny receives a letter from the council. The mayor of Naarden wants to discuss 'irregularities in her identity card' with her and Janny has to report within the fortified walls, in the beautiful town hall opposite the Great Church. On her walk there, across the heath and among the trees, bare but sprouting promisingly, she realizes once again how close they are. To the village and to its mayor, unaware of what is happening in his very own forest.

As Eberhard predicted, Mussert, Hitler and the mayor stare at her unanimously in the meeting room. Janny goes weak at the knees. Van Leeuwen does not waste any time.

'Mrs Brandes, there is something amiss with your identity card.'

Throbbing temples, spots dancing in her eyes, Janny plays ignorant and looks at him sheepishly.

'There are two identity cards, both apparently yours. I don't think that is possible, do you?'

Janny shakes her head, wondering how this might have happened. The one thing she can think of is that her contact at the registry office in Amsterdam failed to destroy her original identity card. That would explain why there are now two – the original and the new one he made with different, false data. Her game is up. It is finished. She tries to swallow but her throat is too thick.

'Mrs Brandes,' says the mayor, 'had I not known your husband, and had I not very much respected him as a civil servant, I would have had to report this. Do you understand?'

At first, Janny believes she has misheard what he said. She stares at the mayor, a puzzled look on her face, but then she pulls herself together. The spots in her eyes disappear, the throbbing sinks down to her wrists.

'I do. Of course. I have no idea how this could have happened, but I'll take care of it.'

'Please do.'

A short nod and the mayor turns around. Their conversation is finished.

Outside, Janny leans against the church wall and tries to steady her breath. She feels light-headed. Laughter wells. She covers her mouth with her hand, aware of her narrow escape, and thinks: how could this have happened?

She remembers a day in winter, last year. She had travelled from The Hague to Amsterdam, Liselotte in the pram, Robbie holding her hand, to collect a parcel for the Party. She didn't know what it was, but it had felt remarkably heavy. She had wrapped the parcel in canvas and hid it underneath the mattress in the pram. On the train, the pram went into storage. Janny took the receipt and her children and sat down in a regular compartment. Upon arrival in The Hague, as she went to collect the pram, Janny could not find the receipt. The memory is still vivid: she was standing on the cold platform in the pouring rain, one child on her arm, the other holding her hand, a railway officer staring at her rummaging through her pockets, the children's pockets, panicking. As she pulled off her glove to search once more, the ticket flew out of its lining. She could have hit herself. Instead she managed a smile, handed the officer the receipt and took the pram with smuggled goods. She put her daughter on the mattress and headed home as calmly as she could.

When she passed a large department store, the

window reflected two men in long raincoats walking behind her. A tap on her shoulder.

'Identity card, please.'

While one of them studied her papers, the other scanned her, head to toe. Janny told herself she was just an ordinary mother, eager to take her children home, but it felt as if she would die on the spot.

'Brilleslijper – are you not Jewish?'

'Not at all. My mother's name is Gerritse; she is not Jewish. My father's name is Brilleslijper. He's half-Jewish and lives in Batavia.'

The silence lasted long and the rain persisted. It no longer bothered her, if only she could get the children out of here. Liselotte started to cry, but Janny didn't want to pick her up from the pram; she was the protective layer of her secret mission.

A nod and she was free to go. Frits Reuter told her later what the heavy parcel was: a dismounted machine gun for the resistance.

After this incident her contact had altered her identity card. The only thing she can think of now is that he did not destroy her original papers at the time.

Back at The High Nest, her father flushes with anger when she tells her story. He waves his finger close to her face.

'Perilous. What you are doing is perilous! What

if that mayor decides to walk up here on a Sunday to have a look around? What if he decides to retrieve your papers at the Jewish Council?'

He paces up and down the living room, opens his mouth, shuts it again. He cannot find the words to express his concern for his daughter.

Janny realizes she hasn't even thought of that; if her contact has not destroyed the original identity card, the Jewish Council also has her papers in their card index. She thinks out loud and upon the words 'Jewish Council', Joseph looks at his daughter, his eyes narrowed.

'Those bastards,' he mutters.

'Calm now,' she says, placing a hand on his arm. 'I'll take care of it.'

The next day, Janny takes the train to Amsterdam and visits Nathan Notowicz, a stateless communist from Poland, who lived in Germany until he fled the Nazis. When the war came, he joined part of a resistance group helping Jewish people to find shelter. Nathan has a kind heart, an iron fist and an intense dislike of collaborators. Janny can usually fend for herself, but as a woman she stands little chance at the Council – and this mission is too important to fail.

Together, they go to the Jewish Council building on the Nieuwe Keizersgracht, where they kindly ask the Jewish administrator in charge to remove Janny's records. He refuses. With a subtle gesture, Nathan sends Janny outside.

She doesn't have to wait long. After five minutes, Nathan calmly pulls the door shut behind him and with a mischievous smile, he gives Janny the thumbs up. She doesn't know what he has threatened to do, and his method was probably not the most elegant, but all of her papers are immediately destroyed.

**And then** there is a brush with the Dutch Nazi heads. In a way, a country house, run by Jews, full of people in hiding, *here* in the forests of Naarden, is something of a Trojan horse; this area is crawling with Fascists, twice as many as the national average. The beautiful villas of Naarden and Bussum often belong to fanatical Nazis.

Most DNP voters are middle-class – office staff and business owners – and upper-class people. Although Nazi ideology is aimed at the working class, the party is far less popular there.

Even before the occupation, the DNP had many supporters in expensive parts of Amsterdam as well as in the wealthy Hilversum area; people living in comfort, reluctant to share their wealth and afraid to be worse off. Anti-Semitic sentiments and aversion to 'foreign elements' come into play as well, even though most Jews are Dutch citizens. To the extent that the more Jews a municipality counts, the more people vote for the DNP. The area between Amsterdam and Hilversum has a relatively large Jewish community, which expanded in the late 1930s, when several hundred German refugees arrived.

In 1942, Dutch Nazis set up the Voluntary Police Support, VHP, a pompous Fascist neighbourhood watch. It is no co-incidence that Hilversum, Bussum *and* Naarden are among the dozen villages and cities where the VHP operates.

Father Joseph has often said: 'We must watch these people here. Mark my words. The rich always turn their heads towards the sun; they have too much to lose to offer any resistance.'

Indeed, The High Nest is literally surrounded by Dutch Nazis. In the same nature reserve where the villa is located lies an estate called 'Oud Bussum'. It is only a short walk from The Nest and owned by fabulously wealthy Nazi Pieter van Leeuwen Boomkamp. Reichsmarschall Göring, also referred to as Fat Hermann, briefly stayed at Oud Bussum when he visited the Netherlands in 1940. And only two and a half miles from The High Nest, both in Naarden and in Bussum, large numbers of German soldiers are stationed. Anton Mussert, leader of the DNP, personally gave a speech at the city gates of Naarden when the war started.

But that isn't all. The very same Mussert chose the wild nature reserve, perfect shelter for Jews, a stone's throw from Amsterdam, as his own hiding place too.

Anton Mussert knew it was coming: war. He also knew that the Dutch would not be able to offer much resistance. But as the May 1940 occupation drew near, he began to worry that fights might break out between the Dutch and members of his DNP in those first chaotic days after the German invasion. So, in a meeting with his party heads in Utrecht, Mussert says he is considering seeking shelter for at least four days – Dutch resistance will not last much longer, he thinks. They all agree that their party leader's safety is of the utmost importance; after the capitulation, the people will desperately need him, architect of a new future for the Netherlands.

For several weeks, Mussert stays with various Nazi comrades throughout the country, looking for the best place to hide. His aide, Tonny Kessler, is searching too and comes up with the perfect location.

Kessler has visited the hiding place several times and has spoken to the house owners, Mr and Mrs Gooijers, both confirmed Nazis. Would they, he asked, be prepared to hide 180 pounds of illegal documents? Their answer is a firm 'yes'. Kessler is certain these people understand the future of the DNP rests upon their shoulders. The one thing left to mention is that he was referring to 176 pounds of Mussert.

**Thursday, 9 May 1940** is a beautiful summery evening. Anton Mussert leaves the DNP headquarters in Utrecht after a meeting and climbs into the Pontiac convertible waiting for him. His chauffeur starts the engine and drives him to Bilthoven, where he is staying.

In the early hours of the next morning, Mussert, like many Dutch people, wakes to the thundering sound of war. He listens to the radio and waits until seven thirty in the morning, when the businessmen of Bilthoven are getting ready to leave their homes, calls his chauffeur and they drive straight to Tonny Kessler in Naarden. From there, they will make their way to the hiding place, the remote house of comrade Gooijer. Even Mussert's wife doesn't know where he goes into voluntary exile.

Three times the car is held by soldiers at checkpoints, but each time they are allowed to pass. The Pontiac stops in Naarden, where Mussert and Kessler say goodbye to the chauffeur and continue their journey on foot. They walk through the vast heath in silence.

Behind them is Naarden, before them lies Huizen. They are walking on the Naarderstraat, the old road connecting the two villages. Both the tramline and all the traffic have been moved to Nieuwe Bussumerweg, parallel to this street, so here, not a single living soul can be found.

The road narrows and along the verges, tall trees raise their thick leaves to the sky. On their right, the men pass an old toll booth, out of use for years. On their left, a bit further on, is their destination.

The aide and his distinguished guest stop at a simple farmhouse, with one floor and an attic. The road is deserted, the house isolated, tucked away in the foliage. It is Friday, 10 May 1940, the German invasion has just begun and Anton Mussert has taken himself to a place of safety.

The house has a small front garden with a hedge hiding the place from view in flowering season. At the back is a wild garden, 300 feet long. Some 600 feet further, the nature reserve forest begins. On one side of the house is a cycle path, running through the forest towards the lake, and on the other side there's nothing but farmland. Apart from a country house around the corner, in the forest, it is completely deserted.

Behind the house, at the back of the garden, a large deadwood hedge serves as a fence. A trench, dug underneath the hedge in the previous war, is overgrown with shrubs. Mussert is very pleased with the place.

Gooijer and his wife have diligently prepared their small attic for their esteemed guest. But Mussert is not at ease; on the radio he hears about nationwide house searches, hundreds of Dutch Nazis being arrested. Instead of barricading himself in the attic, he hides in the trench at the back of the garden – a suggestion from Mrs Gooijer, a woman of German origin, proud to act as guardian angel to the leader.

As the Netherlands are in chaos and the police, in those first days of the war, are fanatically hunting Dutch Nazis, Anton Mussert is lying in a trench, his stomach pressed against the cold soil, catching a severe cold and waiting to see if these days will mark the end of his career, or his first appearance in national history books.

Local police officers search the house twice. They are looking for comrade Gooijer and his brother-in-law, both loyal Nazis, and on the second attempt they find Gooijer and take him. They turn the entire house and the adjacent barn upside down, but don't look in the rear of the garden, where the great Dutch Nazi leader is counting worms in a ditch.

When Gooijer is released that night and looks for Mussert at home, he is alarmed not to find him. Gooijer creeps around his own garden, along the hedge, hissing at Mussert as if looking for a lost cat. He softly whistles the Dutch Nazi song 'Soldiers in Black', the words echoing in his mind:

The fight has flared up
Discord must go away
From our beautiful land
Oppressed to this day
New spirit breaks ground
We are all ready
Let the united front fight
On the streets we are steady
Come, my comrade, come take a stand
For us, people, for our Netherland
Soldiers in Black is who we are
Supporting Mussert in this war.

After a while, Mussert's sandy face pops up and comrade Gooijers breathes a sigh of relief. While the Netherlands are on the eve of five years of death and destruction, Mussert sits down to a meal of baked potato wedges, lettuce and fried egg.

The next day is Anton Mussert's forty-sixth birthday. He considers it safe enough to stay in the room upstairs, where Mrs Gooijer kindly brings him a bunch of flowers and food. The Dutch hold out a day longer than he had predicted, but on Tuesday, 14 May, the capitulation is announced on the radio.

Mussert puts on his best suit, leaves the farmhouse and hoists the Dutch Nazi flag at the Party headquarters in Utrecht. The grim black-and-red stripes, a triangle with the golden lion in the middle, triumphantly flutter in the breeze.

The story of Mussert hiding at the decisive moment is soon picked up and ridiculed in anti-Fascist circles. All sorts of hiding places buzz around – from gypsy caravans to haystacks – and in the following years it will remain a popular topic among cartoonists.

Comrade Gooijer's farmhouse becomes a pilgrimage site for Dutch Nazis, hundreds of them flocking to see where their leader was kept in safety for them. They proudly sign their name in Mrs Gooijer's guestbook with the words 'faithful to our leader' written elegantly on its cover. She puts the clothes Mussert wore on display in the attic; an altar on the place where the leader of the Dutch people was saved.

When the Brilleslijper family seek shelter in Naarden, Mussert is staying close by again – not in hiding this time. Although officially stationed in Utrecht, he will spend most of the war at his mistress' place, around the corner from The High Nest.

Mussert has a special fondness for women he is related to. He has married his aunt – one of his mother's sisters – eighteen years his senior and well into her sixties. Royal dispensation was required for their marriage in 1917, being relatives in the third degree. In addition to his supposed hiding place, the resistance mocks Mussert's relationship: 'for anyone who wants to keep the race pure, marrying their auntie is the perfect cure' is an often-heard joke.

Early in the war, Mussert meets his second cousin Maria 'Marietje' Mijnlieff – her mother, Helena, is a niece to both his mother and his wife. He falls madly in love with the young girl. In symbolic exchange for a diamond necklace, he lends Helena the purchase price of a beautiful villa in Naarden, where, in November 1942, she and Marietje move. Villa *Eik en Linde*, Oak and Lime, becomes Mussert's wartime love nest. He often visits and when in 1943 his own house in Utrecht is cleared for defensive measures, *Eik en Linde*, much to his wife's dismay, becomes his permanent residence.

**One day,** Japie goes out to check his traps in the forest and returns to The Nest not with pheasants for his mother to cook, but with the limp body of a well-fed cat. Fietje is horrified and quickly tells him to bury the beast at the back of the garden, hoping no one will come and look for it.

The day after the cat murder, Janny returns from her resistance work. It is early in the evening and she has had a long day. From the station she takes the tram, gets off at Nieuwe Bussumerweg, walks the familiar route along Ericaweg to the path towards the villa. After a few minutes she suddenly hears a woman's voice ahead of her. She quickly leaves the path and vanishes in the thick bushes along the verge. Cautiously crouching, she carries on as the voice sounds louder and louder.

'Puss, puss, puss!'

Twenty footsteps away from Janny is woman, face turned towards the forest, shaking a bowl of food, calling for her cat.

'Puss, puss, puss!'

She sounds as if her child is missing and looks around in despair.

Janny presses her back into the prickly plants and holds her breath. She curses her younger brother. They have murdered this lady's cat and now of course she's trying to find it. She quickly retreats deeper into the forest, making her way through shrubs and thorns until she's safely home.

When she tells the story, Jaap bursts out laughing,

but Joseph immediately cuts him off and forbids his son ever to use the traps again. Jaap has to stand guard at the grave in the garden – the cat has been dug up by a dog once before – and someone else is stationed as lookout on the first floor. All residents are told not to leave the house, play music or make any noise in the following days until they are certain the danger has passed.

Later, Janny will discover that the cat lady is one of the most fanatical Nazis in the area – a kind of aunt to Mussert. Even when she doesn't turn up on their doorstep, asking for her pet, they find it hard to laugh about what happened.

# 4

# Masks

Eberhard has more time for his music than ever. In their life before the war they had to earn money, but now, hiding in what feels like a sanctuary in no-man's-land, he and Lien have the freedom to practise and play for days on end. He has joined the Amsterdam Music Library under his false name to get piano arrangements based on operas. He borrows as many as he can and spends hours behind the piano. He studies until his knuckles crack and drives the other residents crazy. This has nothing to do with his music – most of the people arriving at The Nest suffer from overstrained nerves because of their flight, the years of not trusting others, the fear of being found. Once they realize their only witnesses are often just deer, foxes and badgers, they surrender to the music.

First, Eberhard and Lien cherish the fortress walls of The High Nest – a beautiful sound barrier, too – but soon their ambition grows. The new regime has condemned the entire country to a spartan existence, but from The High Nest an underground web of artists will arise, livening up the area, and restoring the dazzling pre-war life of Amsterdam and The Hague to some of its former glory.

One morning, when Eberhard is walking in the forest with Kathinka, he notices a figure between the distant trees. Narrow and straight as a bare pine, its head bright white. Eberhard pushes the girl behind his back and they hide behind a shrub as the man comes closer.

'Karel?'

Eberhard steps out of the cover and calls through the forest. A startled bird flaps away.

'Karel Poons?'

The man holds still. His skin seems transparent, his hair bleached. Sharp eyes staring in their direction.

'Yes?'

Eberhard briskly walks towards him, happily surprised. Karel was the star in the Yvonne Georgi ballet; they have often watched him dance in the theatre. Lien came home from shopping one day adamant she had seen Karel walking around Huizen – but Eberhard had not paid any attention. Excited to have met at this strange place, they tell each other about their wanderings.

In 1941, Karel Poons, Jewish ballet dancer, was forced by the Nazis to leave his ensemble and move to a Jewish neighbourhood in Amsterdam. He felt suspicious and decided to vanish from the face of the earth. He bleached his hair with a bottle of hydrogen peroxide and with his steel-blue eyes looked like a Frisian farmer's son. At least, he thought he did, but when Janny sees him, she bursts out laughing. Karel, as she'll tell Lien later, still looks very Jewish to her.

When he and Eberhard run into each other, Karel has already been hiding in a modern villa in Huizen for some time, where the owner, Cecile Hanedoes, had enough space for him to create a dance room. Karel trains every day to keep up his technique and choreographs dances to perform for Cecile.

Eberhard brings Karel to Lien and their meeting results in a plan. In Laren, a village down the road, they can rent a proper dance studio with mirrors and a barre on the wall. Twice a week, Lien and Karel come to the studio to train and devise performances they intend to put on after the war.

Eberhard and Karel become close friends too. The first thing they do is get new forged documents – his fake identity card makes Eberhard laugh when he sees it – and coupons to get through the war.

Their artistic circle widens through Karel. During one of their dancing sessions in the studio, Lien tells him what performances she used to make. They are Yiddish dances, accompanied by Eberhard on piano, and she would love to include them in her repertoire. She is thinking of using masks but wonders how to save herself from looking ridiculous and unprofessional with papier mâché masks straight from a hobby room.

Karel has an idea: his landlady, Cecile, once introduced him to an artist in Blaricum – she is somewhat strange but very talented. She paints and makes sculptures, puppets, marionettes, and when they met, she told Karel she was thinking of experimenting with masks too. Her name is Grietje Kots and, most importantly, she can be trusted.

Lien visits the lady in the forest studio where she lives and works. Grietje prefers not to leave her garden, which she tends with great devotion and where she can often be found discussing life with her invisible forest friends, a bird on one hand, a slice of stale bread in the other. The beautiful little farm with thatched roof, consistently referred to as 'hut' by Grietje, has no kitchen or other bourgeois comforts, but she is very content living there with her trees, animals and art.

When Lien shares her ideas about the Yiddish dances and the masks she pictures, Grietje is instantly inspired. As she studies Lien, from her elegant ballet feet to her striking face, framed by black curls, ideas begin to take shape in her mind. She invites Lien to come back with Eberhard and play for her, so she can get to work.

And so, in the early spring of 1943, Eberhard and Lien find themselves back onstage, performing to Grietje in her 'hut'. She starts sketching and drawing immediately: with fine, black strokes on heavy paper, she portrays Lien as Pierrot. Large eyes with a melancholic look, a straight nose, high cheekbones, her black hair pulled back tightly. On the same page, beside Lien's face, she draws the masks she has in mind for her, each of them inspired by the subject of the song.

She draws a golem mask, for the song based on the Jewish legend of the rabbi who turns a shapeless lump of clay into a living human being. The mask is gloomy and unrefined, close-set eyes sunken deep into the skull, a protruding lower jaw and thick, pouty lips – and yet it's elegantly shaped, both abstract and realistic. Grietje draws Lien in profile as well, with a sharp nose and tormented look, a beautiful death mask in the foreground. It has the characteristic shape of a skull, but the eye sockets are not empty; they have eyelids, round and closed – as if death might change its mind at any moment.

Lien is over the moon with the masks. First, Grietje makes them out of newspapers and baking paper, simple and light with a peachy structure and a wooden stalk for Lien to hold them in front of her face. She later makes some out of plaster too. Eberhard and Lien work on their repertoire of Jewish songs and quickly begin to organize underground concerts. Grietje knows plenty of local artists and enthusiasts, and many resistance friends are interested too.

And so in 1943, when the Nazis have dropped their masks and one train after the other leaves Westerbork filled with Jews, headed for the extermination camps in the east, Yiddish culture and other arts flourish at The High Nest. There is dance, music, song and recitation. Simon drums, Puck plays the violin and Jaap builds Kathinka a little piano. Lien uses the death mask for a Yiddish story and the unrefined mask in a performance on golems. At Grietje's place, the hut in Blaricum, Eberhard and Lien give a series of house concerts too. The proceeds of those soirées always go to *The Free Artist*. Mik tells them others around the country are doing the same: raising money by performing illegal concerts for the magazine to enlarge the print run and to expand the resistance.

Lien and Eberhard are cautious; they never let people arrive or leave at the same time and always have others acting as lookouts. While they freely play music inside and the audience can briefly relax, their watchmen form a cordon around the house, alert to each sound or sudden light flashing in the dark. Afterwards, the guests quietly dissolve into the night – without a single Nazi, German soldier or overzealous neighbour even noticing they were there.

# 5

# Associates

The days are growing longer and the cold leaves the ground. The heath and the trees around the house begin to blossom and Janny loves seeing the seasons change, literally right under her nose, for the first time. She had only seen The High Nest in cold winter months – the house too large to heat, a permanent smell of fire and damp nestled in their clothes. Now, the surroundings are going through a metamorphosis and Janny is amazed to see the villa changing right before her eyes. The IJsselmeer water begins to melt, monotonous charcoal grey giving way to steel blue. Branches, first clawing at the sky around the house, unwind, reach for each other, their buds sprouting. The reeds on the roof begin to brighten, cast off the sombre shadow of the forest, moss green slowly changing into yellow ochre, and the shutters, matte and heavy in dark winter months, seem covered with new gloss, their claret gleaming dramatically in the morning sun.

Before the first sunbeams reach the large windows and brighten the attic, Janny has usually been woken up by birds bursting into song in the early hours of the morning. The sound comes from all sides; the exuberant tweeting and twittering of males attracting mates delights her and she often lies quietly in bed, listening to their concert, the soothing breathing of Bob and the children by her side.

At breakfast they discuss what strange noises they heard in the night. Paranoia has led them to suspect Germans encircle them at night-time, using animal sounds to communicate. Thankfully, there is always someone who knows what kept them awake: that scream was a fox, the low cooing sound an owl desperate to mate, that sharp response his female, not in the mood quite yet.

The Brilleslijper family has established a sort of routine in their underground household, including house rules, places to sleep, shifts for the dishes, schedules for cooking. Jaap has fabricated a radio, which they gather around in the evening, listening to news from London. How much longer will it take? When will the Allies come to bring Hitler to his knees? Jaap is always allowed to sit at the front with Father Joseph when they turn the radio on. Everyone adores the shy boy, his inventions, his dexterous fingers. He has built a beautiful doll's house for Kathinka and Liselotte, with floors and rooms, beds and curtains, and even proper lamps made of bicycle lights. Jaap will fix anything that has broken and can always be found in the shed, stooped over the workbench, his glasses on the tip of his nose.

Because of the disturbing reports Janny brings home from Amsterdam – the fanatical search for people in hiding, the ongoing willingness of citizens to report Jews – Jaap starts to build hiding places all around the house. Beneath and above the built-in cupboards that can be found in most rooms, he makes hiding spaces for one or two people to squeeze in. Some of the floors have cavities, which Jaap turns into storage spaces, and on the top floor, he creates hiding places between the walls of the rooms and the roof. In each room he builds either a crawl space or a cupboard, with a hatch hidden underneath a rug or behind a piece of furniture.

Next, he installs an ingenious alarm system. He mounts little lights in all the rooms and connects them with electrical wire to a small emergency button next to the front door at eye level. If anyone presses the button, all the little lights switch on. This alerts the residents to the imminent danger; they must rush to their designated hiding places. Jaap has taught them how to hide, which foot to use when entering the narrow space, how to shut the hatch. They have rehearsed several times, like a fire drill. Within thirty seconds every trace of their existence can be erased.

On the first floor, in front of the window on the right, just above the name of the house, they put a Chinese vase. The coast is clear as long as this vase is there, in front of the window. If it is gone, this is a sign for resistance couriers or guests of The High Nest that something is amiss.

The constant threat has a different effect on each of them and sometimes subdued tensions lead to conflict. The two young girls, Jetty and Puck, share the maid's room on the first floor and, more than once, boys hiding at The High Nest develop a crush on one of the girls, despite the fact that Jetty is engaged to be married to Simon.

One morning the front-door milkman arrives – they have two, both unaware of the other, so they can buy a lot without it becoming suspicious: the front-door milkman and the back-door milkman. Just as the man is about to put his bottles at the front door at the back of the house, hell breaks loose on the terrace. Two boys, both in love with the same girl, are fighting, a third one is trying to separate them; all three of them are in hiding at The High Nest. The milkman watches the spectacle with his mouth wide open while the third boy tries to save them all by keeping the hotheads away from each other, his arms and legs wide apart. 'Never mind them. Just their morning exercises.' He gives one of them an extra shove.

The milkman, shocked, never returns again.

When they discuss the incident at dinner that night, most of them laugh out loud. But Janny doesn't flinch and gives the boys a serious talking-to. The High Nest might create the illusion of freedom, but, if they are found out, the consequences will be devastating.

**When the** time for spring-cleaning arrives, almost all villages surrounding The High Nest have been declared *judenrein*, cleansed of Jews. Jewish citizens have been forced to move to Amsterdam and were sent to Westerbork from there. Jewish residents of national institutions, such as the foundation for mentally handicapped children and the sanatorium in Hilversum or the children's home in Laren, have all been deported. As the noose around The High Nest tightens, the sisters find an unexpected ally close to home.

As the months go by and the number of guests increases, Janny and Lien have to bend over backwards to feed everyone without attracting attention. Almost every day they take it in turns to cycle to their suppliers in surrounding villages and cities. Some stores or farms are less than a mile apart, others several miles away.

The sisters, like workhorses, do their rounds and to avoid suspicion, they never buy more than one family's needs per shop. They can navigate the paths around the house with their eyes closed. They plough across the heath in all weathers, their face close to the handlebars, back bent, toes stretched to reach the pedals.

They buy their yoghurt at a wholesaler in Blaricum, vegetables and potatoes in two or three different shops. Meat is hardly available any more and the milk is delivered to the house. Soap and detergent come from Bochove, the chemist in Huizen, only a few minutes' cycling from The Nest. One day Lien has gone there to buy toiletries. She is gathering the items on her list; there are no other customers in the shop.

'You have people in hiding, don't you?'

It is a soft voice, but Lien jumps as if someone has beaten a gong right next to her ear. Her hand, reaching for a shelf, freezes in mid-air and she tries to swallow. Then she slowly turns around and stares into the friendly face of Bert Bochove. His head is the shape of an upside-down egg; a wide, high forehead tapering off like an oval into a narrow chin. He smiles at her without a touch of irony.

'You always buy so much toilet paper.'

He points at her basket and Lien feels her cheeks begin to glow. She could drop everything right there and run outside. The man sees the fear in her eyes and changes his tone. He puts his hand on her arm, looks around and leans towards her.

'Don't worry. So do we. Above the shop.'

From that day on they are friends and resistance comrades, just as the darkest hour comes near.

Not long before the German occupation, Bert Bochove lived miles from Huizen. He was running a mill in Finland until, in 1939, his family asked him to come back and take charge of the family business with his brothers. Which he does – for a while. He soon decides he wants to be independent and free, manage his own place. His fiancée, Annie, works as a pharmacist in Amsterdam and in May 1941, one year after the Nazis invade the Netherlands, they marry and move into *De Zonnehoek* – The Sunny Corner – in Huizen. On the ground floor they open a chemist shop; upstairs they have a spacious apartment.

Chemist Bochove soon becomes a household name in

the area. In this time of scarcity, luxury goods such as soap and detergent are rationed. Each family is allowed half a pound of soap per month. Not nearly enough for a former fishing village like Huizen. The creation of the Afsluitdijk dam and causeway may have robbed the village of the sea and its fleet, cutting it off, but the no-nonsense work ethic remains. Hard skin on the hands of the housewives of Huizen reveals their fondness of scrubbing. Bert Bochove quickly realizes: 'In a village like Huizen the women don't just clean their kitchens, they scrub and wax their worktops, make everything shiny and spotless and then keep everyone away so it can stay clean.'

When Bert moves to Huizen in 1941, he starts a business that instantly makes him popular among the reserved community of the village. Jaap van Rijn, an old friend, owns a paint factory. His stock is confiscated by the Germans, but he manages to bury some barrels with thousands of gallons of linseed oil in his garden, just before they arrive. And with this oil, Jaap has a plan for Bert and Annie's pharmacy. Jaap makes highly concentrated twenty-pound blocks of rock-hard soap and delivers these to Bert. Bert then turns the blocks into some 120 pounds of soft soap, which he breaks into pieces to sell. The news on Bochove King of Soaps travels fast and people from the entire area come to his shop to buy it. It is testimony to their kind nature that Bert and Annie never charge anything more than the pre-war price for their soap. This is very unusual at the time and the working class of Huizen love them for it.

Business is thriving until one day Bert arrives at his friend's house to pick up a new load and finds only his wife there. The accountant of the paint factory has betrayed Jaap and reported the missing stock to the Germans. That morning, Jaap had received a phone call – he had to report at the police station for questioning. He put on his coat, got on his bike and told his wife not to worry; the day he would let Germans scare him was yet to come.

Bert is alarmed by the news but not surprised. Jaap has always been a proud man. From day one of the German occupation, he had waved his finger disapprovingly at each passing Dutch Nazi, warning them their despicable behaviour would have serious consequences! But Jaap's wife is frightened and distressed. They have a couple in hiding, wanted for being active members of the resistance. She worries the Germans might come to their house after questioning her husband and she asks Bert to take the couple with him, to Huizen.

Bert instantly agrees and takes the man and the

woman home. They are the first people hiding in Bert and Annie's upstairs apartment in *De Zonnehoek*. Many more will follow.

Jaap van Rijn never came home again.

Bert and Annie Bochove become faithful friends and associates of the Brilleslijper sisters in The High Nest. Janny provides Bert with information from the resistance, often from Amsterdam; Bert gives her news from the village. They even exchange people seeking shelter, such as Hennie Juliard and his wife, Pam, who is heavily pregnant in 1944. For the Bochoves to be accepted into the former fishing community, it is not only exceptional, but it is also, above all, very valuable. The villages of Naarden and Bussum are full of Germans and wealthy pro-Nazis; fear and ambition have turned a great number of dignitaries into National Socialist doormats. But in Huizen the Fascists are met with distrust – just as any new arrival is met with distrust. This curious divergence doesn't surprise Bert. Many people in Huizen help Jews, Bert thinks, because this was a village of fishermen, stubborn by nature, workers who know how to fight their own battles.

In Amsterdam, the hunt for Jews is in full swing. Streets are blocked in the early morning and a superior force of policemen comb the houses looking for hideaways. The raids quickly extend from Amsterdam to smaller cities and villages, also around The High Nest. The information they receive from Bert Bochove suddenly becomes vital.

When they had first moved to The High Nest, Janny would wake up in the night, alarmed by the deep silence. For a fraction of a second, she thought she was gone: vanished from the face of the earth, sunken into a bottomless pit where no one could hear her, not even Bob and the little ones. She would reach for Bob's warm body beside her and wait. After a few minutes there was always the owl calling from the back of the garden; the piercing screams of the foxes who, sometimes curious, came all the way from the forest to their front door, where Eberhard and Lien, returning from a house concert at Grietje's, found them one night.

Then she would think back on Amsterdam, her old bedroom with Lientje lying next to her, the sounds of the city like a mother, humming, lulling them to sleep, their own mother working in the store downstairs. The canals, the market, Carré Theatre, the tram accelerating. Would she ever walk there again? And Father, Mother, Japie? Would they ever be welcomed back in their own city? Was there even a place for them in this world?

It is the most peculiar mechanism: when you hear something often enough – even something as absurd as your entire existence being unwelcome – it eventually plants itself in your head. The only one awake in the large house, with warm, sleeping bodies around her, the smell of burnt wood slowly blending with fresh air, Janny sometimes wondered if she had made it all up: the war, the oppression, the violence. But then the raids reach their area and there is no longer any doubt – not in the night-time, either.

The Bochoves keep them informed. Bert has contacts at the Huizen police who participate in each raid and are given notice one day before a new one is scheduled. As soon as Bert knows, he calls The High Nest and simply says: 'Don't hang out the laundry to dry tonight!' And they know what to do: make sure everyone is ready, suspicious items stowed, hiding places made accessible so they can dive right in – as if they never even existed.

It usually starts at four in the morning. No matter how hard they try to stay awake, be ready when it begins, the approaching convoy always startles them, drowsy and confused. Except for the children, who just sleep through it. The rooms in the rest of the house are packed with people lying stock-still in bed or on their mattresses, holding their breath as they follow the rattling jeeps, the screeching tyres of police cars, with utmost concentration. Sometimes a siren announces them from a distance. They narrow their eyes, clench their fists, prick their ears. Which way are they going? Are they coming nearer or do they turn off? Should they raise the alarm, so everyone rushes to their hiding places, or should they give it a few more seconds? But the column does not drive up the hill. The High Nest is too remote.

Sometimes, when a convoy has stopped close by and the residents of The High Nest are waiting anxiously, they hear gunshots and barking rend the silence. Staccato and piercing, the sounds echo across the heath. When the engines start and the noise slowly fades away, the house breathes out as one and everyone gets ready to rise. The sun announces another day won.

This pattern repeats every few weeks and afterwards Bert, who has been informed by the police, tells them whether anyone has been found or not. In Huizen there seems to be an invisible web of people looking away at the right moment. After Lien sings at Annie Bochove's birthday one evening, Bert runs into his neighbour on the street the next day – the man grumbles they really ought to be quieter with those people they are hiding.

It is nerve-wracking, but each time Janny or Lien

reports at the shop inside The Sunny Corner unscathed, they have a laugh with Bert and Annie. 'At least we need a lot of toilet paper again!' And with the latest news and their panniers filled, they cycle back to The High Nest.

**Mik is** on the train to Naarden looking out of the window, watching Amsterdam fade in the distance. He feels less light-hearted than the last time he was travelling to The High Nest. Much has changed in a short while. Sides have been chosen – neither action nor wait-and-see can keep fluid decisions from turning irreversible and solid. Resistance members are facing the harsh reality too. The initial naive ad hoc approach has given way to an organizational structure and ambitious plans. The Germans have become more violent, but the call for counter violence has grown louder too. First, the resistance mostly focused on forgeries, hiding places, underground presses and acts of sabotage, but the number of liquidations of Germans and collaborators rises – and the number of retaliations as well.

They are losing more and more people, and the choices Mik is facing weigh heavy on his mind. How far is he prepared to go? He still has a lot of discussions with his comrade Gerrit van der Veen about a potential assault on the register – an action with huge consequences. The other resistance group he is in close contact with, CS-6, has shifted its focus to assaults since the deportations started and his friend Gerrit Kastein drew up a list of collaborators to be killed by the group.

Mik knows the sisters will be very upset by his news.

From Naarden-Bussum station, he walks through the ochre-coloured fields to The High Nest without seeing anyone. There is no noise, no traffic, no danger appearing unannounced, but he doesn't manage to keep his dark thoughts at bay. Turn left for the final stretch, into the forest. He has stopped looking around, his gaze focused on the weathered caps of his boots. He marches without following the twists in the path, treads mindlessly, or perhaps on purpose, on mushrooms and grass, his presence leaving a trace, until he stops in his tracks and looks up. Between the trees the shutters of The High Nest are reflecting the light.

Janny is sorting identity cards and Eberhard is playing the piano in the front room when Mik enters the kitchen, greets them curtly and asks them to come outside. They walk into the garden, where he comes straight out with it: 'Gerrit Kastein has jumped out of the window in The Hague. Parliament Square. Head on the cobbles. Dead.'

———

**Gerrit Kastein** was a neurologist with nerves of steel – headstrong, but sadly not strong enough to escape his fate. Janny and Gerrit had been friends since their early twenties when both of them worked for the International Red Aid, offering support to the anti-Fascists in Spain. The Spanish Civil War would turn out to be the dress rehearsal for what followed.

Gerrit and Janny joined the Help for Spain committee, the Dutch department of the International Red Aid. Janny's primary mission was to collect money for dressing material, which was desperately needed in Spain, while Gerrit became the head of a Dutch field hospital at the front.

After three months, Gerrit returned to the Netherlands, returned to his life as a civilian doctor and in 1937 obtained his doctorate at the University of Leiden. But his ideological fire had not gone out; he was an editor of the communist monthly *Politics & Culture* and gave talks on the Spanish Civil War. He wrote articles and in 1938 published a book entitled *The Racial Problem*. It contained a scientific treatise on class differences and anti-Semitism in Germany, which led to his thesis that racism inevitably ends in war. Evidence followed before long.

————

**When the** Communist Party of the Netherlands, CPN, is banned by the Germans in July 1940, the communists go underground to organize acts of sabotage. Doctor Kastein, who lives in The Hague with his wife and two daughters, is present at the inaugural meeting of the illegal CPN branch in his city. Gerrit is also initiator of various resistance groups and takes the lead within Amsterdam resistance group CS-6.

When the deportations of Jews begin in 1942, Gerrit is convinced the resistance must start taking radical measures; Dutch collaborators have to be eliminated. He convinces the members of the CS-6 group to help him assassinate people eagerly assisting the occupying forces, and draws up a list.

**The first** intended victim is Hendrik Seyffardt, the seventy-two-year-old retired general of the Dutch army who, since July 1941, has been commander of the Fascist Volunteer Legion Netherlands, a nationalist vehicle that fights at the Eastern Front as an integral part of the Waffen-SS. He has just been appointed as deputy in the shadow cabinet and it is expected he will soon be Minister of War. He is an obvious target for the resistance.

On 5 February 1943 the doorbell rings at Seyffardt's

home at 36 Van Neckstraat in The Hague, 200 metres from where Kastein lives. The general walks to the front door unsuspectingly. When he opens it, he sees two young men he has not met before: Jan Verleun and Leo Frijda, both members of the resistance group CS-6. They want to make sure they have the right one and so ask the general for his name; 'He had such a beautiful voice,' Frijda would recall later. Verleun shoots as soon as Seyffardt confirms his identity and the two young men run off, assuming their target was killed instantly.

Seyffardt is critically wounded, but tells the *Sicherheitsdienst* that the perpetrators were merely 'two students' and his death is not to be avenged. He dies the next day and, against his wishes, raids on students are carried out immediately. Eighteen hundred boys between the ages of eighteen and twenty-five, including six hundred students, are arrested and taken to Vught concentration camp.

Verleun goes into hiding, still in possession of the pistol he used for the assault. Gerrit Kastein, in the meantime, has chosen the next target. This time he wants to do it himself, so he has to get hold of a new pistol quickly. He goes to a resistance comrade, Lucas Spoor, who lends him one – a move that will mark Gerrit's end.

———

**Two days** later, on 7 February 1943, Gerrit commits the second planned assault, on Hermannus Reydon. This serious jurist is a prominent member of the Dutch Nazi Party and has been named president of the Dutch Chamber of Culture, the state organization for 'healthy art for Aryan people' that all Dutch artists had to join.

In the evening Kastein rings the door at Reydon's house in Voorschoten. His wife answers. Gerrit shoots her in cold blood, closes the door and waits inside in the dark hall for Reydon to come home. After a while he hears the key in the lock; the front door sways open and he fires instantly. Reydon is hit in the neck and Kastein runs off. Reydon is severely injured and will spend six months paralyzed in hospital before he eventually dies.

Gerrit Kastein is the one who pulls the trigger, but unknown to him, Reydon and his wife have deliberately been sacrificed by the Germans with the intention of leading Kastein into a trap, in line with the Nazis' unwritten motto: 'a dead resistance fighter is more important than a living Dutch Nazi.'

Kastein has the misfortune of coming up against a man who equals his ambition, but surpasses his unscrupulousness. SS-*Sturmbahnführer* Joseph Schreieder has, under Heinrich Himmler, risen to the rank of Kriminalrat, and in this role is responsible for counter-espionage of the *Sicherheitsdienst* in the Netherlands. His primary objective is to round up resistance groups – by any means.

The so-called resistance friend Lucas Spoor, who supplies Gerrit with the pistol, is in fact Anton van der Waals, a Dutch spy infiltrating resistance groups for the SD – a man who will be remembered as one of the worst traitors ever, in a time where there was no shortage of such people.

When Kastein asks him if he could get him a pistol the day after the assault on Seyffardt, Van der Waals hurries to his boss, Schreieder, who does not have to think twice: of course they will give Kastein a weapon and when he shoots someone they will have an autopsy carried out and if the calibre of the bullets confirms that their new friend has used their weapon, they may as well assume he shot Seyffardt too.

And so, in the early morning of 6 February, Anton, van der Waals, as resistance man Lucas Spoor, hands the pistol to Gerrit. At the SD-headquarters, Schreieder and his colleagues anxiously await the outcome of their game of Russian roulette. Who will die?

Schreieder does not have to wait long for his bodies. Reydon ends up in hospital, critically wounded, but thankfully they can do a post-mortem on his wife's body. Schreieder is very pleased when he receives the reports: the shots have indeed been fired with the pistol he had given his infiltrator. It is a shame that the general and his wife fell, but, he reasons, there are plenty of Dutch Nazis left.

When Anton van der Waals comes to his boss to report, an unpleasant surprise awaits: Schreieder does not want to arrest Kastein. Quite the opposite, he wants Van der Waals to bond with Kastein and gather more information on actions and comrades in the resistance. Van der Waals, having witnessed the cool-headedness of Kastein, does not like this idea at all. He might be a productive traitor; he is not a very courageous one. He fears he might end up losing this game. Van der Waals tries to convince Schreieder, but his superior will not even consider putting the operation on hold. Indeed, he sees it as an interesting confrontation between his top infiltrator and that fanatical communist Kastein. If Anton comes off worst, that will be the conclusion and solution in one.

**On 19 February 1943,** Van der Waals has a new appointment with Gerrit Kastein and, there, the problem solves itself – an SD-assault squad arrests Kastein just before they are due to meet. Schreieder is furious and suspects his cowardly spy is playing him off against someone else.

Meanwhile, Kastein is clapped in irons and lead to a service car that takes him to the Binnenhof, where the headquarters of both *Sicherheitzpolizei* and SD are located; the political investigation department and the secret service.

But Gerrit is considered a formidable opponent for a reason; he will not have the Germans transport him meek as a lamb. When he gets out at Parliament Square in the Binnenhof, he sees his chance: with his hands cuffed he fires a small calibre gun from a special inside pocket in his trousers. One officer is hit in his leg, another bullet ricochets before they can snatch the pistol from him.

Inside, four men are already waiting to question Gerrit. After a while two officers leave to get coffee and the third to use the bathroom. One SD-man is a joke to Kastein. He floors him, kicks down the window and jumps from the second floor.

Aged thirty-two, the doctor is brought down after all, as his head hits the cobbles of the Binnenhof – on the exact same spot where, one week before, the first victim on his list, Lieutenant-General Seyffardt, beneath a row of outstretched arms, received a grand funeral.

———

**At The** High Nest everyone is devastated by the news. Bob comes home from his work at the food office in Weesp to find them sitting in the dusky front room with tight, pale faces. Janny takes her husband aside and tells him what happened. Bob and Gerrit were close friends from the communist circuit. When Janny shares the story of Gerrit's death, the bizarre circumstances of the accident, Bob's briefcase almost slips out of his hand. Of course they knew Gerrit carried out dangerous orders for the Party and played a crucial part in the assaults on Dutch collaborators, but in some strange way they had imagined him untouchable.

After dinner, when the children have gone to bed, they reminisce about Gerrit. They talk about the years of the Spanish Civil War, his work in the resistance, the sections he brought together since the occupation began. About his strategic insight and organizational talent, which were never an excuse to not dirty his own hands.

They also speculate about his motive for jumping out of the window. Most likely, Gerrit had tried to outwit the enemy one more time; the injuries of the fall would have forced them to take him to hospital, where perhaps he could have escaped. Not only because it was a different location with new circumstances, but also because he, as a neurologist, knew the way there. He did not care about wrecking his body, his mind was what he needed to preserve for the battle. But he took such a nasty fall on that damned Binnenhof that he did not live to tell his tale.

Gerrit's death is tangible proof of the new phase the occupation has reached: on either side more victims will follow at alarming speed.

Shortly before Mik leaves for Amsterdam, he takes Lien and Eberhard, Janny and Bob aside in the hall. Serious eyes in a youthful face; the war pressing heavier than time.

'Be careful not to take *too* many people in. It might go wrong eventually.'

'Mik,' Lien responds indignantly, 'if someone is in need, we have no other option but to help him!'

'I just want to warn you: be cautious.'

They kiss Mik goodbye, a last embrace, and follow him with their eyes as he walks down the garden path, into the dark forest.

**Summer arrives.** The new residents of The High Nest have never seen this spectacle before; it is breathtaking, like fireworks. They move around the grounds, admiring it from different angles each time. The grass turns thick and green, and it feels like a velvet carpet underneath their feet. They pack lunch in a large basket and settle down somewhere on the large lawn almost every day. The rhododendrons, the fig at the front of the house, the blackberry bushes on the side, the pear trees and apple trees in the orchard at the back, the rose bushes crawling up the shed, the beech hedge protecting the garden against wild animals – rather unsuccessfully – the weeds growing to shoulder level in just one night, the vine with its sprouting tendrils, the trees all around folding out like umbrellas, the deep purple heather in the distance, and the water of the IJsselmeer shimmers like a thousand tiny mirrors glued together as one. It is a constantly changing show, free and for their eyes only.

Each morning, Joseph and Fietje sit down on a bench at the side of the house with a cup of tea, huddling closely together. They don't speak as much any more and mainly try to make themselves useful in the enormous household. It is a bit like working in the shop: the stock, the coupons, the shopping, the consumption, the kitchen duties and other chores. Since the temperature carefully crept above 18 degrees, they sit here for a short while each morning, catching the first sunshine, listening to birdsong. The stone wall safely at their back, the thatched roof fatherly above their head, the shell path at the front a crackling alarm in case anyone is approaching.

Reports from the rest of the country are alarming. The 'evacuation' of Jews is running smoothly; the provinces of Friesland, Groningen, Drenthe, Overijssel, Gelderland, Limburg, Zeeland and North Brabant have all been declared *judenrein*. On the other hand: the battle at the Eastern Front takes longer and is a lot tougher than Hitler had anticipated. German reserves are seriously affected and from the summer of 1943 onwards, the Red Army keeps pushing the Germans further back.

This unfortunately has consequences for the Netherlands: to produce military equipment and supplies, the Nazis need more workmen. From May 1943 onwards, all men between the ages of eighteen and thirty-five must report for *Arbeitseinsatz*, forced labour, in Germany. Neglecting the call is punishable and large-scale raids will follow to send more young men to the Third Reich. Those reluctant to report go into hiding too – fear and chaos are now everywhere.

The streets of Amsterdam have changed beyond recognition in just a few years. The historical centre has not been destroyed, as it has in Rotterdam, and the river still streams stoically from Centraal Station to

Carré Theatre, but most of the people who coloured the city are gone. The merchants, the workmen and the clerks; the actors and the musicians, the intellectuals and the night owls; the librarians, the slurring regular and the quiet zookeeper – with tens of thousands of others at the time, they were taken out of their homes, put on the train, transported to Westerbork, as simple as that. A quick change trick has taken place in the *Zentralstelle für Jüdische Auswanderung*, where the index cards of registered Jews are kept. The 'Amsterdam' box has almost emptied over the course of 1943.

The last large raids are held in May and June. On 26 May, the Jews from the city centre are rounded up at Muiderpoort station. Children pressing their favourite toys to their chest, women wearing beautiful hats, men in their best clothes, grandmothers with freshly curled hair. After hours of waiting a train arrives to take them to Westerbork. *Storm*, the SS weekly, reports extensively on the event in its 4 June edition:

We have had to say goodbye, goodbye to people who have 'shared' our bread for centuries, always keeping the best pieces for themselves. We have sent them off and bid them a last farewell in Amsterdam-East, at the Polderweg site. They were wearing badges, six-pointed stars, proving their membership of the party travelling to Poland [. . .] The amount of blood as yet contaminated by Jews, the amount of bastards walking our streets could only be understood upon witnessing these scenes. Dead numbers came to life. Practice confirmed science. Worse even. We were heading towards the creation of a nice blond type of Jew with almost Aryan features. There they were, those Jewish men and women. A well-known fair-haired woman was there, platinum blonde, so no one would suspect her Jewish blood. Dozens of them there could easily have married a nice Aryan boy, without him realizing he was marrying a Jew. There was a danger there and that danger was very large. It is a good thing active measures were taken. And thus the Jews have gone. We saw them leave on the trains. We were not sad to part.

On Sunday, 20 June 1943, the large raid in Amsterdam-South and Amsterdam-East follows. The last Jews above ground are deported to Westerbork that very same day, five and a half thousand in total. They are followed, in September, by the members of the Jewish Council, which then officially ceases to exist.

On 1 October, the Henneicke Column with its Jew hunters is disbanded and the very last transportation with Jews, drawn out of their hiding places, leaves the capital on 19 November 1943. Less than three and a half years after *Heeresgruppe B* invaded the Netherlands under the command of General Fedor von Bock, Amsterdam is *judenrein*.

# 6

# Unwelcome Encounters

P anic in The High Nest. The Jansen sisters intend
to pay them a visit. It is the height of summer, a
time usually spent in their country house in nature,
not in the stuffy city; they are desperate for a day out.
Of course another – unmentioned – reason for coming
over is to see if their house and garden are treated well.

After the alarming phone call, they have a few days
to get ready. Mother and Lien set everyone to work
cleaning, while the men start dragging mattresses away
and reorganize beds, cupboards, chairs and tables,
making it seem as if only two families, the official tenants, live there with their children: Janny and Bob with
Robbie and Liselotte, and Lien and Eberhard with little
Kathinka.

On the day the visitors are expected, the illegal residents are hidden in the forest like Easter eggs. They will use special signs when everyone can reappear. Thankfully, it is a warm day.

The tram delivers the ladies right on time at the stop closest to the villa and when they arrive at The High Nest, they receive the warmest welcome. The sun is shining brightly and the house upon the hill, surrounded by a sea of flowers, is basking in its light.

Lien and Janny take the sisters inside, to the living room, for the next scene in this absurd play. Indeed, such a delight to live here, changing of the seasons simply overwhelming, no problems with the rent hopefully, and perhaps would they like something to drink?

They do. Enter Red Puck to perform another audacious act. Lien rings a little bell and the maid arrives wearing a starched white apron and a cap, carrying a silver tray with a teapot, cups and a plateful of cookies. Puck, her fiery hair bound sideways in two braids, curtsies while Janny and Lien bite their lip so as not to burst out laughing.

'Afternoon, madam,' she greets the visitors twice. 'Do you take milk or sugar?'

Puck neatly pours the tea as the Jansen sisters watch her, visibly impressed and curious.

'Are you from around here, girl?'

'Yes, madam.'

'What's your name, then?'

'Aagje Honing, madam.'

One of the sisters puts down her cup on a side table and claps her hands with joy.

'How lovely! We know the Honing family in Huizen! Are you related to Auntie Betsie Honing?'

Puck doesn't flinch. 'I'm afraid I'm not, madam. There are two Honing families here.'

Lien quickly steers the conversation in a different direction while Janny rushes Puck out of the room.

'Well,' Lien says softly, pointing at her temple, 'the child is a bit simple, but ever so diligent and sweet.'

After tea, the ladies want to have a look around the house. Visibly pleased, they pass the shiny, clean kitchen and the fresh hall and walk upstairs, where there is not a trace of little children playing, let alone dozens of people sleeping, in any of the rooms. Downstairs, they have a look at the antique cupboard with the expensive porcelain service.

Janny and Lien hold their breath. This winter one of their guests had pushed a pile of crockery through the kitchen hatch with a little too much force. It landed on the other side with a loud bang, shattering into a thousand pieces on the wooden floor. It was as if the pressure in the entire house completely dropped, they were in such shock. The noise seemed to break straight through the walls and echo between the trees. When, after an eternity, neither Germans nor Dutch Nazis appeared at the door, they all stood there laughing nervously before getting on their knees to collect the shards. From that moment, Janny and Lien made a game out of picking up china – begging and stealing – anywhere they went. Each new plate they dug up from their handbag and added to the multicoloured collection in the cupboard was welcomed with cheers.

But now the Jansen sisters are staring into the same cupboard with narrowed eyes. Lien placed the remaining cups and saucers from the original service at the front to cover the mishmash of porcelain replacements behind them. If they make it through the war alive, they will repay all of it and more – for now, this beautiful display will have to do.

The Jansen sisters turn around, smiling broadly at Janny and Lien, who smile back with their buttocks clenched.

After a few exhausting hours of sitting outside on a bench in the sun, watching the shadow move across the grass stalk by stalk, the ladies finally get up, smooth down their skirts and say a fond farewell. Janny and Lien wave them goodbye from the hill, laugh off their nerves and then hurry into the forest to free everyone from their hiding places.

———

**Summer seems** to last forever. Lien and Eberhard focus on the house concerts, developing new shows and writing articles for *The Free Artist*; Janny and Bob work hard for the resistance. On top of that they have the daily shop, a full-time job in itself.

The constant threat becomes the new norm. They are less keen to listen to the radio and hardly speak about the so-called progress of the Allied forces. They all try to find an internal pause button enabling them to survive this uncertainty. One year ago, most of them were firmly convinced the war would be over by now. That they would have returned to their own homes, shops and jobs. That they, if only they hadn't lost anyone, could resume the thread of their lives. But so many family members and friends have been deported to an unknown destination. They can only endure all of this by focusing on the horizon. Stop dreaming. Think in terms of months instead of days.

Janny has never longed for winter, cold, darkness and short days before, but now they seem like an attractive hole in which to disappear. She cannot wait for summer to be over; the sun drives everyone outside and there are more people on the streets, in the villages, on the train. The colours and warmth all around make the residents of The Nest feel dangerously carefree, careless even, while the enemy is no less ruthless. Among each other, they keep insisting: you must trust no one.

One day, Eberhard is walking towards Huizen with Kathinka. As Father Bos and his daughter, both very blond, they are relatively free to go where they want. They are walking hand in hand across Naarderstraat, when a troop of German soldiers turns the corner and heads straight towards them. Their knees move up as one and the road seems to tremble as their boots all hit the ground.

Eberhard freezes and squeezes Kathinka's hand. They are trapped. The next side street is past the soldiers and turning their back on them is not an option. All they can do is walk on. Eberhard breathes out softly, drops his shoulders, trying not to let anything show to Kathinka, happily skipping along by his side.

The unit is only a few dozen feet away from them and led by an officer. When their eyes meet, Eberhard stands rooted to the spot and jerks Kathinka's arm backwards. The officer is his old friend Kurt Kahle.

The man looks away, leading his German men past father and daughter as if they do not exist, but Eberhard realizes this is the end. For him and everyone else in The High Nest. There is no doubt Kurt recognized him and, any second now, he will have them arrested. Kathinka is talking to her father, pulling his arm, but he presses his hand against her mouth and stares at the soldiers' backs. They march on with Eberhard watching until the ground beneath his feet has stopped trembling and the men become black dots, dissolving in purple heather.

As soon as his knees are willing to move, he runs back home with Kathinka to warn the others.

Kurt Kahle was part of their artistic group of friends in Amsterdam. A photographer from Berlin who, like so many other Germans, fled the rise of National Socialism and came to the Netherlands in the early 1930s. Kurt was one of the people walking in and out of Mik's place at Keizersgracht. He and Eberhard became friends, discussing recent developments in their fatherland – they were both extremely outraged, then.

Eberhard thinks back on his own call from the Wehrmacht to join them. The conversations with Lien, the fear, the doubt, Rhijn, the failed starvation cure and then the most important question of his life: to desert or not. *Fahnenflucht.* Kurt received the same call and faced the same decision. Can Eberhard hold it against him that he turned another way?

Kurt gave no show of recognition, but they cannot take the risk. Eberhard discusses the situation with the others at home and they all agree: there is a chance

Kurt has defected, in which case he might come back and look for him in the area of Naarderstraat. The only person who can give them a decisive answer is Mik.

As fast as she can, Lien cycles to Laren, where one of their contacts, who is due to go to Amsterdam, lives and explains the situation. He promises to discuss everything with Mik and get back to them as soon as possible.

That night they have an emergency meeting at The High Nest. There is a chance they all have to leave within one or two days. Where can they go? Bochove in Huizen can accommodate one or two people, some other contacts might as well, but no one can take in the entire group.

After a sleepless night, Mik's answer brings great relief. Kurt Kahle is one of them. First he was stationed at the military command in Amsterdam Centraal Station where he was supposed to provide information to travelling Germans, but in fact spent months helping the resistance distribute illegal anti-Fascist pamphlets. Early 1943, he was conscripted after all and assigned to *Sicherungsregiment 26* at Crailo camp in Laren. From there he currently funnels munitions and weapons to the resistance. Mik's message is very clear: they need not worry.

———

**On 2 October 1943,** Lien stares at the newspaper on the table in front of her, the letters on the front page slowly becoming illegible. She blinks a few times, but the letters melt into one another until only large headlines remain. THE SITUATION AT THE EASTERN FRONT is one on the left side. Her eyes carefully move to the right. ANNOUNCEMENT it says, a bit closer to the middle, some judicial order on turning in radios. It is the column next to that one, bottom right, which initially drew her attention. She sniffs loudly and forces herself to read it again: PUNISHMENT FOR MURDERING GENERAL SEYFFARDT, MINISTER POSTHUMA AND OTHERS.

As announced by the *Höhere SS-Polizeiführer Nordwest,* the *Polizeistandgericht* Amsterdam has, on 30 September 1943, sentenced the following Dutchmen to death.

This is followed by a list of nineteen names, most of which she recognizes. Medical student Leo Frijda from Amsterdam. Biology student Hans Katan from Amsterdam. Three times the name Boissevain. Anton Koreman, guitarist, also an old friend of theirs. But in between, at number twelve:

Journalist Maarten van Gilse from Amsterdam, born 12 June 1916 in Munich [. . .] The death sentences have, after consideration of clemency, been executed in the early hours of 1 October 1943.

When everyone comes home that night, Lien takes the family aside in the garden and tells them what has happened. They stand in the tall grass in silence. Father stares at his shoes, Mother has put her hand on her pursed lips. Bob reaches for Janny's hand then drops his arm instead. The sun slowly disappears behind the trees, pulling a shadow across the ochre roof of the house. Fietje shivers. Joseph takes her hand. 'Come,' he says and walks towards the house, the rest of the family following in his wake.

Janny will learn from her contacts what happened. Mik and his girlfriend had found shelter in the studio of a sculptor friend at a Prinsengracht attic, close to Westertoren. From here, he coordinated his work for *The Free Artist*, resistance group CS-6 and the identity card centre. They worked day and night. When the house was surrounded by police, they hastily barricaded the door and stoked the stove to burn as many papers as possible: forged documents, resistance contacts and addresses, his notebook – everything. By now, police were banging on the door and Mik jumped out of the window, onto the roof, just as officers stormed into the room and arrested his girlfriend. Mik was shot and hit, slightly injured, then caught. Prison, hours of questioning, but word has it, he did not reveal anything, not for weeks. And then the death penalty: a bullet straight through his heart, on 1 October, in the dunes near Bloemendaal.

The November issue of *The Free Artist* includes an extensive obituary and Eberhard reads it out in the evening when all are gathered around the dinner table:

Maarten Van Gilse Dead
Mik was young, young in years, young in his ideals, in his faith in people, in his expectations, in his sincerity and his drive [. . .] Born and raised cosmopolitan, restless by nature, he travelled many countries, earning his keep with his pen, making friends wherever he went, fully enjoying the good life [. . .] We cannot speak of his wartime activities yet; but we can say he fought like a man, his unflinching courage and indestructible optimism were a great support to many, his perseverance accomplished what others, confused and despondent, gave up on. There were many of Mik's generation who shared his beliefs, many with the same ideals, who until 10 May 1940 took great pride in their

open mind and deep understanding. There were very, very few however, who accepted, like he did, the consequences – even the most extreme – when the hour of need came, who persevered when the storm rose, who risked their lives, day after day, who stopped at nothing – no ordeal, no danger – to carry their highest good through fire and death towards a better future.

# 7

# The Kestrel

A Saturday in November. Jetty has celebrated her birthday and everyone has been in high spirits all day. Lien sang a few songs, Eberhard played the piano for everyone and with the scarce resources at their disposal – some dough, preserved apples from the orchard and a pinch of cinnamon – they had produced something that could pass for a cake.

Around half past ten in the evening – when the children and some of the adults are in bed, the fire is burning, some are reading a book and a few other guests are still chatting around the dining table in the living room – they suddenly hear rhythmic stamping. It is soft and far away, as if a drill deep in the ground is thrusting upwards, causing the earth beneath the house to tremble. They urge each other to keep quiet. Faces tighten. They hold their breath and listen.

The noise comes from outside. It swells. They recognize it and rise to their feet, almost in slow motion. At first, there is panic, but then the well-rehearsed emergency plan takes over.

The marching boots are now quickly approaching, hold still on the shell path, make a few crackling steps and then turn off towards the house. Someone presses the emergency button next to the front door and they fly apart, each to their designated hiding place. Fietje, Joseph and Japie will take the children out of bed and hide with them. Lien, Janny, Bob and Eberhard smooth down their clothes, straighten their backs and brace themselves for the confrontation.

'Bram is still on the toilet!' Loes Teixeira de Mattos grabs Janny's arm. She hisses that Loes has to go upstairs anyway, but there is no time. With a curt nod, Janny sends her to a hiding place downstairs, underneath the storage bench beside the fireplace.

The pull handle of the bell at the front door moves back and forth; the tinkling sound cuts through the silence.

'*Aufmachen!* Open up!'

Janny and Bob are still rushing to clear suspicious items away. Too many glasses on the table, a carafe of

water, too many cigarette butts in the ashtray, an underground magazine lying around. Lien walks through
the hall to the front door and stands on her toes, opens
the square hatch at the top and tells the men outside:
'Please be so kind as to walk around the house. I shall
open the door to the kitchen for you.'

Another few seconds gained.

With a lot of rattling, clumsily tugging at the bolts,
she opens the locks to the kitchen door. When she looks
over her shoulder, Janny gives her the thumbs up. Lien
swings the door open and a German soldier in uniform
is standing right in front of her. His leather belt glistens in the dark, a cloud of breath running ahead of his
words.

'Sorry to disturb you, madam. Could you point us to
the path towards the sea, please?'

Behind the man are more soldiers, nodding politely.

Lien forces herself to smile. 'But of course,' she answers.

'We got lost, our group. Any chance you would have
a glass of water for us?'

Lien is searching for words, steps aside, opens the
door fully.

'Not a problem. Do come in.'

And so they all end up in the same kitchen; over a
dozen German soldiers with their foreman, plus Janny,

Lien and Eberhard. They shake the captain's hand and introduce themselves. Piet Bos. Antje Bos. Janny Brandes. Bob is still busying himself in the living room.

In addition to a glass of water, they offer the boys fresh yoghurt, left over from breakfast.

'Please don't go out of your way,' the captain says initially, but then they all eat with relish.

The men look cold and worn out.

'We're on a drill tonight and must find our way to the water,' their leader says between two bites.

'Well, you are almost there, then.' Lien tries to sound as friendly as possible. She points at the kitchen door, towards the back of the garden, the dark forest and the water behind. 'Just follow the road, through the forest, across the heath, straight on. Keep walking on the narrow path; it leads right to the water.'

'Can't you come with us, show us the way in the dark?' The soldier asking looks at Eberhard, who answers in fluent Dutch.

'No, I'm sorry, we really can't. We're past curfew now.' He lifts his hands apologetically, but the soldier starts fumbling around in his bag.

Janny and Lien exchange a worried glance.

'Then I will just give you a permit,' he says cheerfully, placing a sheet of paper on the kitchen worktop.

'Mr and Mrs Bos are permitted to leave their house during curfew,' he says as he writes down the words.

The scratching of pen on paper is absorbed by the ticking of spoons.

'Signature, stamp, done.'

With a big smile, he hands the paper to Eberhard, who folds it and puts it in his pocket. They get their coats and off they go, down the path, into the forest.

When they return half an hour later, Janny and Bob have freed everyone from their hiding places and calmed them down. The residents had been terrified, not knowing what was going on downstairs while they heard so many deep voices in the house. Lien and Eberhard have to tell all about their walk.

'So there we were,' Lien says, still a little shaken, 'a German deserter and a Dutch Jew leading a German military unit of twenty soldiers, at night, across the dark heath towards the lake, which was once a sea.'

At that moment the toilet door opens and Bram appears – the poor old man has haemorrhoids.

'What is going on?' he stammers, and they all burst out laughing.

The permit, with a false date, would often be used that winter.

**Their second** spring in the house arrives and Janny realizes there is no other place where they have all lived this long together – not since the war began. She feels at home in The High Nest, despite the exceptional circumstances. Of course there is the constant threat, the fear of being found putting their lives on hold, a permanent pressure on their chest. But there is also the freedom of the forest, the heath, the water. There are days, sometimes weeks, when no one comes near the house. When there are no loud noises except for the music rising from various corners of the house at any given moment. And there is Jaap popping his dust-covered head out of the shed to show yet another construct – something one of the residents ordered or a new invention. They have food, water and tobacco; pretty much all they need.

It sometimes pains her to look at the little ones: Liselotte, Kathinka, Robbie. The girls are two and a half and Rob is already a big boy; he is four and a half, but in his own mind almost five. They feel the tension, are forced to grow up in world where there is no place for them. But when she thinks of all the other children she meets – in hiding with her non-Jewish resistance friends or spending a day at The High Nest when passing through – whose parents have been deported or killed, who are separated from their brothers and sisters and housed with perfect strangers, she finds comfort in the thought that at least their children are together, with their parents, their grandparents and their uncle Jaap.

The presence of so many grown-ups has made them rather smart. A little while ago, Lien went shopping with her daughter and they were in the queue at the grocer's, when Kathinka burst into an old folksong. The customers had looked at the little girl with endearment as she hopped up and down, singing 'Hop, Marjanneke', 'Hey ho, Marianne', perfectly in tune. But someone had taught Kathinka new words and instead of French soldiers chasing the Dutch prince away; there were now 'bald-headed Krauts'. Lien was shocked and quickly covered her daughter's mouth with her hand. The women in the shop looked at each other and burst out laughing. When Lien told Janny the story, she thought it was funny too. Nonetheless, Lien asked Eberhard never to teach their child such lyrics again.

They have become children of the forest. They climb trees, jump over trunks, run around the heath with their arms open wide, build huts in the back of the garden. On warm days they walk to the lake at the other side of the forest, bringing towels, fruit and water. The children are only allowed in calf-deep, but on their way home it feels as if they have conquered a sea. They go to bed all drowsy and sleep like a log under freshly cleaned sheets.

In the morning, when Janny arrives downstairs to find her mother coordinating breakfast shifts, she looks at all the people they are housing – young and old, alone or with their entire family, all those different characters, voices, dialects – and for an instant it feels as if, right in the middle of the forest, she is back in Amsterdam.

She has a bite to eat and a brief chat with her parents, then she puts Robbie's coat on and leaves the house for work, sometimes taking Liselotte with her too. She takes the tram or walks to the station, then gets on the train to either Utrecht, The Hague or Amsterdam, depending on what instructions she has received. She collects a package, delivers identity cards, distributes underground pamphlets or brings someone waybills, stolen from Bob's office. She never knows if her contact will be there, or whether they have been betrayed, arrested, deported. When she gets to the meeting point and finds no one or someone she doesn't expect, Janny kneels down as if to arrange her child's coat, looks about to assess the situation and makes herself scarce, back to the station, then home.

As she's walking, it always feels as if someone is following her, but she must remain calm. Not give in to the constant urge to run for it, to drag her child along and scoot off to . . . indeed, to where? There is no escaping it. If she gets caught, everything is finished and until then, she had better act normal and stay focused.

She always makes it home, back at The High Nest. Just like the kestrel at the back of their garden, where dark forest swallows the open grass. Each night after sunset he informs her with his clear cries that he has returned too. Janny keeps an eye on him, kindred spirit. In the daytime he goes hunting, slowly taking in the area, making speed with his short, pointy wings to then hover in the sky until he dives into action. Sometimes she is lucky and catches him suspended in the air – one of the most beautiful things she ever has seen. Calm, waiting for the perfect moment, which he picks intuitively. His tail and wings spread wide and in one straight line with his back and neck, as if time and heaven stand still. His back a beautiful reddish-brown, his head grey like the tail with its deep dark tips. Then, suddenly, he swoops towards the earth as if plunging to his death and reappears in the sky, seconds later, with a field mouse or a chick.

One night Janny is lying in bed, staring at the rafters.

Sometimes all the commotion in the house overwhelms her, but all is quiet now. Too quiet. She squeezes her eyes shut, tries to filter out Bob's soft snoring beside her, and listens. She suddenly realizes she has not seen or heard the kestrel for some time. Was it yesterday? The day before? She has been so busy, she has no idea. Tonight, she definitely has not heard his cries. Janny begins to feel nervous, as if this is not a good omen.

She falls asleep, with one ear alert to the sounds outside, and at sunrise creeps outside on bare feet. The rest of the house is still fast asleep. A sweet smell is lingering between the walls. In the half-light of morning she crosses the garden. The dew on the grass feels cold at her feet. She passes the gazebo, where she sees the children's doll's house and its miniature set of china, and through the orchard she walks to the back, where the dark edge of the forest is looming. She vanishes between the trees. Thick stems of ivy curl around old barks. Here and there are heaps of dry autumn leaves, yellow and crisp after hot summer months. Branches scratch her skin, a thorn tugs at the cotton of her nightgown, but she carefully walks on, her head leant back and her eyes focused on the thick treetops above.

After a couple of feet, she holds still with bated breath. There he is, perching on the rim of a large nest, once made by crows. His claws clasping the branches, his beady eyes focusing straight on Janny, ready, it seems, to attack. Behind him in the nest, a female is brooding; her broad back is speckled beautifully.

Cautiously, Janny backs out of the forest, turns around, walks briskly to the house across the lawn and crawls back into bed with Bob, a smile playing around her lips. Everyone is where they ought to be.

# 8
# Autumn Song

Each time she returns to Amsterdam, Janny finds the city emptier. When she takes the tram from Centraal Station and looks out of the window, it seems as if nothing has changed. The stately canal houses, the bridges and the awnings with names of old familiar shops – it is all still there. But the people are gone.

It is like passing through a ghost town; dark memories everywhere. The family with three daughters she was at school with – gone. The cheesemonger and the butcher – gone. The wealthy businessman and his family in the house with those heavy burgundy curtains – gone. All the market people she knew through her father – gone. Sometimes their places, curtains and all, have been taken by strangers. Her stomach churns as she watches a mother feeding her child on a chair that is not theirs. A former classmate used to live *there*, a girl Lien danced with used to live *there*. And 'used to' is only one year ago.

When she has to pick up something in the old Jewish Quarter, Janny walks along the Amstel river and Waterlooplein. The streets are deserted. It feels like walking in an architectural plan of the city, the cobbles clean and untrodden as far as her eyes can see. Nothing reminds her of the roaring, busy life that made this area so beautiful, the life she and her parents, her sister, her brother so fully enjoyed. In this version of the neighbourhood, houses seem empty, curtains are closed and the only people she sees are policemen. All life is drained from the Jewish Quarter; hundreds of years of heritage have been destroyed.

One day, in the spring of 1944, Janny returns to The High Nest after another day in lifeless Amsterdam. Even before she has walked around the house, she is welcomed by the chatter of women fluttering through the kitchen door. She instantly relaxes. Further down the garden, at the gazebo, the children are playing with their doll's house and the sounds of a piano well up from deep inside the house. Boys are playing marbles on the terrace. As she approaches, Mother waves at her through the kitchen window. Janny wipes her feet and when she enters the kitchen, she realizes their neighbourhood is not dead. They have brought a little Amsterdam to The High Nest.

British aircraft pass overhead at night, more and more of them. The next morning, they listen to the radio and tell Mother: see. Things are looking up at the Eastern Front. The Red Army is gaining ground and the Allied Forces will land soon. It won't be long now.

In Joseph's room is a large map, where he marks the progress at the Eastern Front after each news item. When someone at the table says anything about the troop movements that is not right, he corrects this person and drops names of places they had never heard of before the war: Kursk, Vyazma, Bryansk. Joseph closely followed the Battle of Kursk last summer and each victory on Fascist troops he reported, no matter how small or insignificant, was celebrated by the residents as a step towards liberation. Of course, Allied troops on Sicily are marked on the map too, as well as the surrender in May 1943 of German and Italian troops in Tunisia. But those are – literally – pinpricks compared to the bloody battles in the east. So much time has passed since then – and there is still no second front.

Each week the Brilleslijper family try to come up with something to lift everyone's spirits, such as a music night or a treasure hunt in the garden. Anything so as not to descend into anxiety, boredom, or, worst-case scenario, panic. With the opera sheet music Eberhard borrows at the Amsterdam library, they still create shows to perform at The High Nest. Eberhard studies the scores, Lien sings and Eberhard covers the bass or tenor parts when necessary. And so they put on their favourite pieces of Mozart, the operas *The Marriage of Figaro* and *The Magic Flute*. When they play *Fidelio* – the only opera by Beethoven, about Leonore who, disguised as prison guard, Fidelio, saves her husband, Florestan, from a political prison – the atmosphere at The High Nest is highly charged. The residents gather in the living room and sit around the dining table, in the comfy chairs or cross-legged on the floor. Outside it is dark; a few candles on the piano light up the room. Lien sings about the battle for justice and Florestan's fears in prison. The release follows when the prisoners' chorus sings their ode to freedom: 'Oh what joy, in the open air. Freely to breathe again! [. . .] Hope whispers softly in my ears! We shall be free, we shall find peace.'

On 1 May they cook each other a special dinner. Red Puck has made menus with elegant flowers and they have prepared no less than seven courses. The food is no more exciting than usual – mainly potatoes, vegetables, fish and a tiny bit of meat for everyone – but their creativity makes all the difference. They serve *salade* de prolétariat, viande rouge, pouding à la Révolution, and a tarte des plongeurs for dessert.

The beautiful front room underneath the rafters looks like a proper restaurant. The large dining table is full of stolen crockery, glasses, candles, menus and toilet paper folded into flowers serving as napkins. After dinner Eberhard plays the piano, the others sing or hum along, and for just one night they forget about the chaos outside the brick walls of the house.

They aren't fooling themselves saying it really is almost over; there is good progress at the Eastern Front. Mussolini has surrendered and the Allied forces have moved up to Southern Italy. Since 1941, Stalin has been calling for a second front to relieve pressure on the east. It can't be long now, they are sure of it.

Reports from the concentration camps have spread across the whole of Europe now and if even they, in their hiding places, have known what is happening for such a long time, surely the world cannot look away for much longer? Janny and Lien first heard about Auschwitz in 1942; that countless numbers of Jews were gassed – there were radio messages about exhaust fumes, later about gas chambers. Tens of thousands of Jews transported from Amsterdam to Westerbork, train after train. Freight trains with over 1,500 prisoners left Westerbork for Auschwitz each week. On Radio

London they also heard about camps in Majdanek, Treblinka and other Polish places. Last autumn they already worked out that at least 70,000 Dutch Jews had been deported within a year. It was beyond comprehension. All those abandoned houses, empty schools, shops. All those people in trains; a journey which, according to their calculations, must have taken at least one or two days. In freight wagons! They convinced each other that most of the deported had ended up in weapons factories. They clung to the thought that it was impossible to kill so many people in such a short amount of time.

Although they never talk about it, the residents of The High Nest know that with each day they are not saved, they are in more danger. Bert Bochove keeps them informed on local hideaways that are discovered. Apparently, the area was less *judenrein* than initially supposed; shelters are discovered in Naarden, Bussum, Laren, Blaricum, Huizen and Hilversum, and Jews are deported to Westerbork, non-Jews to camps in Vught or Amersfoort.

And so, in the spring of 1944, The High Nest feels like a pressure cooker with too many people under too much pressure, trying to find ways to let off steam. Jaap has quickly found his way: he is digging a tunnel from underneath the house to the garden. In the spare room on the ground floor, at the back of the house, where the garden meets the forest, he makes a hatch into the heavy wooden floor – its seams are invisible and it can be covered by the carpet. It is the room where Lien, Eberhard and Kathinka live, where they sleep and have their breakfast together, in the privacy of their family unit.

As soon as they have left their room, Jaap gets to work, day after day. To make better progress, he asks two boys hiding with them to help him. They dig the sand from underneath the house and carry it to the heath in buckets, one by one. There, they have to spread it again, to avoid attracting suspicion. It is hard, strenuous work and progress is slow, but Janny knows Jaap will not stop until he can proudly show her his job done.

'Janny, this can't go on.'

She is walking in the dunes with Frits Reuter. A breeze passing over the heath summons a purple surge towards the horizon. They walk a little uphill, warm air and loose sand pulling at their legs. On top of a dune they hold still and she feels him staring at her. He is expecting an answer. She wearily brushes a wisp of hair from her face.

'I know.'

They walk down, digging their heels in the sand, and Janny knows Frits wants to hear her plan. But there is none. So many people in the house, all those faces, each with their own story, all those hopeful eyes looking at her when she comes home: it is almost over now, right?

Who could she ask to leave? They all pass her mind's eye; little Red Puck with her apron, her jokes. Jetty with her cheeky smile, turning all the boys' heads. Dear old Bram and Loes, always together – she remembers the astonished look on Bram's face when those soldiers had turned up in their kitchen. She thinks of her friends who have fallen: Gerrit, Mik and all those others whose fate she does not know. As soon as Frits arrived, he told them they had lost Janrik van Gilse too. On 28 March, half a year after his younger brother, Mik, was shot, he was killed by the *Sicherheitspolizei*.

So much has happened in such a short amount of time. Sometimes Janny thinks they will all meet again after the war, drink coffee along the canal and talk about the future. She wishes she could just keep taking everyone in, all the Jews not yet deported, all the resistance people not yet executed, and they would all live together at this place in the forest.

They walk towards the lake and Frits is getting impatient: 'How will you go about it?'

Janny sighs.

'I'm working on it, Frits. We have already placed two people elsewhere. I'm asking around for the others. With Bert and Annie in Huizen, Grietje in Blaricum, my contact in Laren. Amsterdam is no longer an option, but there are vacant houses further down in the forest. Karel Poons' host might know a place for one, perhaps two people.'

She looks aside. Frits does not seem impressed.

'We'll work it out,' Janny says. 'I know we have to, I'm doing the best I can.'

Laughter sounds from behind the final hill separating them from the water. Lien, Eberhard and Bob have taken the children to the lake, while they turned off towards the forest to catch up. Cor Snel, Frits' girlfriend, is with the others too. When they reach the top of the hill they see her waving enthusiastically, the sun reflecting against her blonde hair. 'Come!' she mimes, moving her mouth like a fish. Janny laughs and runs down the hill.

**They have** almost given up hope, when suddenly it is there – 6 June 1944. D-Day. The second front they have been desperately waiting for. Radio London transmits the first two lines of 'Autumn Song', the poem by Paul

Verlaine – a cryptic message announcing the invasion is at hand.

| | |
|---|---|
| *Les sanglots longs* | The long sobs |
| *Des violons* | Of violins |
| *De l'automne* | Of autumn |
| *Blessent mon cœur* | Wound my heart |
| *D'une langueur* | With a monotone |
| *Monotone.* | Languor. |

And it happens; the Brits and the Americans land on the Normandy coast. In terrible weather, waves crashing against the steep cliffs, steel landing crafts lower their ramps for thousands of soldiers to break loose in the waves, their backs covered by battleships firing away. Bombs would hit craters in the sand for the front-line soldiers to seek cover, but visibility is poor; thousands of rockets miss their targets and end up in the water. The young men must walk across over 500 yards of sand unprotected. The journey has made them seasick, the landing soaking wet. Loose sand is tugging at their combat boots and their kit weighs heavy on their backs. For over a quarter of a mile, they are live targets for German tanks.

From a German perspective, the water is black with

Allied marine ships. Viewed from the sky, however, the beach is quickly colouring red with blood. Hours later, when the sea advances and waves, little by little, re-conquer the beach, the sand turns yellow again. Heavy losses are suffered, but the Allies force the Germans back and march towards Paris.

People in shelters throughout Europe are thinking exactly the same: it is only a matter of time before our liberation is a fact.

When news of the invasion reaches The High Nest via the radio, a tight belt around their bellies seems to snap. For the first time in months, the residents breathe freely again. They cheer and hug each other, freeze to the spot or burst into tears. Lien grabs her sister's arm to dance for joy, but Janny wriggles free after a few steps. She walks to the beautiful wine cupboard in the corner of the front room, grabs a knife from the dining table and prizes open its wooden doors. The cupboard is filled with bottles of expensive red wine with yel-lowed labels and elegant letters; she takes four of them, puts them on the table and asks Jaap to get glasses from the kitchen. Joseph and Fietje exchange a quick glance, then shrug and begin to pour. They bring a loud toast – '*Mazzeltov!*' – sniff the bouquet until it makes them dizzy, take small sips, swish the wine around in their mouth. The alcohol goes straight to their heads, colours their cheeks as they stay glued to the radio.

While the others are drinking and listen intently, Janny walks to the cupboard with a note for the Jansen sisters: after the war they will replace the missing bottles. She will later regret not finishing the entire stock that day.

# 9

# The Chinese Vase

Bob and Janny get up early. The rest of the house is still in peace, muffled noises rising from some of the rooms. They sit in the kitchen in silence, drink a cup of coffee, eat a crust of bread. The cool of the night lingers between the heavy brick walls, but when Janny opens the door to the garden, sultry air presses her skin. Another warm day. They kiss each other goodbye; Bob is leaving for the office and she has a special assignment in Amsterdam.

Robbie is coming with her, happily skipping along by her side; children offer a certain protection during police checks. They take the train from Naarden-Bussum to Amsterdam, where they first stop by at the register to pick up a few identity cards. Her contacts there request new, real cards in the names of people who have passed away – those deaths will have to be registered after the war. Identity cards are so hard to forge that this is the safest way.

With the cards in her bra, she continues her journey to Roelof Hartplein in Amsterdam, where she has arranged to meet her friend Trees Lemaire, who still works for the Identity Card Centre. She will take the documents from Janny and further distribute them underground.

Janny is standing on the square connecting Roelof Hartstraat, J.M. Coenenstraat and Van Baerlestraat, holding Robbie's hand, and waits. She has a good view of all the streets, but Trees is nowhere to be seen. Robbie is getting impatient, starts whining, tugging at her skirt, and Janny is getting nervous. Her friend is never late. None of them is ever late; they simply cannot afford to be.

Seconds creep by, but nothing happens. There is no one else on the square – she feels unprotected. The sun steadily climbs to the highest point above the city and beneath her hot crown her head starts to pound. The identity cards are burning on her chest. She peers across the street, where an imposing building folds itself around the corner, numerous windows looking out on her, and she starts pacing up and down.

She thinks back on the day after the house search in

The Hague, when someone demanded the keys to the printer and she had agreed to meet him in front of the Willem III statue at Noordeinde. Krauts were waiting behind each pillar.

Robbie really begins to cry now. His cries fan out across the square, into the three streets. Janny resists the urge to press her hand on his mouth and instead tries to quiet him. 'We'll be back on the train again soon, that will be nice.' She looks over his head, scanning the surroundings. At least ten minutes have passed. This feels all wrong. She pulls Robbie's hand and starts to walk, fast, away from the square, in the direction of the Concertgebouw.

She rushes until Robbie stops protesting, focuses on placing his feet next to his mother's without falling, steadied by her painful clasp. Janny already feels the *Sicherheitspolizei* breathing down her neck, a hand reaching out to tap her shoulder. She is expecting cars to appear from all side streets, sirens wailing, to close her in, and she walks on without looking back, her chest rising in synchrony with the step of her feet.

A tram is waiting – they get in. Centraal Station. Through the station hall with Robbie, who is dragging his feet and says nothing. There are mutes everywhere, she knows that. Act normal, calm, or else some Kraut with an unusual sense of morality might arrest her for child abuse. She holds still, kneels down and folds her hands around Robbie's face, 'It's all good, right?' She gives him a kiss, gets up, looks around and composedly walks to the platform, where the train to Naarden is ready to leave.

As fields pass them by outside, Robbie steers an imaginary car through the air, his feet dangling high above the floor. Her heart is still racing, the sticky documents on her chest are moving along. She listens to the slow cadence of the train, tries to breathe on the beat. Would Trees have been caught? And if they question her, would she talk? Tell everything, speak about The High Nest? No, Janny will refuse to believe it. Trees would rather die. But still, there were others who . . . a knot in her stomach blocks her breathing, a clenched fist just below her diaphragm.

Weesp station, get out, they still have shopping to do.

Robbie is skipping along, holding her hand; he seems to have forgotten everything. To the farmer for a large bag of wheat. With the coffee grinder they turn it into flour for bread. It is still early in the day, but when she walks back to Weesp station with two heavy bags, Janny feels the soles of her feet burning.

A few more minutes on the train to Naarden. The carriages are almost deserted and as the train speeds up, her breathing returns to normal. No one has followed them and alternative scenarios replace her previous dark thoughts. Trees simply overslept. Or was given the wrong time. Wrong location, perhaps. It has happened to Janny as well. She will distribute the documents some other way. She rests her head against the seat and sighs.

When they arrive at Naarden-Bussum station, the tram is just about to leave. Robbie races ahead, Janny is slowed down by the load. They catch the tram – a little bit of luck. Sometimes they walk home across the heath, but not today, not with all these groceries.

They get off at Ericaweg, then walk for ten more minutes along the unpaved path, narrowed down by nature until it ends at The High Nest, just past the edge of the forest. The bags pull her arms down; they almost drag across the ground. She can only take a few steps without pausing. The sun is high in the sky, heathers draw the last water deep from the ground, but the tips of their shrubs have dried out already and rustle like scorched grass.

Almost home. Janny feels a sense of relief, lowers her bags and wipes her forehead. Robbie runs ahead, stops, turns around and waits for his mother.

'You go,' Janny calls, 'and ask if someone can come help me carry. I'll wait here.'

And off he goes. She smiles when she sees him run

as if the morning hasn't happened. The boy dashes off the path and disappears into the forest, out of her sight.

Janny plumps herself down on the bag of wheat and waits. It takes long. Too long. Five more minutes. She parks the bags behind some young oak trees, a wall of shrubs between their slender trunks, pulls the identity cards from her bra and hides them underneath the groceries. She notices her hands are shaking wildly.

She follows the path with brisk steps and then begins to run, dry clods of soil slow her down, she sprains her ankle but hurries on. All her tiredness is gone. The edge of the forest. Not a sign of Robbie. The shell path crunches underneath her feet, the house appears between the trees and her gaze shoots up to the shutters flanking the window, first floor on the right, above the name of the house. The large Chinese vase is gone. Her knees give way and her hand reaches for a grip that is not there. A thought flashes through her mind: if she turns around *now*, runs into the forest, she has a chance.

*Liselotte. Robbie.*

In slow motion, she opens the gate and walks down the path to the back of the house, where the front door is. The ground beneath her feet is rolling, seems made of rubber foam. She takes giant steps, but hardly moves forwards. Only now does she notice the quiet. All the doors, all the windows are shut. No people in the garden, no music, no one sawing in the shed. Even the deafening birdsong has stopped. The house is on its hill, unaffected, but all the life has run out.

She is standing in front of the deep red door with the square window and the small white bars. She looks back one more time, scanning the bright blue sky. The kestrel is not there. Then she rings the doorbell.

**The door** flies open; a man with a shaven head and piercing eyes is standing in the doorway. It is Eddy Moesbergen, one of the most successful Jew hunters of the Henneicke Column. The group was disbanded in October 1943 when Amsterdam was declared *judenrein* and Moesbergen has since joined the Amsterdam police, who work for the SD. On his own initiative and the reward of the double rate of fifteen guilders per Jew, Moesbergen has continued the chase.

One of his informants is a pension keeper from Amsterdam whom he once arrested for hiding Jews. Since her release, Moesbergen has threatened to send her to a camp, unless she feeds him information. The previous day, on 9 July, the desperate lady had given him a crumpled note, which read 'Bos, The High Nest Villa, Driftweg 2, Naarden'. She had received the address in September 1943 on an Amsterdam terrace, where an anonymous Jewish resistance worker had passed it on as a potential shelter for people in need, but she had never used it.

Moesbergen took the note and this morning he travelled to Huizen with two colleagues: Harm Krikke and Willem Punt, both SD. At the local police station they asked two officers in civilian clothes to accompany them and set off to have a look. To his astonishment, Moesbergen discovered a whole group of Jews hiding in the remote country house, and now there's another one calling at the door.

Janny stares Moesbergen in the face and in a flash she sees Robbie, standing in the hall behind him, a terrified look on his face. Before she can call her son, the man grabs her arm, roughly pulls her inside and barks in her face: 'Who are you?'

Janny, in her bewilderment, says: 'Why don't you first tell me who *you* are?'

The man lashes out – several times – hitting her full in the face with his flat hand.

Robbie starts to scream: 'Mummy, Mummy!'

Janny staggers, the walls are spinning, but she manages to keep standing. Moesbergen drags her to the front room; Robbie grabs her leg as she passes. The door opens and there they are, sat on the wooden floor. When they see Janny and Robbie, they gasp for air. Not them! They had hoped the vanished vase would work.

They are all here. Lien and Eberhard with Kathinka. Jaap. Red Puck with – thank God – Liselotte on her lap. Jetty. Simon. Loes and Bram, a red stripe right across his neck. No, they are not all here. Janny quickly counts. Four are missing: Father, Mother, Rita, Willi.

When she sees the distorted face of her younger sister, red from the beatings on one side, Lien puts her hand to her mouth with a loud sob. Eberhard presses her close. Bram Teixeira de Mattos looks at Janny intently, slowly shaking his head. She reads his lips: 'It is not your fault,' and then another man hits him to the ground.

'No talking!'

Janny is thrown on the floor too, Robbie quickly nestles against her. She sits up, cross-legged, gives a reassuring nod to Liselotte and Puck, staring at her with large eyes and trembling lower lip, her arms wrapped tightly around the little girl.

The sound of heavy footsteps is all around the house; on the stairs, in the rooms, while the police are turning everything inside out with great force. The lamps above the dining table are shaking. They watch in silence, then quickly avert their eyes. One of the SD men, Detective Punt from Amsterdam, has been put on guard with them and after the nasty blow to Bram's head, they don't want to provoke him.

Through the hatch to the kitchen they hear Moesbergen and another colleague eat their provisions.
They shout at the officers upstairs, chuck something
to eat at them, eat noisily, laugh and continue their
house search. They are yelling obscene threats to drive
any remaining others out of their hiding places. Janny
closes her eyes and thinks of Father and Mother, lying
underneath their hatch without knowing what is happening and who has already been caught. With her fingertips she brushes her cheek, which is slowly swelling.

While she sits on the ground and tries to remain
calm, she listens to the noise of the men, repeating their
names like a mantra:

Moesbergen
Krikke
Punt
Hiemstra
Boellaard

Had they ever believed they were untouchable? That
the hill where The High Nest stood had its own atmosphere, off the radar during raids, overlooked by the
authorities, time and again? No, they did not live in a
fantasy world. They had always been watchful and very
aware of the risks of their work; they had conducted a

drill with the emergency button and the hatches only a few days ago.

Everybody had told them it was madness; Jews running a hideaway for Jews. Bert and Annie Bochove from the village. Mik, each time they saw him. Frits and Cor, Jan and Aleid, Karel Poons and numerous others. But to Janny and Lien it was always beyond question: not only would they themselves and their families survive, but they would also help as many others as possible. They had done what they had to do, what they *could* do.

Inundated with people seeking shelter, resistance members passing by, they really had taken security measures. People had relocated, they no longer accepted guests they did not know and they developed a protocol for underground contacts visiting the house. They had a secret alarm, hiding places for each resident, an underground tunnel, a web of informants with the authorities. The vase in front of the window was a good enough sign to warn people that something was amiss from afar. But they could not arm themselves for betrayal.

Lien, Eberhard and Kathinka had just finished breakfast in their room, downstairs at the forest side, when suddenly they heard loud noises outside. It was just before nine – Bob and Janny had already left, but the rest of the house was still waking up; most people stayed in their room for some peace and quiet before immersing themselves in the noise of the day. Lien and Eberhard froze and looked at each other, and from the corner of their eyes they saw the picture that had often haunted them in their sleep: strange men walking across the grounds.

Eberhard immediately came into action. He rolled up the carpet, opened the hatch and shoved the chest with prohibited goods into the hole underground: illegal newspapers, Yiddish lyrics, resistance pamphlets, books on Jewish Culture Lien studied with Leo Fuks and much more. Kathinka was watching, a puzzled look on her face, and Lien quickly whispered: 'Don't tell anyone, darling!' Shut the hatch, cover it with the carpet, put table and chairs on top.

Banging on the front door.

'Open up!'

Eberhard squeezed Lien's hand and opened the door from their room to the hall. He walked towards the front door, pressed the emergency button, praying everyone upstairs was awake and would do as they had so often practised. As the banging and shouting persisted, he fumbled with the lock to buy time. As soon as the door opened, a man stormed in, red-faced and wild like a bull.

'*Sicherheitsdienst!*'

A second man followed on his heels and behind him, Eberhard saw another three standing in the garden, attentively looking around. Their civilian clothes frightened him; for some reason he found men wearing uniforms less threatening, as if their task was imposed and could therefore be put aside again. The men spoke Dutch.

'Where are they?' the leader of the pack shouted straight to Eberhard's face. A fountain of spit accompanied his words.

Eberhard looked surprised. Lien tried to make herself small, pushing her back against the wall of the hall while she held Kathinka close so she wouldn't have to see.

'Who?' Eberhard asked.

'To the front room with you!'

The man walked back to the front door, leaned outside through the doorway and beckoned to the men on guard. In the hall they received their orders.

'Punt: guard those three. Hiemstra: come with me.'

And off he went, up the stairs. Hiemstra, a fragile-looking man with cold eyes and pale scaly skin, ran after him with large steps. The SD-officer who had entered earlier was searching the ground floor.

Eberhard, Lien and Kathinka were sitting in the front room, with Detective Punt as their guard, anxiously awaiting what the men would find upstairs. Puck and Liselotte were brought into the room first. The little girl had a fever and crawled onto Puck's lap like a kitten. The men continued their search.

'I would swear I saw a young boy standing at the window just then, when we were outside,' they heard somebody upstairs say through the wooden ceiling.

Lien held her breath – it must have been Willi. When he saw the alarm lights flash on, he must have glanced outside, curious to see what was happening. They had urged each other never to do that. Alarm meant: hide, *now*!

From time to time, Moesbergen came downstairs to yell at them. He took them out of the room one by one to threaten them into talking – but they kept their mouths shut and so far the men had not discovered anyone else in the house. Lien was glad at least Bob, Janny and Robbie were not at home, and then she suddenly remembered their sign. The vase in the window on the first floor, it had to go! She did not know what Janny was up to today – they deliberately never told each other – or what time she would be back. Perhaps she was already on her way home.

When Punt briefly left the room, she whispered into Kathinka's ear: 'Run upstairs, to the large front room. I'll follow you. Go!'

She gave the child a push and Kathinka ran into the hall, up the stairs, into the room at the front, her mother close on her heels. The SD-officers started shouting, at her and at each other, but Lien faked a nosedive for her daughter and swept the vase from the windowsill with her arm. The deafening tinkle of porcelain shattering on the floor was drowned out by Moesbergen roaring at his men. Kathinka had no idea what was happening – she burst into tears as Lien quickly scooped her up in her arms.

Officer Hiemstra drove them down the stairs, where he handed them back to an embarrassed-looking Punt. Lien, quieting Kathinka, shot Eberhard a triumphant look. The vase was gone.

'This is your very last chance: where are the others?'

Lien was staring at the face of Moesbergen – a vertical vein was bulging in his neck, a horizontal one on his forehead. He leant towards Lien.

'I know there are more people hiding here. Where are they?'

Lien turned pale with fear. Had they been watching them? Had they known all along they were here? In that case they were lost. One of their resistance contacts must have been arrested, must have talked. Or perhaps one of their former residents. Hardly anyone could endure the torture; they knew, they understood. But who on earth was it?

'I have no idea what you are talking about,' she answered calmly.

Neither Eberhard nor Puck said anything either, but when Moesbergen took Kathinka out of the room, they panicked. Five minutes later the girl came back and proudly said: 'He said I could have chocolate, but I said no. I said nothing, Mummy, only that he is a very bad sir.' Lien pressed her daughter to her chest.

After another hour had passed, they heard stumbling on the stairs. The door flung open and Bram and Loes Teixeira de Mattos were thrown into the room, bowed heads and lowered eyes. Moesbergen briefly stared at the group gathered before him on the ground, then ordered Bram to get up again and come with him. The old man rose with difficulty and followed him to the hall. The door was shut, but they could hear every single word.

'So, you are a Jew?' Moesbergen screamed as if he were shouting down a crowd.

'No, sir,' they heard Bram say, his soft voice muffled by the heavy walls. Loes lowered her head and cried, covering her face with her hands.

'Here we have a Jew who doesn't even know that he's Jewish!'

Laughter. Then there was stumbling in the hall, disturbing sounds, furniture moving, a scrimmage perhaps, and they all stared at the door, their faces tight with fear.

'Are you still not a Jew? Do I have to make you a Jew?'

The group in the front room flinched at each word.

Suddenly, the door flew open. Bram staggered inside, his hands around his neck, his eyes bloodshot, breathing heavily. With difficulty, he sat down on the ground next to Loes, who moved towards her husband, but he recoiled and stared at the floor, gasping for breath with his mouth wide open. And then there was just silence.

One hour later: Jaap, Jetty and Simon.

'Look!' Moesbergen said with a smile and a theatrical gesture as he pushed them into the room. 'We found the next lot. You will go to prison. All of you.'

They had torn down the panelling, the wooden floors, and discovered their hiding places.

Around two in the afternoon, the crushing blow: Janny and little Rob. The broken vase had not averted their fate.

———

**They have** been in the front room for a while and it seems the others are too hard to find. Janny starts to think clearly again. The earlier panic has gone; she feels icily calm. A few things are urgent at this moment. Bob needs to be warned at work. Those who are not yet found must remain in their hiding places. And they have to get the children out of here. She looks straight at Lien and knows she thinks exactly the same. They have been able to postpone it for so long, but now the time has come: they have to part from their children.

'Sir,' Janny calmly says to Punt, 'my daughter has a fever.' She points at Liselotte, slumped against Puck, red cheeks and drowsy eyes, like a little clown. He shrugs and looks at her questioningly.

'She has to go to a doctor. She won't survive prison.'

Punt averts his gaze and stares outside. He doesn't want to hear this.

Janny looks at Lien and nods.

'Don't be scared,' Lien whispers into Kathinka's ear, and she begins to squeal like a pig.

Kathinka jumps away from her mother, who falls back on the floor, wildly flailing her arms around, her head shooting from left to right as she keeps screaming.

Everyone in the room is in shock, including Punt,

who looks as if he sees a ghost. He gets ready to lash out, but cannot decide who to target first.

'Not the children! Not the children!'

Lien screams and cries. She fakes the fit, but her despair is real. She spits, drools, rolls across the floor. Punt has to jump to the side and shouts at her to stop, but Lien just adds a little extra.

'Take me! But not the children, please not the children.'

Janny's eyes fill with tears. The rest look on – they understand it is a ruse, but they also feel what's at stake here.

'Stop it, woman! Where do the children have to go then? Stop it!' Punt looks at the door, afraid Moesbergen will come in to establish once more that he cannot handle the situation.

'They can go to the doctor,' Janny says calmly from a corner of the room.

Punt turns around. 'What?'

'There is a GP close by. I am sure he will take the children in. Please. I can call him now.'

Lien moans like a wounded animal and keeps murmuring: not the children. Punt fears she will have another fit any moment. He briefly nods at Janny, but then Moesbergen enters.

He gives Punt orders to take the whole group,

except for the elderly couple Teixeira de Mattos, to Huizen police station. No one knows why Bram and Loes are not coming – perhaps because they have difficulty walking, perhaps because the officers think they can pry more information out of these fragile people. The two local officers who have helped the SD men all day, Hiemstra and Boellaard, will escort Punt.

'Go. Now.'

The three men chase them outside and line them up in front of The High Nest. It is clear that their discovery was a complete surprise; nothing is taken care of – no transport, no backup, no plan.

The party sets off to Huizen on foot, but Lien and Janny keep working on Punt along the way; the children are half-Jews – bring them to the doctor, take us with you. When it turns out we are lying, you can always pick them up later. The doctor lives just around the corner from here, we are almost there, look, there's his house. Come on, please.

Punt gives in. He sends one officer to the station with the rest of the detainees and asks the other one to escort him to the doctor. They turn off towards Nieuwe Bussummerweg, where Doctor Van den Berg lives, and ring the doorbell.

The doctor opens the door and is shocked to see the two women, white as chalk, on his doorstep. They are

Mrs Brandes and Mrs Bos, holding their three little children tight; he has helped them before, knows both women are Jewish and have people in hiding at The High Nest. Behind them are two men. Punt introduces himself as an SD officer; his colleague is with the Huizen police. Can they come in? Before the doctor can answer, the men are in his house.

From there everything goes fast. The doctor and his wife are prepared to take in the children for the time being. Punt commands that the children remain at the disposal of the SD at all times: provisional examination shows that both mothers have married Aryans, so it seems the children are not fully Jewish. If, however, they do turn out to be, they shall be collected and deported.

Robbie is almost five and suddenly realizes what is about to happen. He looks from the strange men to his mother, presses his fingers firmly in her flesh and is about to burst into tears. Janny kneels down and folds her hands around his face. She presses her nose against his, looks him straight in the eyes and whispers: 'Don't be afraid. I'll come back, I promise. Daddy will come and pick you up, and then you tell Daddy I'll come back to you. All right?'

His body is shaking and his eyes are wide, but Robbie nods slowly and lets his mother press a last kiss on his snotty lips. Janny gives him a little shove and the police officer takes him. Then she picks up Liselotte, still glowing with fever. Lien does the same with Kathinka. Both girls are almost three and they whimper softly, unable to understand what is going on but fully aware that something terrible is about to happen.

'Be good, stay calm, all will be well,' Lien whispers in Kathinka's hair.

Janny presses Liselotte to her chest one more time and then the doctor takes the three children into the living room.

It is dead quiet when the front door has shut behind them. Janny and Lien walk down the path to the street, look back one more time. The three little ones appear in front of the window – they do not wave.

Then a push in their back and they are gone.

# 10
# The Bullet

Indeed, the SD had not expected such a big catch; hardly any Jews are left in the country. One Jew, perhaps two, they thought, but − not counting the children − they found no less than eight: Janny, Lien, Jaap, Bram, Loes, Jetty, Simon, Puck. Plus the German deserter, the traitor. Even Moesbergen has not often made such a substantial discovery.

All of them, except for Bram and Loes, are imprisoned at Huizen police station. Punt instantly returns to The High Nest to help his colleagues Moesbergen and Krikke, who stayed behind, with the search. They are certain more people are hiding in the forest villa, with all its expertly built secret spaces. They demolish floors and panels, tear away carpets, shout profanities to chase any people left in hiding out of their shelters, and knock on walls with hammers.

But all remains deathly quiet, the stones of The High Nest do not speak. The men threaten to riddle the entire house with bullets, pretend to give up, pull the front door shut and sneak back inside, but: nothing. They are furious. There *must* be more of them. They have counted the mattresses in the rooms, the toothbrushes at the sinks.

In the meantime, the group of nine must be taken to the SD headquarters in Amsterdam for questioning. How, though? Since they were unprepared, no police vans are available in Naarden nor Huizen. The SD officers telephone around for vans to hire, but to no avail. Could they take the group on the train? Too risky. Eventually, they have to wait for one of their Amsterdam SD colleagues to drive down with a van and collect them.

Meanwhile, Janny has scribbled the number of Bob's office on a piece of paper and waits for the right person to pass it on to. She knows from experience that there are good people at the Huizen police; officers who turn a blind eye at crucial moments, even pass on information to the local resistance and people in hiding. She slips the note into the hand of one of the officers who was with them all day. 'Please call: do *not* come home!' She says it between her teeth, barely audible. The officer clenches his fist around the paper and says nothing. Now, she must hope for the best.

It is already late afternoon when the SD van from Amsterdam arrives. They leave the police station and stop at The High Nest along the way to pick up Bram and Loes; the couple look ashen-faced and fragile. They don't know what happened to them in the meantime, but the last four people – Joseph, Fietje, Willi and Rita – have, apparently, neither been discovered nor betrayed.

On the way to Amsterdam, all of them are quiet; they fear that each word they say might give one of the others away. Lien and Janny can barely look at each other, defeated after leaving the children, sick with worry about Father and Mother underneath their hatch.

As soon as they reach Amsterdam, they sit up. For everyone but Janny and Eberhard, it is their first time here in a very long while. They enter the city via Weesperzijde and drive towards the south, where the SD headquarters are. Amsterdam feels numb. No hustle and bustle, just very many soldiers and policemen on the streets. Even at the end of this bright summer day, when the inner city would normally explode with noise and activity, a cloud seems to hang above the people and the houses.

Cross the bridge and onwards across Amstellaan, they pass Rijnstraat, then the prominent building on Apollolaan – The Tower of Labour as they used to call it. A skeleton of steel with glass armour, the proud sky-scraper of the Social Security Bank. Only a few years ago the sisters had watched with open mouths as the window cleaner dangled in his cradle; the very first one in the Netherlands. They thought it was dead scary, but the man had waved at them, cheerfully. Now, the Wehrmacht has graced the roof of the tower with searchlights and anti-aircraft guns. In The High Nest the occupation was mainly tangible, here it is visible.

And then: Euterpestraat, the old school building.

'Get out!'

From the bus via the main hall to a dark basement. Narrow wooden bunk beds against the wall. The door slams shut as they stand pressed together, lined up as if this were a post office. Damp darkness, a single light bulb at the ceiling. They sit down on the cold floor by touch, feel the presence of other people in the room. No one speaks.

That evening, a police van takes them to a slightly more modern building on Marnixstraat. After a rest-less, anxious night, they are brought back to the Euterpestraat basement in the morning. The interrogation bunker.

Together, they have discussed several escape options, but the SS guards never leave their side. They are taken out of the basement one by one. SS-*Sturmbannführer* Willi Lages, the German head of the SD in the North Holland region, is an experienced torturer and has been involved in several executions. Promises, blackmail, profanities; he pulls out all the stops, but they all keep their mouths shut. He threatens to pick up the children to get them talking; Janny and Lien fear they may not remain silent when he does. Lien is terrified they will find out she and Eberhard are not at all married, which officially makes Kathinka fully Jewish and eligible for deportation.

When they return to the Marnixstraat station that night, Bram and Loes Teixeira de Mattos have been taken away, sent to Westerbork camp. In low spirits, Janny and Lien walk through the corridors towards the cells, and then cannot believe their eyes: Joseph and Fietje are standing at the end of the hallway. Old, fragile. A hand briefly touching an arm, eyes meeting just long enough to catch the despondent looks. Father has protectively wrapped his arm around Mother, knowing full well that it will not be enough.

'We have held out as long as we could,' Joseph whispers apologetically. He lowers his eyes. 'They have discovered the others too. And Eberhard's documents.'

They must walk on, to the cell. Lien staggers, tries to find Janny's eyes: it's all over now.

As soon as they had moved into The High Nest, Eberhard had buried his German papers, including his original identity card, in a chest made of lead at the back of the garden. After D-Day, all optimistic, they had dug up the box to see what state the papers were in. They were wet and warped. In one of the bedrooms was an out-of-use fireplace; Eberhard had put the papers out to dry in there. He had intended to wrap them up better, bury them again, later. Now, they know who he really is. Jean-Jacques Bos stood a chance. Eberhard Rebling will hang.

Meanwhile, everyone at the SD headquarters is thrilled with the catch: sixteen stowaways, including two children. Those will be left in peace for now; *Mischlinge* do not have to go on transport. The third child is a different story. Because they found the German's papers, they now know he never married the Jewish woman; their daughter is fully Jewish.

Moesbergen is pleased with the news and commands Doctor Van den Berg to deliver the child in person at the SD office in Amsterdam as soon as possible.

All the adults, except Janny, Lien and Eberhard, are

taken to the House of Detention at Weteringschans on day three. A few months earlier, their friend Gerrit van der Veen, Mik's companion at *The Free Artist*, committed an assault on this same prison in an attempt to free other resistance fighters. The assault on the Amsterdam register in March 1943 had only been partly successful, but that did not stop Gerrit from trying the lion's den again. He stormed Weteringschans in May 1944, was shot in the back but escaped.

A few weeks later he was arrested, after all, and was executed in the dunes near Haarlem in June. The Brilleslijpers and their residents are unaware of this news. At the time they are imprisoned at Weteringschans – two out of three founders of *The Free Artist* are dead: Mik van Gilse and Gerrit van der Veen. The third partner, composer Jan van Gilse, Mik's father, already in poor health, succumbs a few months later. The light of *The Free Artist*, standard-bearer of the artists' resistance, has gone out for good.

Lien and Eberhard spend the night of 12 July with just the two of them in one cell. It is their last night together. They hold each other in silence, prepare for their farewell, think of Kathinka without speaking her name.

'If we survive, we will meet at Mieke and Haakon's on Johannes Verhulststraat, all right?'

Eberhard looks at Lien questioningly and she nods.

Those are the only words that count, although they describe a highly unlikely scenario. As Lien cries, Eberhard cradles her in his arms. Janny has given her a Luminal, a sedative that can knock down a horse. Lien breaks the pill in two and gives one half to Eberhard so he can get some sleep. He has to be fit to endure the questioning the next day. They sleep as if anaesthetized and the next morning, Thursday, 13 July, they are separated.

Shortly after, everyone but Eberhard and Janny are put on the train to Westerbork: Joseph, Fietje, Lien and Jaap. The girls, Puck and Jetty. Simon. Bram and Loes. Their daughter, Rita, and their son-in-law, Willi. They are no longer required.

**From now** on the SD focuses on the German deserter and the Jewish resistance woman. Together, they have done pretty much everything the Aryan bible forbids and the only question is: who must fall first?

The Dutch officers of the Marnixstraat police station, however, are good to them, even seem to pity their fate, and Janny takes the chance: perhaps can they purchase their freedom? The officers say they would help if they could, but it simply is not possible. The SS are everywhere – they trust no one and are keeping a close watch on them too.

The pattern remains the same: they sleep at Marnixstraat and are questioned at the SD headquarters at Euterpestraat. There, *Sturmbannführer* Willi Lages interrogates them in turns. He is on good form, this tall man with his egg-shaped skull, thin lips and pointed nose that seems permanently pinched. Janny cannot bear looking at his face; his features are too sharp. She is beaten to get Eberhard talking. Eberhard is beaten to get Janny talking. Both remain silent and are laughed at by Lages.

'Your fate is sealed anyway,' he sneers at Eberhard. 'Death penalty for *Fahnenflucht, Landesverrat, Sabotage und Rassenschande!*'

He spits the last word in his face with disgust: race defilement. A child with a Jewish woman – his fellow countryman could not have fallen any lower.

'You will appear in front of the military court tomorrow and then you are finished.'

One last night Janny and Eberhard stay at Marnixstraat police station, knowing that execution awaits him the next day. Janny tosses and turns, worries all night, feverishly trying to come up with a way to save Eberhard from the bullet, but her mind is blank. When at last she falls asleep, she dreams of tumbling backwards into a deep well, her fingers failing to find a hold, not yet reaching the bottom when the guards collect her from her cell in the early morning of 14 July.

When they take her behind Eberhard to the police van waiting outside, Janny's head almost bursts with a migraine. The morning sun climbing a cloudless sky is already burning brighter than her eyes can bear. The doors at the back of the van are wide open; they see wooden bench seats on either side. The officers push them inside the vehicle, where an older detainee is already waiting, staring at the caps of his shoes. Two policemen in civilian clothes take their place beside them and shut the doors; the windows are opened to let in fresh air. Eberhard, Janny and one officer on one bench, the other detainee and the second officer opposite them on the other. When the van starts to move, all five of them turn their face to the windows at the back, staring at the Amsterdam streets they are leaving behind.

Oddly enough, they are driving north. The SD headquarters at Euterpestraat are in the south part of the city. Haarlemmerstraat. Janny and Eberhard exchange a brief glance. Spaarndammerstraat.

'Where are we going?' Janny asks. She hears her voice somewhere in the tin space, as if it is not her own.

'Amsterdam-North. We have to collect someone else first,' one of the officers responds.

They drive on in silence. Black spots dance before Janny's eyes; her head is pounding against her temples but she does not want to close her eyes. She wants to see her city, because she does not know when she will be back. If she will ever be back.

The car stops. Spaarndammerdijk police station. The officer next to Janny gets out – 'Be right back' – and slams the door shut behind him. Janny blinks, one time, ten times, to chase away the spots. Eberhard turns towards her, tries to meet her gaze, looks at the door handle next to her. Would she . . . ? Then Janny leans forwards, close to the face of the officer opposite her. There is a gun in his lap. She starts to talk to him with a velvety voice.

Eberhard sees what she is doing – he has to act, *now*. But he freezes. Suddenly, Janny throws herself into the arms of the guard. 'Out!' she cries. Eberhard flings himself behind her back, through the window, out of the van. A hand gropes for his ankle, tugs at the tail of his raincoat, the fabric rips, Eberhard transfers his weight forwards and runs across the pavement, away from the van, his coat flapping behind him.

The officer has roughly pushed Janny from his lap and is on the street, firing his gun in the air – 'Stop!' – but Eberhard is already too far. Noise everywhere, people gathering around them. Janny gets out and sees

Eberhard dissolve into the city. The pounding in her head is gone; she suddenly feels as light as a balloon blowing over the heath. Then everything turns black and she collapses on the paving stones.

**Janny is** unconscious when they carry her into the police station. She comes to, passes out again, comes to, passes out, but always that tingling sense of triumph: Eberhard has got away.

In the first instance the Dutch officers take her under their wing, but then the Germans come and fetch her. They load her into the van, back to the SD headquarters at Euterpestraat. They are all livid. With her, with each other, with the German deserter. And then, SS-*Sturmbannführer* Willi Lages appears.

They start in the elevator to the basement. They thrash her, beat and kick her everywhere. When she has gone down, Willi Lages puts his full weight on her legs; others hit her through the bars of the elevator with anything they can get their hands on. Lages just continues relentlessly – he has a whip; there are fists, clubs. They throw her into a closet or a cellar, a pitch-black space. Janny cannot see a thing, not a crack of light – the darkness is suffocating.

Out of consciousness, awake – a minute has passed, or an hour. The pain, the dark. Footsteps above her head, stabbing pain in her entire body. She feels for the walls with her fingers, calls for help, falls back into a deep sleep. Now and then she comes to, hears people walk, far away, and cries with pain until she loses her voice; no one comes.

In the night all is quiet.

A day passes and the door finally opens. Willi Lages is in the doorway, legs wide apart.

'We'll get you. You'll meet the firing squad.'

Light softly shines around his silhouette on her legs – one bloody mass. Janny carefully touches her skin: there are wounds everywhere, and her body is bruised, head to toe. Then she glances up at Lages and looks him straight in the face. The tiniest sparkle in her eyes, a sense of triumph dispelling the pain. She is certain that she'll be shot now, but to her surprise she is cuffed and taken to the prison at Amstelveenseweg.

Stumbling and exhausted, Janny is taken to a cell, her handcuffs are removed and the door closes behind her. A cell for two, peopled by six. She receives a warm welcome; voices are asking what has happened to her. There is tapping on bars and heating pipes all around to report on the new arrival. Other prisoners help her, gently clean and look after her wounds, and within a few hours a bundle of clean laundry arrives via another cell, especially for Janny. A clean pillowcase, such luxury. There is a note inside. She opens it, makes her eyes move across the letters: 'Eberhard is safe and so are the children. Bob.' A cry escapes her throat; her eyes well up. She covers her mouth with her hand; her shoulders are shaking. She doesn't want to cry, but these are tears of joy.

**They share** the two-person cell at the House of Detention II at Amstelveenseweg with six, sometimes eight people. In the first days, Janny is terrified Willi Lages' face will reappear behind the cell door and she will be taken to the firing squad. But nothing happens. Apparently, nobody talked; they suspect a lot about her resistance work but they know nothing.

But the betrayal is gnawing at her. Who knew about The High Nest? She spends hours going over the names in her mind; the residents, resistance people, people in hiding, contacts, shopkeepers where they got their supplies, passers-by on the heath, police officers, Dutch Nazis, chance meetings, old friends who were taken away.

At night her head crackles as if a thousand insects walk inside her skull with their crawling feet; she hears them ticking against the bone. She makes herself crazy, mumbling the names until she falls asleep, almost deliriously:

Moesbergen
Krikke
Punt
Hiemstra
Boellaard

Days turn into weeks as another uncertainty gnaws at her: how would Lien be doing, Jaap, Father and Mother, all the other residents? What happened to Kathinka? Bob's note says 'the children'; does he mean all three of them? Or have the Germans taken Kathinka? Her fellow prisoners are suffering under similar questions about their beloved ones and it does not do the atmosphere in the narrow cell much good. They quarrel about the tiniest things. Some lose their self-control while others keep making themselves smaller. Aunt Betty from the Amsterdam Jordaan is in their cell too. She is highly offended to have been arrested – she merely has two Jewish grandfathers – and airs her anger day in, day out. But each morning when they get a cup of water to wash themselves, Aunt Betty cries: 'Girls, don't forget the fannies!' and they cannot help but laugh.

Meanwhile, in the centre of Amsterdam, a mile or so away, another group of Jews is found who, like the residents of The High Nest, saw the end of the war glistening on the horizon.

On 4 August 1944, the SD discovers a large shelter behind a revolving bookcase in a canal house at 263 Prinsengracht, with eight people in hiding. The premises house the Dutch head office of Opekta, a German company producing pectin – an ingredient for, among other things, jam. On 6 July 1942, the Jewish director, Otto Frank, his wife, Edith, and their two teenage daughters, Anne and Margot, went into hiding in the annex of the business premises, a small space spread across two floors. They were soon joined by a colleague, his wife and child, and another refugee. They hold out for over two years, but on that summery Friday morning, a group of Dutch SD officers shows up at 263 Prinsengracht for the house search that will lead to their discovery.

# 11
# Westerbork

Westerbork. *Judendurchgangslager* – Jewish transit camp. The camp may seem more than a temporary accommodation, with a hospital housing almost 1,800 beds and 120 doctors, a dental clinic, a daycare centre and a school, an administration office and a camp shop, where people pay with special camp money, but no one is expected to stay here.

Ironically, the camp was established in 1939 as Central Refugee Camp Westerbork, a safe heaven for Jewish refugees from other European countries. After the SS took over in spring 1942, it became the gateway to the many concentration camps across the border. Dutch contractors built an extra number of very large barracks, each 275 by 32 feet, within the existing camp, so that at the height of the war there are twenty-four draughty wooden sheds, filled to the rafters with people.

In order for the deportations to run smoothly, days in the camp are modelled on normal life: the Germans maintained the *Jüdischer Ordnungsdienst*, the Jewish camp police. These 'Jewish SS officers', as they are called, were often young men, wearing green uniforms and a band around their upper arm: OD. A controversial honorary job, life-prolonging but maddening. In the first few years the OD is assisted by Dutch military police, but officers from the Amsterdam police force have come in their place, just before the residents of The High Nest arrive.

The crucial task of the Jewish camp staff lies with their administrative department. Each week, camp commander and SS-*Obersturmführer* Albert Gemmeker gives them the number of people to deport and the administrative assistants then draw up the dreaded transportation lists. Gemmeker himself does not select or deport a single man, woman or child; he leaves it up to the Jews.

When trains from Westerbork started running east in July 1942, there were weekly transportations on Monday and Friday. Towards the end of the year, 39,762 people had been deported, most of them ending up in Auschwitz. From early 1943 until Tuesday, 15 February 1944, a new transportation left each Tuesday, week after week. The desired outcome became visible; the Jewish community was drying up and trains from Westerbork became less frequent. Trains would leave every ten days, on Wednesday, Friday, even on Sunday – with less and less people on board. No longer well over 1,000, or even 2,000, as in previous months, but 809, 732, 599, 453. In 1943, 50,919 people were deported from the Netherlands.

Between June 1942 and September 1944, a total number of 107,000 people – Jews, Sinti and Roma, resistance workers and homosexuals, men, women and children – were taken in ninety-three transportations by Dutch National Rail; removed from Dutch society and taken straight to the German border, with utmost efficiency and logistic vigour.

Each time the rhythmic pounding had evaporated and the train had moved beyond the horizon towards the east, the square terrain on the heath was clouded by an eerie atmosphere. A toxic mixture of relief and despair. From the moment the train had left the camp, the tension gradually grew until, in the days just before the new lists were disclosed, it literally made people sick. By the time the names were announced per barrack, those who were told to pack almost felt liberated.

The preceding uncertainty was perhaps crueller than the verdict itself.

**The betrayal** of The High Nest, the past weeks in Westerbork, worrying about Eberhard, Kathinka – they still don't know what happened to her – and about her sister in the Amsterdam prison – it has all left Lien completely dispirited. Each night, after a long day at the filthy tables of the battery workshop, it takes all of Fietje's energy to instil some courage in her eldest daughter. Because they are in the *Strafbaracke* (punishment barracks), they are not allowed to work outside the camp. People in the punishment block have offences to their name, committed in Westerbork camp or before. They are the ones who tried to hide, to escape, the ones who, one way or another, dared to violate German rules.

Camp life is deliberately structured as it would normally be, so people are not aware this is the waiting room for the extermination camps and will not kick up a fuss, but conditions are still abominable. In The High Nest they had been under great stress too, always anxious for discovery, betrayal, but they had all the home comforts as well as quiet, space and fresh air. Even when they were hiding with over twenty people, they could always seek solitude; in one of the rooms, the gazebo, the shed, the forest. In Westerbork, everyone is packed into overfull sheds that swell like corpses in summer. Every inch is taken up by people, trapped in a stench of sweat and bodily gases. They are stacked up in triple bunk beds, people gazing at them, breathing upon them, everywhere they turn. Laundry is hanging out to dry underneath the ceiling. In Westerbork there is no place to be alone; each bit of self-determination has been taken from them. Even when they put their head underneath the blankets for a hint of privacy, the tickling of flees and lice reminds them that there is none. Those days are over. The only question that keeps them going is: how much longer still?

From behind the fence between the punishment block and the other barracks, Lien can overlook the rest of the camp. Sometimes she sees Jetty, Simon or one of her other former housemates on the other side; they aren't forced to wear overalls with a white band with an S for *Strafgefangener*, convicts, like Lien and the rest of the Brilleslijper family are. Those with an S are at the top of the deportation list. On Lien's side men and women are separated, but across the fence they are not; they even have special family barracks, small ones, where people can live with their families. They can buy groceries at the camp shop and people in the regular barracks are also more likely to be sent to Bergen-Belsen or Theresienstadt instead of Auschwitz, camps where prospects are said to be better. Rumour even has it that from Bergen-Belsen, a camp on the German forehead, the Red Cross can move you further up, towards Sweden, where Jews are exchanged for German prisoners of war. Some wealthy families have paid a small fortune to end up on such an exchange list – the results are as yet unknown.

All prisoners are keen to work; not only because anything is better than idly watching time pass by until the next train arrives or departs, but also because everyone knows that the least useful ones go first. Lien is lucky that she and Mother were placed in the battery workshop. Sam Polak, younger brother of Ben and Hans Polak, their close friends from The Hague, helped them to get the job. The work is filthy and heavy. First, they split the batteries with hammer and chisel, then they pry out the tar and the carbon stick, which they throw into separate baskets, and finally they must use a screwdriver to remove the metal cap, which they chuck in a third basket. After a while their fingers have become so black that it is impossible to tell where the battery stops and their hand begins.

What's worse is the nasty dry cough caused by toxic chemicals flying around and nestling in their lungs.

Coughing fits that fracture ribs slip out of the barracks through cracks in the wood and float across the heath, even at night. But at least the prisoners can talk in the workshop and every day not spent on an eastbound train counts – ruined lungs or not.

Lien fills her days with working, worrying and waiting. Everyone in the camp is anxiously anticipating new transportations from Amsterdam. Sometimes someone suddenly stops in the middle of the grounds, looks at the dry soil with bated breath; was that a vibration of the track? Is there a train coming? They so wish for the last undiscovered ones to make it to the end of the war, for them to outwit the Germans.

Unfortunately, as the years of occupation go by, it seems as if people get better at finding hidden Jews. Even with liberation in sight, Dutch Jew hunters feel the need to keep on searching, all by themselves, and Dutch civilians still feel the need to turn in neighbours, friends, strangers. All this is deeply humiliating, incomprehensible, but there is optimism in the camp too. Other prisoners, who have been in the camp longer, tell Lien that only one transportation left Westerbork towards the east in April. The next one wasn't until May. Another one in early June and the next is not due till the end of July. And so the softest of whispers starts to spread through the camp: we are going to make it.

In the Brilleslijper family, they each have a different way of dealing with the situation, with the stories reaching the camp. Japie has met a girl and after a few days of exchanging furtive glances, he is now brave enough to walk the main camp street with her. His eyes twinkle behind his dust-covered glasses for the first time in a really long while.

Fietje keeps her spirits up, like she always has, and each night in the women's barracks she tries to give courage to her eldest daughter. They have endured so much already and the children are safe; they must keep the faith. It really cannot be long now. But Lien will not have any of it and she is not the only one. Joseph spends his days in the overheated barracks; his eyesight is too poor for him to be allowed to work with the other men in the cable-repair workshop. He mumbles and grumbles to himself and fulminates at the Jewish supervisors, how filthy and corrupt they are to do this work and get privileges from the camp staff. Being guarded by his own people here has taken his last bit of faith in humanity.

One late afternoon, Lien is walking towards the punishment block, tired and filthy from working on the batteries, squinting her eyes against the bright sun, when she suddenly spots her father in the distance, sitting in the men's barracks. No more than a dark shadow, shoulders hanging, thin little neck. She thinks back on the time when her parents went to see operas – at the Carré Theatre, the Palace on Frederiksplein, the Flora Theatre on Amstelstraat. Her father always seemed four inches taller when they came home, his chin up, his chest puffed out. He was so impressed by Shakespeare's *Merchant of Venice* that he memorized Shylock's monologue and recited it time and again in their tiny apartment upstairs:

And what's his reason? I am a Jew. Hath not a Jew eyes? Hath not a Jew hands, organs, dimensions, senses, affections, passions? Fed with the same food, hurt with the same weapons, subject to the same diseases, healed by the same means, warmed and cooled by the same winter and summer, as a Christian is? If you prick us, do we not bleed? If you tickle us, do we not laugh? If you poison us, do we not die? And if you wrong us, shall we not revenge?

Staring at the shadow of the man her father once was, Lien realizes that the worst humiliation is not that his humanity has been taken from him, but knowing he will probably never revenge the wrong that has been done to his family.

―――――

**One day** Sam Polak comes to Lien and asks her to accompany him to the gates of the family barracks; someone wants to see her. Lien is alarmed. In all those weeks they have not heard from Janny – but no news is good news and each day without a train from Amsterdam is another one gained. She hopes her sister will not come to Westerbork but will stay in Amsterdam until the liberation. Reluctantly, she follows Sam to the gate.

To her surprise she sees Lily approach from the other side, young Anita holding her hand. Lien's tight face breaks into a smile as her hands automatically reach for her friend. But there is a fence between them and Lien drops her arms again. The women are six feet apart, facing each other, glad to reconnect but saddened by the circumstances.

The last time they saw each other was in the House of Detention at Weteringschans. The Amsterdam prison was a repository for people dragged out of hiding and leading figures from the resistance. The morning Lien had said goodbye to Eberhard, 13 July, he was again taken to the SD headquarters for questioning and she was thrown into a cell with five other women and a young girl. She could not care less. She had lost her child and her man would be facing the firing squad th*at* day.

The cell door shut behind her with a metallic ring and Lien found herself a place between the other women. One of them took pity and began to put courage into her – although she had herself and her little daughter, eight years old but nonetheless imprisoned with them, to worry about. They were Lily and Anita, and as long as they were in the same cell, the women clung together.

Carolina, 'Lily', Biet-Gassan, had been married to Samuel Gassan, from a renowned family of diamond-cutters. Two years before, in 1943, Lily had divorced Samuel and he had escaped the Germans just in time to flee to Switzerland. All the while Lily and little Anita had been hiding, first crammed into a tiny side room with another family, in the house of a family with five children. They had to be dead quiet day and night, so those five would not notice the illegal sleepover. After a while, mother and daughter moved to a boarding house, and there they were betrayed and arrested.

Lily and Lien gave each other courage at a time they could no longer draw on their own reserves. Lien cheered Anita up by recounting the fairy tales she would read Kathinka before bed. She sang songs to the girl, very quietly so the guards would not hear. Lily, in turn, did something for Lien that perhaps would save her life.

Lien spoke about Eberhard, the father of their little daughter, Kathinka, whom she had not been allowed to marry because of the Nuremberg Laws. To stop Jews from escaping deportation, on 25 March 1942, a ban on all mixed marriages was introduced in the Netherlands too: Jews could no longer marry non-Jews. This made Lien and Kathinka outlaws, whereas Janny, who had married Bob *before* the new measures, was now the mother of two *Mischlinge*.

Before Lien had finished her sentence on the impossible marriage to Eberhard, Lily grabbed her hand and leaned forwards.

'We must get you a false marriage certificate as soon as possible. You might stand a chance. I know someone!'

Lien stared at her with bewilderment.

'You are going to write down this story and then we have to smuggle that letter outside, get it to someone who can go and see Nino Kotting for you. I know him; he is a great lawyer, here in Amsterdam. Nino has helped countless Jews this way.'

Lily had a bit of money and the right contacts; she knew exactly who among the guards was no Nazi, and she arranged for Lien to be given a piece of paper and a pencil. Lien got to work. She addressed her letter to her dear friends, the Stotijn family in Amsterdam, and tried to phrase her message as briefly and cleverly as possible.

My dearests!

This is my last chance to write to you. Please try to pick up my English marriage certificate and take this to Mr. Kotting. Try to get me out of here, look after the child and send me a package with clothes, food, etc. I have nothing, please help me. J [Janny] is at Avw [Amstelveensweg prison]. Try to have my S [*Strafgefangene*] removed too.

Greetings to you all and lots of kisses, Lien

At four o'clock one morning, the women were taken from their cell and brought to a tram. When Lien walked past the tram driver, she dropped the unstamped letter into his bag as inconspicuously as possible.

From Centraal Station, the journey continued across the rails, eastwards, further and further away from civilization. On the wasteland of Westerbork the train came to a halt. Lily and her daughter Anita were led to the family barracks – probably as a result of her wealth – and Lien had to go to the other side of the fence, where the *Strafgefangene* lived. She did not know if her last cry for help had found its way, or whether it was for ever lost between the papers of an anonymous tram driver.

But now, Lily is standing opposite her on the other side of the fence and Lien hopes for good news from the lawyer.

She has come to deliver a very different message. Lily has spoken to Lien's old friend, Ida Rosenheimer – the pianist who accompanied her when things became too dangerous for Eberhard and one of the first to warn her about the end goal of the Nazis: the gas chambers. Unfortunately, Lien had never believed her. Lily has come to tell her that Ida and some other friends in Westerbork have raised money to free Lien from the *Strafbaracke*, get her to their side of the fence and place her on the list of the privileged, the ones who will be deported to Theresienstadt, a concentration camp in Czechoslovakia.

Lien listens, touched that her friends can think of another person even in these conditions. Then she quietly shakes her head.

'I'm sorry, but I'm staying here. I won't leave my little brother and my parents. Also, I'm not sure if Janny is coming – if she is, she will certainly end up at this side of the fence too.'

Lily opens her mouth, shuts it again and lowers her

head. In the distance, a camp police officer is approaching; they must finish their conversation.

'I understand,' she whispers at last, barely audible.

Lien nods gratefully. Then she turns around and walks back to her mother.

# 12

# The Last Train

At the beginning of August 1944, the cell doors finally open. It is early morning when, for the first time in weeks, Janny is led outside. The cold of the night is still lingering, but the fresh air in her lungs is a delight. Amsterdam is still sound asleep and the sun is slowly warming the streets. Janny looks around; the Vondelpark starts over there – she knows this neighbourhood well. Guards escort her group of people to a tram that will take them to Centraal Station. She stares out of the window, watches Amsterdam-South passing by, the canals, the centre, the beautiful city. Everyone is quiet, afraid of what is coming – only squeaking steel and crunching switches disrupt the silence. She engraves the images on her memory, absorbs every detail – step gables against the blue sky, cobblestones on the pavement, a coot floating on the water.

The station square, get out, side entrance, to the platform. A cold shadow tumbles over Janny as they enter the dark building. At the exact same moment another group is led inside and walks to the platform too. In silence, they shuffle in the same direction; one-way traffic at Centraal Station – it all feels very surreal.

Old and young, men and women, parents with children. Janny sees a family in sportswear, the parents looking dejected, two teenage daughters carrying rucksacks as if they are going on holiday. Closed in by walls, guards, companions in misfortune. The trap. All those years she tried to keep people away from here, from the gates of this trap, as many people as she could. She climbs the final steps to the platform and slowly emerges from the stairwell. The passenger train is already waiting, its doors opened wide.

**Get off** the train. Hot air hits Janny in the face. The camp is large, much larger than she had expected. A village on desolate heathland. People everywhere. Men, women, children; seen through narrowed eyes, this place is almost normal – a village square in a Western. But reality is in the details. Everything is angular, wooden, compartmentalized. The terrain is square, enclosed by deep trenches and tall fences with barbed wire on top. Watchtowers like lifeguard platforms on long legs. Large barns in straight rows. Wooden hangars enormous enough to house actual aircraft, standing side by side with smaller versions. The soil is dry and dust clouds rush across the grounds, wriggle between the slats of the sheds, give everyone's skin a dull shine.

Uniforms are waiting for them. Caps pulled down deep, cigarette butts glowing where eyes should be. To her astonishment, Janny does not hear a word of German, only Dutch. Some guards seem to be Jewish, not Dutch Nazis or police officers. She is taken from the central part of the camp to an isolated section behind the tracks. A prison within a prison. The punishment block.

Finally, Janny joins her family. The reunion is tearful but quiet. Twelve out of the seventeen permanent residents of The High Nest are now in Westerbork. Father, Mother, Lientje, Jaap: the entire Brilleslijper family is here. Red Puck is with them too. The other six have ended up in the family barracks on the other side of the fence; Jetty and Simon, the whole Teixeira de Mattos family: Bram, Louise, their daughter, Rita, and her husband, Willi. When she sees the faces of her family, tense but unharmed, Janny's shoulders drop.

The open wounds on her legs are starting to heal, the bruises on the rest of her body have turned from bright blue to deep purple to yellowy brown. But her ankle is smashed and she can barely put her weight on it. It is clear to the rest of the family what Lages and his men did to her after she helped Eberhard to escape.

Janny tells them the great news she received in prison, that Bob and the children are safe – she assumes he meant all three of them. Apparently, the police officer in Huizen warned Bob at work. These are sparks of hope; the idea that some of them have kept one step ahead of the Germans, as well as knowing there are still people brave enough to think and act autonomously.

Lien refuses to accept that Eberhard is safe. The scenario is too rosy to be true and naive optimism is a luxury they have not been able to afford themselves for years now. Lien believes he was caught while he ran from the police, or was unable to find shelter, or was betrayed once more – she is convinced it did not end well and Janny cannot make her see the opposite is true.

With the arrival of the new transportation, barracks fill up again on both sides of the fences. It is easy to spot who is new. Large eyes in tight faces, people dressed in clean clothes with carefully packed bags and suitcases searching for an empty bed, their eyes nervously moving back and forth as they take in the barracks, the site, the Jewish camp police. Some newcomers have been in hiding for months, or years even, and they stand out with their bloodless faces, their rubbery and yellow skin.

The journey, to them, was the first time they had been outside, in fresh air, for a really long time. They had sat on the seats of the passenger train, stretched their legs and watched the Dutch landscape pass them by. Reality only kicked in when the train reduced speed, the sound of joints beneath the wheels slowly fading, and passengers on either side were staring out of the window anxiously. No-man's-land as far as their eyes could see. And then a watchtower, announcing the first corner of the camp as the train entered Westerbork station.

The people who, only a few days before, were discovered by the SD behind the bookcase at the grand building on 263 Prinsengracht end up in the punishment block too: father and mother Frank with their two daughters, Anne and Margot. The girls and their mother, Edith Frank, are put to work in the battery barracks. Janny is placed in this workshop as well.

And so the paths of two Jewish hiding families cross and their faces collectively grow black with the tar dust flying around in the shed. Because the work is so simple and mind-numbing, it allows them to chat. Edith voices her concerns about the fate of her daughters. She tells Lien they have been hiding in the annex of a large building for two years and one month, eight of them staying in five secret rooms. On the ground floor was a warehouse where employees knew nothing, so in the daytime each shift, each cough, each object that was moved could be the end of them. A maddening thought, particularly for her young girls, only fifteen and eighteen years old. They had almost made it and the raid had come as a complete surprise – just as it had in The High Nest.

**Then two** things happen that give the entire family, Lien in particular, hope. First, a letter is delivered to her name in which, to her surprise, she finds a copy of an official English marriage certificate.

Eberhard Rebling and Rebekka Brilleslijper, 26 and 25 years old, married on 28 March 1938 in London

Signature, stamp, everything. She turns the sheet of paper over and over, as if she does not trust it, but it really says so. Not only the Huizen police officer, but also the Amsterdam tram driver has risked his life to help a complete stranger: he delivered the letter to Haakon and Mieke. The document is trembling in her filthy fingers, her black nails contrasting with the spotless white. She will never be able to thank this man, does not even know his name. And how can she ever thank Lily, who has given her the name of the lawyer with this administrative trick up his sleeve?

To assist with the 'Final Solution to the Jewish problem', the Germans had set up a department for disputable cases. When someone thought he was wrongly registered as 'Jewish', he could lodge an appeal at the *Abteilung Innere Verwaltung* (General Internal Administration). The head of the department is Hans Calmeyer, a German lawyer, who has to deal with thousands of appeals – often a matter of life and death. Lawyer Nino Kotting and his co-worker supply all sorts of false documents for their clients – they believe that unjust laws need not be observed – and Calmeyer turns a blind eye when checking the papers. In a remarkable dance between these two lawyers, one Dutch, the other German, thousands of people are thus 'un-Jewed'.

Lien is over the moon that, thanks to Kotting, her relationship is now registered as a 'mixed marriage' and she now has the same status as her sister, Janny – hopefully reducing the chance of being separated. She quickly takes the documents to the camp administration, where they are added to her file.

Another package for Lien is delivered at the gate. As soon as she arrived in Westerbork, she had written a letter to Mieke, urgently requesting her to send blankets, towels, toiletries and a few Yiddish songs. She cannot believe her friend has responded so soon and quickly tears the paper from the box.

Fietje is sat beside her on the bed, curious to see what will appear. Indeed: blankets, some other things she had asked Mieke for, and then, at the bottom: written sheets with lyrics and notes. Lien snatches the papers from the box, then carefully holds them up, her hands completely still as if she's weighing gold. She reads the scribbles; her mouth tightens and her eyes widen as she mumbles the Yiddish words: '*Rajsele, wer der erschter wet lachn.*'

Lien briskly turns her head to Fietje.

'It's Eberhard!' Her finger presses into the paper. 'Eberhard has written this! It's his handwriting, he is safe.'

Lien leafs through the sheets searching for another clue from Eberhard. She finds an old satirical Yiddish song they rehearsed together at The High Nest – sadly, she never had a chance to perform it in front of an audience. She reads the first lines out loud:

*Wos bistu Katinke barojges,*
*Wos gejstu arobgelost di nos?*
*Un efscher wilstu wissn majn jiches*
*Un fun wanen un fun wos.*

She quickly reads on:

*Si is baj di fun 't hof,*
*Di mame ganwet fisch in mark. . .*

These lines are new to her – they don't belong to the song. She glances at Fietje, who shrugs her shoulders. Lien narrows her eyes; what is Eberhard trying to tell her? *Si is baj di fun 't hof.* She is with the people from the court. The court of justice? De la Court! Their friends Albert and Cilia de la Court from Wassenaar with their five children. Kathinka is the sixth child in their house. Lien presses the paper to her chest, closes her eyes and breathes out.

Since she said goodbye to Kathinka, she had forced herself to think about her as little as possible, afraid that otherwise she would not be able to get up in the morning. If she allowed but a fraction of the thought that her little girl was taken from the doctor in Huizen by the Nazis, she went weak at the knees. Then she would shake her head, press her nails into the palms of her hands until she almost bled, and focus on the continuous crying and coughing around her until she had driven her daughter out of her system.

But now that she knows both Eberhard and Kathinka are safe, a strength returns, which helps her to believe again: we are going to make it.

It is a fact that the Allies are making progress. Since D-Day, their troops have moved up towards the east and the north and in August 1944, they free several major French cities. The Red Army is victorious in Romania, reconquers Belarus and the east of Poland. On 25 August, an important victory follows when Charles de Gaulle marches into Paris and declares the French capital liberated.

Sobibor, a small camp on the right side of Poland, exclusively designed for extermination, is closed by the Germans after a large prisoners' revolt in October 1943. But not before at least 170,000 people – including most of the 34,313 Dutch deported to the camp – were killed in a highly mechanized process, in less than eighteen months' time. There will never be an exact number of victims, because almost no one has managed to leave Sobibor alive.

Each new day the Brilleslijper sisters, just like the Frank sisters, walk from the *Strafbaracke* to the workshop, where they count the number of batteries they split, hoping these will be the last ten, twenty, hundred before the liberation.

In the meantime, they talk a lot. Someone speaks about the victory march from Paris to Belgium, says the British troops are almost in Arnhem now. Someone is certain the transportations have stopped and someone else claims to have heard that *if* another train leaves, it will not go to Auschwitz but to Wolfenbüttel, another labour camp. Sam Polak tells them that even camp commander Gemmeker is getting nervous, because the Allies are said to have reached Limburg.

The only one who refuses to be carried away by all the optimism is Joseph Brilleslijper. Their father is not well, neither mentally, nor physically. His bad eyesight has depleted him, he has lost weight and he barely endures the stay in the sweltering hot barracks, with the presence of so many other prisoners. When, one night, he hears his daughters building castles in the sky about the imminent liberation again, he has suddenly had enough.

'Stop that nonsense, stop fooling yourselves! Do you really think they will just let us go when the Allies turn up? That there won't be revenge before they arrive here at the gate?'

He snorts and shakes his head, frustrated by the

naivety of his daughters – or perhaps by his own incapacity to change their situation.

Joseph is not alone in his nervousness; the entire
camp is in the grip of the forthcoming liberation. At
night, when the prisoners are piled onto their triple
bunk beds and the dust settles in the barracks underneath the starry sky, most are wide awake on their
straw mattresses. They are kept from sleeping by the
heat burning between the wooden slats, by the stench
of sweat, by the crying of children. They worry about
deported family members and about what might be
awaiting them. They wonder how they ended up in this
situation, or what they have done to deserve this fate.
They are wide awake because they keep counting the
days that have passed since the last trains left Westerbork on 31 July on their fingers as if, with each extra
day, they drift further away from the final verdict, and
instead float towards a new horizon.

One of those last trains ran to Theresienstadt and
took Jetty Druijff and Simon van Kreveld, who lived in
The High Nest with them. A second, with destination
Bergen-Belsen, had Lily Biet-Gassan and her daughter
Anita on board.

It is Saturday, 2 September when the verdict is
passed – 1,019 names are called for transportation.

Except for Willi and Rita, they are all on the list.

Brilleslijper, Joseph
Brilleslijper-Gerritse, Fietje
Rebling-Brilleslijper, Rebekka
Brandes-Brilleslijper, Marianne
Brilleslijper, Jacob
v.d. Berg-Walvisch, Pauline
Teixeira de Mattos, Abraham
Teixeira de Mattos-Gompes, Louise
Frank, Otto
Frank-Hollander, Edith
Frank, Margot Betti
Frank, Annelies Marie

The last train to Auschwitz will leave Westerbork the following morning.

# 13
# Kidnapped

The villa on the hill looks forlorn. Inside, nothing is the same; furniture has been moved, mattresses are turned upside down, curtains pulled off their rails. In the kitchen, a plate covered with crumbs and a knife with some butter testify in silence to the impertinence of the police.

Doctor van den Berg was not prepared for the arrival of three young children. He asks the SD if he may transfer two of them to Doctor Schaaberg, one of his colleagues in the village. He promises to keep the Kathinka girl and watch her closely. Van den Berg also asks permission to gather some children's things from the house. The SD approve, and he takes Robbie and Liselotte to the other address.

While their wives mind the children, the two doctors go to The High Nest to collect the children's beds and some clothes. While they lug the stuff back home, they discuss the situation.

'Those officers made me swear I'll keep the children until they are certain they aren't fully Jewish,' Van den Berg says pensively. 'Make sure those two don't run away, or else the SD will come after me!'

Schaaberg nods in silence. He understands what is at stake. They hold still in front of Van den Berg's house and rest. Inside the house is little Kathinka, exhausted by the events of the day. She is waiting all alone for that strange man to return. Schaaberg picks up his stuff, says goodbye to his colleague with a wave of his hand. Then he walks to his own place, a quarter of a mile further along, where Robbie and Liselotte are quietly sitting on the sofa in the living room.

As soon as Jan Hemelrijk learns that The High Nest has been betrayed and the children, for the time being, have been accommodated elsewhere, he knows that every minute counts. Robbie and Liselotte, both half-Jewish, are safe, but it is only a matter of time before the SD figures out that Lien and Eberhard are not married and Kathinka is fully Jewish. Which means she will be deported.

Hemelrijk instantly contacts Doctor van den Berg and asks him to hand the girl over to him as quickly as possible. Van den Berg refuses. He has given the SD his word and knows what awaits him when he helps a Jew go into hiding – even if she is barely three years old.

Jan Hemelrijk calls upon two friends of the Brilleslijper family who live close to the doctor. The first is Karel Poons, the peroxide-blond ballet dancer. When he and Lien trained each week, Karel became a close friend to Eberhard and the rest of the family as well. The second is a young woman named Marion van Binsbergen.

The war brought Karel and Marion together by chance. He was hiding in Huizen, in the garden house of Cecile Hanendoes, and Marion, a recent graduate from Amsterdam in her early twenties, moved into the house next door in 1943. Daughter to a free-thinking judge and an English mother with authority issues, Marion was encouraged to think for herself from a very young age. When the German occupation began, she studied Social Work in Amsterdam. A few encounters with Fascists made such an impression on her that she quickly joined the resistance.

One of those decisive events took place on a beautiful day in spring 1942. Marion cycled past a Jewish orphanage just as it was cleared out by the Nazis. The raid was in full swing when she stopped on the street. All the children of the home were crying. Marion saw them being chucked into a truck one by one. Babies, toddlers, eight-year-olds – they were literally thrown into the trailer, flung over the tailgate like bags of potatoes, by an arm, a leg, a ponytail.

Two women approached, saw what was happening and pounced on the Germans without any hesitation. They were both overpowered and tossed into the truck with the children. Marion stood there watching and decided then and there that she would offer resistance – even if it would kill her.

She registers Jewish babies as her own then finds them hiding places throughout the Netherlands. She has a two-year-old boy stay with her for months, pretending he is her son. She helps a heavily pregnant Jewish woman whose host family does not want to hide babies. Immediately after the birth she takes the newborn from Amsterdam to Rotterdam, where she has found a family with four children who are willing to adopt the baby. Her most courageous act, however, follows the request to find a safe place for Freddie Polak and his young children of four years, two years and two weeks old.

It is August 1943 when the youngest one, Erica Polak, is born. Her mother is a member of the resistance and soon after giving birth, she is arrested and put into prison. Marion finds the family a hiding place just outside Amsterdam, in the village of Huizen – as it happens, right next to where Karel Poons is hiding. Marion soon moves in with Freddie to look after the children while he works on his thesis. Marion is like a mother to the little ones and makes the neighbours think they are her own, Christian children. Still, she is very worried they will be found. Underneath a few floorboards and a carpet, she creates a crawl space, where Freddie and the children must hide when yet another raid is imminent. To keep baby Erica quiet at such critical moments, they sometimes give her a sleeping pill.

Nonetheless one night it goes wrong. Four SS officers barge into the house under surveillance of a local police officer, a notorious Dutch Nazi. The men search the house, find nothing and leave again, but the local officer waits around as dusk begins to fall. Marion is familiar with this tactic and urges Fred to stay in the hiding place.

Then the little ones become restless and she has to get them out – no one was given sleeping pills this time. The officer walks around the house, lets himself in and comes face to face with the three Jewish children. Marion has one second to decide. She grabs a gun from the bookcase beside her and fires.

A web of silent helpers comes into action. Marion

panics; she worries what might happen to the Polak family if the murder is discovered, and calls on her friend and neighbour Karel Poons for help. Together, they come up with a plan. Marion wants to bury the body in the garden at the back, but Karel has a better idea. He ignores curfew, races through the dark to the local baker, whom he trusts, and asks him to come and collect the body with his van. The baker is willing to help and brings the body to the local undertaker. Marion begs the undertaker to help her get rid of the body in order to save the lives of three children. He does. The dead police officer is put in a coffin with a recently deceased person and is buried the following day by unsuspecting relatives.

Days, weeks, months go by while Marion is anxiously waiting for someone to show up on her doorstep, looking for the Dutch police officer who has disappeared off the face of the earth. Family members, colleagues or the four SS officers who accompanied him that day; surely someone has to miss him? But no one comes. Apparently, Marion was not the only person who was relieved that she no longer had to fear this man.

It is this twosome Jan Hemelrijk calls on to save the life of little Kathinka before it is too late. He tells them that he has asked Van den Berg to hand the child over to him. When the doctor refused, Jan had tried to get

Kathinka out of the house himself. As soon as he was inside, Mrs van den Berg started crying like a wailing siren, whereupon the doctor called the police and Jan quickly had to make his escape. The police now stand guard at the house.

Marion and Karel instantly approve, although Marion thinks she should go alone; if Karel gets caught, he, as a Jew, is done for, while she stands a chance of getting away with a prison sentence. Karel will not have any of it. Kathinka is the daughter of his dear friends Lien and Eberhard, who got him his false documents; he is determined to help save the girl from being deported. Jan Hemelrijk gives them instructions; it has to happen the next morning.

On 14 July 1944 at half past eight, Karel and Marion head to the village together. While Karel is chatting to the police and the doctor at the front, Marion slips into the house via the back entrance to search for Kathinka. She finds the doctor's wife and her children in the bathroom upstairs, immersed in their morning rituals. Kathinka is there too, all dressed and ready. As the woman sees the intruder, she begins to scream again, but Marion pushes her into the bathtub with no mercy.

Marion grabs the girl, runs down the stairs, through

the backdoor to her bicycle. She puts the child in a basket on the rack, takes a long run-up and peddles away like a maniac. Echoes of moaning and commotion shoot across the street from the open windows, but the girl on the back of the bike is completely silent – as if she understands what is at stake.

Marion races for almost two miles in one straight line to Blaricum, where she delivers the girl at the address of two resistance friends. At a leisurely pace, she cycles back to Huizen, relieved that the child is safe. In the meantime, Karel, amid all the panic, has made his escape from the doctor's house.

Half an hour later, the Gestapo arrives at Van den Berg's house to collect Kathinka for deportation.

The Germans found Eberhard's papers in The High Nest. Willy Lages understands that the couple are not married and orders his men to get Kathinka. Before he deports her, he plans to use the girl to get her father talking.

The SD officers fly into a rage when they learn that the child has just been taken by an unknown woman on a bicycle. Doctor van den Berg has to face the full fury of the officers, but eventually he goes free.

Everywhere in Huizen posters are put up with a picture of Kathinka and underneath, in bold letters:

### WANTED!
### Kathinka Anita Bos
### Born 8.8.1941

Not a single tip comes in; the child is gone.

Robbie and Liselotte stay with Doctor Schaaberg in Huizen for a few weeks and are then taken to their non-Jewish grandparents in The Hague. On the day of the raid Bob was indeed warned by the officer from the Huizen police station. After work he did not go to the The High Nest but straight to Trees Lemaire in Amsterdam. Eberhard, after Janny helped him to escape from the police van, has gone into hiding with Eva Besnyö at Leidsekade, also in Amsterdam. The men meet in secret at Eva's place. Bob shares with Eberhard that Kathinka is safe – Jan Hemelrijk has told him everything. Eberhard in turn relates to Bob how Janny saved his life.

Shortly after the rescue operation, Karel Poons and his landlady, Cecile Hanedoes, sneak to The High Nest through forest and heathland in the middle of the night. They want to secure personal belongings and any incriminating documents that might have remained.

While Karel, nervously giggling, is on guard outside the house, Cecile shins up the drainpipe, smashes a window and searches the house. She tries to take everything that might incriminate the abducted residents, including the chest with sheet music and songs, hidden underneath the floor by Eberhard and overlooked by the Germans. Via Bob, they end up with Eberhard, who sends part of the music – with a hidden message – to Lien in Westerbork, hoping it will help her keep courage.

Bob, Robbie, Liselotte, Eberhard and Kathinka; they are unsettled, they are spread throughout the country – but, miraculously, they are all safe. Bob and Eberhard pray that their women, the rest of the Brilleslijper family and their former housemates will stay in Westerbork until the imminent liberation is a fact.

# Part Three

# Surviving

'We were so sad, we were tired, we were cold, we had gone without food for days, we were faint with – we were not even sure if we were hungry or not, because it goes away, I do not know if you ever . . . Thankfully, you will never know, oh God, please may you never know.'

Janny Brandes-Brilleslijper

# 1

# The Journey East

More than 1,000 people have been summoned and after a short moment of disbelief, panic spreads in the camp. Where is this transportation headed? Chaos everywhere. Some run around, trying to get hold of the right people, looking for exemptions or more information. Others gather their family, not sure what to do. Stay together? Try to escape tonight? Getting out of Westerbork is out of the question. They had better wait until they are on the train, jump off underway. What about the children, is there anywhere they can hide them? But if – best-case scenario – the train goes to a labour camp, would they not rather have the children with them, wait out the liberation together? Others consider faking symptoms of illness or beg doctors in the camp hospital for help. There are Jewish doctors in Westerbork who go to great lengths to save people, but for the Brilleslijper family that route is no option. Because they are in the punishment block, they cannot move around as freely as others; it would take several detours to get in touch with a doctor.

From the moment all of their names are rattled off, Fietje Brilleslijper has been adamant: they must stay together. Whether they go to Bergen-Belsen, Theresienstadt, Wolfenbüttel or Auschwitz, what matters is not being separated.

The five of them sit close together, hold each other, discuss scenarios. Auschwitz seems least plausible; the Red Army is in Poland, and it is said that Lublin is liberated, a city in the south, merely 250 miles from Auschwitz. But Janny is realistic as ever.

'We must not make any assumptions. Not about other camps being better, either. Everyone is talking about Theresienstadt as if we would be lucky to go there, but how can we be sure? How many people have you seen coming back from Theresienstadt?'

Father lies down on his bed, paralyzed with powerlessness. The others walk around the barracks nervously, with no particular purpose but nonetheless searching for a solution that might save their lives. Japie seeks the company of the girl he met here in Westerbork. Otto Frank rushes past several times, running back and forth to gather information. He believes they will indeed go to Theresienstadt, so things will work out.

Time is their enemy. With every passing minute, the train that will collect them is creeping closer across the tracks, sleeper after sleeper.

After a long day, during which some prisoners have run around in despair and others were quietly packing their things, everyone gathers in and around the barracks at dusk. The heat is less intense than in August and the ground cools faster at night. Families sit together, children on laps, arms wrapped around each other. Fietje is sitting on her bed and has gathered her husband and children. She wants to speak to them before each of them gets ready for the night that will end in the start of their journey. She leans forwards to rise above the noise, but when she speaks everything around them falls silent.

'Make the most of every last moment we have left. Make it as good as it can be.'

Fietje looks at her daughters and son intently, emphasizes each word, her expression as gentle as ever. The folds between her nose and her cheeks have deepened.

'And remember: this, too, shall pass.' She squeezes Joseph's hand. Then she turns to her girls. 'Janny, Lientje: make sure you stay together! Don't worry about your father and me, the two of us will look after each other.'

She looks at Joseph, her eyebrows raised, and he nods affirmatively. Then he looks from one daughter to the other, a sudden determination in his eyes, revealing a glimpse of the man they had so dearly missed.

Fietje continues: 'Jaap will be fine. He is young and strong and has enough stamina for all of us.'

As she speaks those last words, she tries to smile to her youngest, who is leaning against a bed, his arms crossed on his chest. But Japie's face remains tight; he cannot oblige his mother, not even for the sake of politeness. Of course he will be fine, but he is worried sick about his sisters and parents.

Then, when there are no words left, they get up and hold each other. They assume it will be complete chaos tomorrow, when more than one thousand people are put on the same train, and there will be no chance to say anything – let alone say goodbye.

## 3 September 1944

Sunday morning. It is still a little dark outside, but when the *Ordnungsdienst* storm into the barracks, screaming, no one wakes up with a start. People are ready to leave, some wearing five pairs of trousers, double jumpers, some hiding compact powder in a bra, a lipstick in a shoe. Pictures and letters of loved ones, carefully sown into the pocket of a shirt.

People lower themselves from their bunk beds, the sick and the elderly move with difficulty, little ones rub the sleep from their eyes. Fathers and mothers grab children's wrists – all the colour drained from their fingers, even before they have left the barracks. People grab personal belongings, hurry outside, urged on by wildly gesticulating guards.

'Move!'

'Hurry!'

'Don't take too much stuff!'

From the punishment blocks to the train track, they see hundreds of people approaching from the other side of the camp. Even camp commander Albert Gemmeker is present at this early hour – the shine of his boots is hard to ignore. With his SS officers and a couple of large dogs, he is watching from the side, relaxed but hawk-eyed, cracking jokes but dead serious about the job at hand.

Janny and Lien cling on to each other, try to stay close to the rest of the family, search the crowd for faces of friends who will attempt to jump out of the train along the way – hoping they might be able to follow them. But then names are called and chaos ensues. People go against the stream, family members shout at

each other. One last touch, then they part ways: Janny
and Lien to one side, Joseph and Fietje to another. Jaap
disappears into the crowd – his surprised face with the
arched eyebrows is the last they see of him.

The train. No passenger train with seats and aisles
and windows, like the one that took Janny from Amsterdam Centraal Station to Westerbork, but heavy wooden
cattle wagons, mini barracks on wheels, boarded up
to the roof – there are no visible vents. The carriages
spread a pungent odour. A sour smell that stings the
insides of their noses.

The train seems endless. People swarm together
in front of the rails; there is pushing, stumbling, but
Gemmeker and his men are content to see how everyone, slowly but surely, is divided and disappears into
the carriages. The sisters see how Fietje and Joseph
are ushered to the same wagon as the elderly couple
Teixeira de Mattos, then they lose their parents from
sight. They can only hope that Jaap is with them.

Dozens of people per carriage – sixty, seventy,
eighty, plus their baggage – until the shack is crammed,
toes and noses sticking out. People in the outer row face
the platform, but their eyes do not register the ground,
a few feet below, about to glide away underneath their
feet. Then the door slides to, right in front of their
faces, and both the camp and the sunlight are gone. An

iron bar turns 180 degrees, locking them in, and the number of prisoners is chalked on the outside of the carriage. On to the next.

People help each other climb into the train, Lien and Janny clutch to each other's clothes, afraid they will be separated at the very last moment. But they are not. They go to the same carriage, probably because they are both labelled 'political *Häftlinge*' – prisoners.

They are inside the carriage, wedged between strange bodies. Everyone tries to shuffle and shift, elderly people struggle to keep their footing, children disappear between their mothers' legs, grown men stick to each other like glue, and everything is held by four wooden walls that do not have any give.

Some thin slats at the top allow for a breath of air to enter, but the closeness is tangible even with the door still open. They are given one empty barrel and a bucket of water. 'Hands! Feet!' a guard shouts and the front row tries to shuffle back another inch. Then the door shuts.

The carriage is left in pitch-darkness; it feels as if they've been buried alive. Everywhere around them is crying, heavy breathing, children panicking because they cannot see a thing. Someone is standing on someone else's foot, a persistent cough in the corner is getting on people's nerves. Lien is scared, her chest is heaving and when she tries to move, she finds that even her feet are stuck between those of someone else. She squeals, starts panting, but Janny pinches the skin of her sister's hand, right between thumb and index finger, where it hurts the most.

'Stay where you are, don't move. Stay calm,' she repeats quietly to Lien until she is distracted and her sister pulls back her hand.

They hear shouting outside, heavy footsteps on the platform, a few Germans laughing at jokes. The noise fades and slowly it grows quiet, inside the train as well. They just stand there and wait for what seems like for ever. And then with a massive jolt, they shout like one, would fall over like dominoes if it weren't for the walls holding them up as the train begins to move. The steel arms slowly begin to grind; even the children are silent. A bump, and another one, faster and faster until the wheels pass the joints in a steady cadence.

While the sun above Westerbork is climbing the sky, the cattle train crammed with 1,019 people slowly disappears into the distance.

Although they try to make themselves smaller and smaller, the contents of the carriage seem to multiply. A few people try to sit, on their bag, on the ground, but most have to stand. Every inch that was empty when they left is now taken and the little bit of oxygen seeping through the cracks seems to be sucked up by more and more mouths. And they have only been going for one, perhaps two hours. A few elderly people cry softly without anyone knowing how to comfort them; mothers tell their children to stop crying, stop wriggling, and no, you cannot have a pee. Someone vomits. The stench is nauseating, but they get used to it.

Then the train slows. Janny and Lien squeeze each other, try to catch each other's eye, but it is too dark. The train jerks to a halt. Everyone in the carriage is dead silent, holds their breath. Now? Already? Is that a good sign?

There is noise outside, shouting in German, the same heavy footsteps stomping back and forth as if they have never left Westerbork. Fumbling at the door, iron creaking and then: bright sunlight. They narrow their eyes and open their mouths. Fresh air streaming into the carriage in buckets and they suck it in, gulp down the oxygen as if it were water. It is cool for the time of year, 15 degrees or so, and they can feel their softened muscles and bones slowly toughen up in their bodies.

The relief is only short-lived. Guards arrive, pushing people ahead of them; familiar faces from the camp. They hold still in front of their open carriage and shout orders – climb in. Confusion – not possible, no space, murmuring at the back, but they must. They shuffle backwards, a few inches, half a handbreadth, people pull themselves up on outstretched arms and as soon as they are in, their faces almost touching those of the front row, the door is shut behind them. What happened? The newcomers tell their story.

There has been an attempted escape from one of the carriages at the back. Successful for some: a few prisoners have managed to jump out of the running train through a hole in the front of the carriage. Someone had smuggled a small bread saw and they had taken it in turns to scratch the blunt knife to and fro, until they had made a notch in the wooden wall, close to the coupling between their carriage and the next. Then another saw-cut, until there was a hatch large enough for a person to squeeze through.

The first put his legs out, found his footing on the steel buffers between the carriages while the sleepers of the track flashed beneath him at dizzying speed. He did not hesitate, dived into the hole like a swimmer and disappeared under the running train. The next one, once outside, stood on the buffers, his legs shaking, until someone hissed he should jump and make way for the others. He jumped. No one could tell if he got caught by the wheels or not.

Then a woman. She stuck her feet through the hole, slid outside on her buttocks until she sat on the cold, smooth buffers. The wind whipped against the carriages of the train shooting through the land and she just sat there, her eyes wide open. They had stopped believing she would, but then she just did it; she fell down on her back as the train moved on.

And so, six or seven people in total had escaped from that cattle carriage – dead or alive, no one could tell – before the Germans noticed and made the train stop. The remaining passengers were beaten out of the carriage, now with a gaping hole in its front, which was uncoupled and they were divided over the rest of the train.

As the wheels begin to move, one of the newcomers mentions that the escape and the stop must have been near Zwolle – someone who knows the area said so. Discussions about their destination flare up again. Were they not supposed to go east? Then why did they go to Zwolle? Janny listens and says nothing. She knows all trains from Westerbork first have to get on the Assen–Zwolle railway line, where the journey to Poland starts. Still, she does not believe they will go all the way to Auschwitz, or even Wolfenbüttel; surely the Red Army has almost reached Berlin? No, they will not travel very far.

In the hours that follow, they all lean against each other in the overcrowded carriage rushing along the track. At first, everyone tries to be mindful of the people closest to them. If a neighbour needs to sit for a while, you stand up, and if a child wants to crawl between legs to his older sister, a few bodies away, you try to let them pass. If someone almost faints because they cannot breathe, you let them gasp for air underneath the steel slats, and if you accidentally kick or push another person, you say 'sorry'. But civilization is merely a matter of circumstance and before long, pleasantries make way for self-preservation. Janny and Lien still cling to each other and as aggression in the close space increases, the sisters form their own protective shield.

As the day progresses, some people can no longer stand on their feet and slump down, another person gets trapped and begins to shout. The ones who found a space on the ground or, better yet, on a bit of straw are stuck, get kicked or hit in the face with a knee. When one child is quiet, another begins to cry and gradually the mood turns grim. First, they were all in the same boat, but most feel so miserable that their only goal now is to survive this journey, by any means necessary.

There is a wooden barrel the size of a bucket where they can relieve themselves, but in the first few hours only the children use it. When evening falls and the train shows no intention of slowing, the grown-ups give in to the pressure on their bladder, one by one. Wedged between strangers, they sit down on the bucket and cast their last bit of dignity aside. The barrel almost overflows and the air is heavy with a smell so pungent that they can taste it on their tongue.

When night falls they lose their bearings completely as they dip into a black layer of oil. There is nothing they can do but surrender and, gradually, the carriage falls silent. Janny and Lien have found a way to doze. They are standing upright, back to back, balancing each other. The feeling of their bodies pressed tightly together reminds them of Amsterdam, home, their old bed. It is literally all they have to hold on to.

## 4 September 1944

A jolt, the wheels glide on, another jolt, the train comes to a halt. Bodies jerk along with the carriage but are unable to move by themselves. No more noise, no more crying, the past twenty-four hours have worn everyone out. The bolt lifts, the door opens. Morning sun. No one moves, they sit, lie, stand where they were, stare ahead of them, their eyes half-shut.

'Out!'

No response.

'*Dalli, dalli!* Quick!'

They begin to move; some twenty prisoners are allowed to walk to a platform, empty the barrels with urine and fill the water buckets. Back into the carriage, shut the door, slide the bolt. Everything is dark again, smells like it did yesterday, as if nothing happened. The train accelerates and soon they are listening to the steady sound of joints beneath their feet again.

Janny has discovered that, apart from the slanting cracks near the ceiling of the carriage, there are two wire mesh grids in the wall that let in some air. Very slowly, she and Lien try to move closer to those grids; they manoeuvre themselves in that direction with their faces turned towards the ceiling, as if taking the fresh air in advance. The packed bodies move: there is oxygen near the grids, but also a draught. Lien makes an inch of space for Janny, Janny makes an inch of space for Lien, and so they move up.

There is a third little hole close to the door bolt. With a bit of luck, you can peer outside through this gap. When Janny finally presses her cheek against the wood and sees the world, she exhales deeply and imprints each image, each colour, each outside sound on her mind. There is not a cloud in the sky and the bright blue stands out against the ochre yellow of the cornfields. Someone tries to push her aside, but she does not give way. Before her one eye everything is so sunny, colourful and peaceful that for a few seconds she forgets the desperate circumstances the rest of her body is in. Then she is shoved aside and her moment has passed.

The sisters try counting the hours, but their minds just refuse to work any more. They are wedged between people in the middle of the carriage; every sense of time and space has drained away, along with the feeling from their limbs. They had a stale piece of bread, but they are so tired and the stench is so sickening that they could not eat if they wanted to. People around them are rambling, children are whimpering softly, the switches are groaning and the iron is screeching, until sound and surroundings blend into another endless night.

## 5 September 1944

They lie over and under each other like sandbags on a pile – a leg ends in a hand in a head in a foot. A chest slowly goes up and down, then stops moving. Each time they change track they all shake as one, hairs brushing the filthy floor like fans. They no longer use the barrel. They no longer peer through the door. From time to time the sisters look up at each other. Wolfenbüttel is not that far, surely they are not . . .

In the third night, the train stops. Doors are unlocked, floodlights shine into the carriages from the dark sky high above. Dogs barking, orders in German, screaming in the distance. Hands groping around in their carriage, searching for dead bodies. A tinny voice sounds, as if this were a stadium, louder than everything else.

'*Alle raus, schneller, schneller!*'

Everybody out, faster, faster!

'*Austreten, alle Koffer hinlegen!*'

Get out, leave all suitcases!

The sisters can barely get up, they are blinded, their legs and eyelids feel heavy, so heavy. They trip over a body on the train, lose their balance when they are on the platform, but they are steadied by a strange pair of hands; a man in a striped uniform whispers: '*Ihr seid gesund. Lauf. Nicht auf die Wagen gehen!*' You are healthy. Walk. Do not get on the cars! They do not understand, grab each other's hand and walk on, trapped in thick beams of light, tiny particles of dust drifting down on them like snow.

Lien looks back; the new blanket Mieke has sent them is still on the train. But as they pass the other carriages, they see bags torn from hands, thrown on the platform in large heaps. '*Alles gepäck liegen lassen, nichts mitnehmen!*' Leave all luggage, take nothing with you. Next to the heaps of luggage, piles of bodies rise, tossed out of the carriages by guards as if it were a game. Alsatians are standing on their hind legs, the leads to keep them in check tightly wrapped around hands sticking out of uniforms with high leather boots underneath. Bare teeth come terrifyingly close. Quick, walk on, further down the platform.

Lines are formed. Men on one side, women and children on the other. An SS officer is standing on a raised platform, his tall, dark figure defined against the bright light. His mouth opens and shuts, veins swell up in his neck. What is he saying? What do they have to do? Janny and Lien do not let go of each other's hand.

'*Alte und Kinder auf den Lastkraftwagen!*'

Elderly people and children must go to the trucks. People of fifty years and older, struggling to keep on their feet after the exhausting journey, get picked out of the line and are pushed towards the vehicles, as are the children, staring vacantly into space. Mothers run after their offspring.

The sisters scan the crowd for familiar faces. Lien raises a hand, thinking she saw Jaap in the distance, his arched eyebrows above a sea of dark crowns, but she is not quite sure and then the boy is gone. Janny thinks she sees a glimpse of Father and Mother near a truck, but then they are forced to move on.

'*Dalli, dalli! Schneller!*'

Together they stand in line, squeeze each other's hand, try to forget the stench of the train, and then they smell it. They smell that scent they will never forget and they know.

In the night of 5 to 6 September 1944, following Mad Tuesday, when the Dutch pull out their nation's flags and banners because they expect to welcome the liberators any time, the Brilleslijper family arrives in Auschwitz.

**The SS officer** shouts above their heads. Their line is thinned out, but hundreds of people are still swarming across the platform.

'*Ruhe!*' Quiet!

They look up, prick up their ears, but there is so much noise and chaos.

'I am calling fifty names! *Extra Schutzhaftbefehl!*'

Protective Custody Order. Suddenly, all is quiet. The man lowers his head and reads the names from his sheet of paper.

'Brandes, Marianne . . . Rebling, Rebekka.'

They are together; the result of the forged marriage certificate. The men who were called are taken away immediately – the women must go to a *Scharführer* (squad leader) with a clipboard, who checks their names again. Their group is only small. They wait and with each breath notice the smell of burning. The sky above the floodlights is still pitch-dark. Then they have to walk too.

Watchtowers. Concrete poles rise high above them –
a bend in their top making them seem to be greeting
everyone. Rows of barbed wire between the poles are
under high voltage. Janny and Lien look at each other
and think the same. This is not a labour camp. Goose-
bumps, perhaps owing to tiredness. They had no idea
one could be this exhausted without dying. Lien can
barely lift her feet off the ground, it is as if she is walking on melted asphalt. Her knees collide and her ankles
give way, tears are running down her cheeks. She is
giving up. Quickly, Janny grabs her upper arm, props
her sister up, keeps her in step. Lien wipes the snot
from under her nose and lets herself be dragged along.

The old woman in front of them is on the verge of
collapsing as well and they support her by each taking
one of her arms. She is light and fragile as porcelain,
she must be at least seventy years old. 'Thank you,'
she whispers. They try to keep her from fainting, ask
for her name. 'Luise Kautsky.' It is barely audible, but
Lien and Janny recognize it. 'Karl Kautsky's wife?' A
nod and a hint of a smile as she remembers. Her husband was a well-known Czech–Austrian politician and
theoretician of social democracy. The sisters know he
died in exile in Amsterdam shortly before the war; Bob
and Eberhard often talked about his work. The strange
moment of human contact and the memory of their

past lives pulls them through the final final few feet. They are rushed into a low building, where they lose sight of Luise.

A long stone hall, cold and grey. SS officers in uniform and prisoners in striped clothes everywhere. Long tables, as if they were here to register for a swimming competition.

'*Ausziehen, alle Kleider hinlegen!*'

Undress, leave all your clothes!

The voice of the SS officer sounds tinny, his order echoes in the space. None of the women in the group takes off any clothes, they look at each other questioningly. There is no separate space, no curtain, there are people everywhere.

'*Dalli, dalli, schneller!*' the man shouts once more.

'*Ihr werdet desinfiziert!*' You will be disinfected! a prisoner in striped uniform calls.

Janny and Lien look at each other anxiously, but other women begin to undress and they reluctantly follow their example. They do not have the energy to resist and they are surrounded by guards waiting for an excuse to lash out. They take off the clothes they so carefully selected in Westerbork, hoping to be well prepared. Westerbork. The name suddenly seems an echo from a distant past, like the street where you lived as a child. Shoes off, socks, vest. Hesitation.

Bra.

Underpants.

They stand barefoot on the cold floor, hands crossed in front of their chest, their gaze towards the ground so they do not have to see themselves through the eyes of strangers.

'Move!'

Along the tables, faster, SS officers rushing them with whips and dogs. So much shouting, it scares them again each time, they pull their head between their shoulders and raise their hands up in the air in defence. Janny is further along and Lien speeds up, makes sure she stays close to her sister. Prisoners in camp clothes are waiting with razors, a blank expression on their face. They are spread. Wherever you end up, they shave you – no matter if it is done by a man or a woman. Arms up. Armpits. Legs apart. Pubic hair. Turn. Their hair is grabbed and cut short in one movement.

Walk on, even more naked than before. More tables. Someone grabs their arm and puts a needle in. They feel no pain. The tip of the scratching needle slowly leaves a series of five numbers on their skin, on the top of their left forearm. As the man pierces her skin with his needle, injecting drops of ink, Janny looks aside at Lien, staring vacantly in the distance with one arm stretched out, straggly hair and her mouth sagging.

88420.

Janny only needs to see the number once; it is engraved in her mind for ever.

A shower room. The tiny trickle is alternately piping hot and ice cold. They shiver, a draught is howling along the walls. Between the other women's bodies, they try to catch some drops in their cupped hands, scrub their skin with moist fingers, but the dirt is everywhere. Arms and legs are shaking so violently that their movements seem like convulsions. Some women seem drunk, stagger through the room and are corrected by guards using their whip both to rush them and keep them at a distance.

'*Schneller!*'

Luise Kautsky, the old lady, falls on the ground and remains on the stones. Another woman manages to get her back on her feet. Everywhere are groups of women with cupped hands underneath at the showerheads in vain. Steam gathers around their heads and for the first time hides the guards from view. Janny and Lien look at each other, hold each other tight, together, briefly, like they used to.

'We must get through this,' says Janny.

No sound, lip-reading. A decision. They both nod.

# 2
# Do You Know the Mussel Man?

A late summer evening in Amsterdam, dinner with Mother and Father. After taking the train from The Hague, Janny walks towards her parental home through the streets where she knows each stone in the pavement, every bump in the road. She waves at familiar faces. Shops are closing, her old friends are on their way to the pub and the Amstel water laps against the riverbank. The bustle on Waterlooplein is coming to an end and crowds make their way towards Carré Theatre. A ship horn, out of tune, sounds from an open basement window; behind a music stand a boy practises his brass instrument. Cyclists toil up the steep Magere Brug, some get off and walk up, amused by their own incapacity.

Janny turns left onto the hidden corner of Nieuwe Achtergracht and enters at number 14/II. Lientje, already there, is being lectured by Father on her absurd dancing career and she rolls her eyes as her sister enters. They embrace. When Japie's absent-minded face appears behind the door, they greet him in unison. Mother is in the kitchen, pans steaming, an order. Janny helps her. Fietje asks Joseph to open a window. A sultry breeze blows in and the sounds of the city centre become a buzzing backing track.

At the table. So many stories, plans and dreams to discuss. The trade, family, money worries. Jaap has almost finished his evening classes and is contemplating further education. Lien pushes some potatoes to the side of her plate. 'I am too fat,' she sulks. 'You are not fat, we are small,' Mother parries without looking up from her plate. Janny grumbles a bit about work; she does not know what she wants to do. These past few months she has worked as a nanny with a distinguished family in The Hague, some De Brauw aristocrat and his offspring, but doesn't enjoy it at all. Her work at the International Red Aid, now *that* is useful. How can she babysit children when Fascists are seizing power all around them? The world is on fire! How can Father do business with the Germans when that horrible man is their leader?

She is still angry with Joseph for selling a bulk of fruit and vegetables to a German steel factory; they have had flaming rows about it. Partly because of this, and also because he thought her Red Aid work was too dangerous, she has left home and moved in with her sister in The Hague. Father shakes his head, thinks his daughter is grossly exaggerating, yet again, but does not want to ruin the atmosphere; they have had this argument too many times already. He does not want to know what Janny is up to in her 'battle against evil', as she consistently refers to it, and believes it will all work out. He has a business to run and that is hard enough these days.

'And I'm going to be a star!' In the midst of the conversation, Lien throws both hands in the air and breaks into song, stretching the letters of the last word into a festoon. They all burst out laughing, dissolving the tension at the table. Outside, the copper bell of the ice-cream van tinkles to the rhythm of 'Do You Know the Mussel Man?' – instantly, they look at their mother, three pairs of eyebrows raised enquiringly. The sound grows louder, he is approaching from the canal. Fietje looks stern for a moment but then her face lights up. She nods and they dash away like little children.

Get up, get outside, quickly. They almost trip each other up in their haste, one behind the other, side by side, overtaking someone so as not to end up on the outside but in the middle of the crowd that is beginning to form. It has started raining. No glistening spring drops holding off but a heavy shower, a dump truck pouring out over their heads. Grey clouds gather above them, rapidly colouring the sky as dark as the soil.

Janny takes her place in the line, looks quickly for Lien. Right behind her. Good. She looks ahead again, moves along. The water is already trickling down her face, drops falling from her eyelashes. Within minutes her clothes, still damp from the previous shower, are soaked. She shivers underneath the thin rags that have not dried for days. Her clogs sink into the mud and start to fill up. They were so pleased when they got them and they held up well for the first month, but nothing can withstand these circumstances. She has sunken into the sludge up to her ankles now and tries to pull the clogs out, one by one, very carefully, so nobody can see. Every move can be one too many. The *Kapos* shout, women still come running, too late, they are slapped, fall over in the mud. You must not be one of the last, you must not end up in the outer lines, you must not stand out, you must have nothing sticking out. She and Lien are lucky to be so small.

Hours pass and the counting continues. One mistake, start again, all over, hundreds of heads lined up on a giant chessboard. Sometimes someone collapses, causing a hole in the pattern. Janny stares at the back of the woman in front of her, fighting her urge to resist the ongoing shouting of the *Kapos* and *Aufseherinnen*, the female guards, ignoring the rain, the hunger, the tingling pain in her shrinking body. Peeled off, they were, layer by layer like an onion, until nothing but the essence of their existence was left. First, they had taken their work, their schools, their homes and their city. Their neighbours and their friends. Then their families and their freedom. Ultimately their clothes, their hair, their reflection. But not the essence, that is what they need to focus on, they shall not have that.

They can tell what happens otherwise, by looking at the living dead drifting across the grounds. The *Müselmanner*. They have given up on themselves and surrendered even before the Nazis pushed them over the edge. The comatose look of the *Müselmanner* is perhaps an even bigger triumph for the Fascists than the smoking chimneys on the site. They lie, hang, stumble across the grounds, men and women. Exhausted and emaciated, numbed and mute, jaws like iron clamps and eyes like marbles no longer registering anything. During the selection, the *Müselmanner* are the first ones sent to one side with a sweep of the hand, even before the sick, the pregnant, the children and the elderly; in their minds they have already made the journey to the gas chambers. They do not scream and do not cry, are no longer aware of their environment, or perhaps only too aware of its hopelessness. Which is precisely why the other prisoners avoid them.

Rain pounds on Janny's head, the drenched clothes have dissolved into her skin. She shivers in her chemise. No underpants, the wind blows straight through her. Her feet are so numb with cold that the wooden clogs seem to grow straight from her legs. But each time their essence threatens to slip away, they find what most others here lack – someone to turn to. The other helps them to remember who they are, because the other reminds them who they once were: two sisters from Amsterdam.

# 3
# Lien's Violet

The sisters soon realize that the camp runs on a pyramid of humiliations that pits everyone against each other. Although at first sight Auschwitz-Birkenau seems like chaos submerged in mud, it is in fact a perfectly orchestrated killing machine, designed in great detail on SS drawing boards – gas chambers and crematoria included – and built on the marshes around the Polish village of Brzezinka. Constructing the camp already killed prisoners by the dozen. When the foundation was laid, the marshy soil swallowed the workers. With Hitler's mandate, *Reichsführer* SS Heinrich Himmler then organized his perfect extermination camp there.

Himmler's approach was not exactly experimental; he already had extensive experience. In 1933, he opened the first Nazi concentration camp for political prisoners in Dachau, near Munich. This neat man with his clerk-like oval head, tight lips and rimless glasses had more loyalty to Hitler than love for his own mother, and an obsession with creating a purely Nordic breed, picturing himself as the ultimate racial hygienist. Unsurprisingly, he focused mainly on women. Swift extermination of Jewish women was key, because they would produce the next generation of Jews, intent on avenging their fathers, and Aryan women had to reproduce as fast as possible. This concept, with Auschwitz-Birkenau as one of its final destinations, is where Janny and Lien have ended up.

From the SS camp commander at the top, the ranks run all the way down into the barracks. Chosen prisoners exert the last bit of power there. Kicking down as hard as possible helps to maintain your position – and this position is of vital importance. A higher status means an extra piece of bread when others are starving, or exemption when others are sent to the gas chambers. Deploying prisoners for surveillance saves money and pitting victims against each other is an effective way to destroy the community, or whatever is left of it, from inside out.

There is a *Stübenälteste*, head of the barracks, who has to obey a *Blockälteste*, head of the block, who has to bow for the *Kapos*, who account to the *Aufseherinnen*, who set the tone with their violent approach, each in their own way. One stoically smashes her whip on prisoners, another batters the skull of a girl until her brains are lying at her feet. Prisoners are not only crushed along vertical lines; divisiveness is encouraged everywhere. Poles are set up against Russians, Russians against Hungarians, Hungarians against Western Europeans. The sisters soon notice that most *Kapos* are Polish women with a specific dislike of French and Dutch girls.

Janny and Lien are in a separate block with other political prisoners, women of all sorts of nationalities; they are from Greece, France, Italy, Russia and Denmark. They are all hungry and exhausted, they all miss their children and their families. Despite feverish attempts to get information on their relatives, the sisters have not yet been able to find Jaap, Father and Mother. Not a trace of Red Puck and the elderly couple, Loes and Bram Teixeira de Mattos, either, but that does not have to mean anything: Birkenau camp alone is larger than 350 football pitches with tens of thousands of prisoners in hundreds of barracks. Then there is the base camp, Auschwitz I, and, further away, Auschwitz III. There lies the industrial site with, among others, chemical company IG Farben, where slaves of the Third Reich help to produce synthetic rubber. When, as often, they cannot sleep at night, crammed between other restless women's bodies on their wooden shelves, they try to picture Father, Mother and Jaap in the assembly line. Tired and filthy but with a beating heart. Or perhaps they have ended up in one of the forty smaller camps in the area and are now working on the land. Optimistic scenarios present themselves in the long nocturnal hours, but during roll call in the dark morning, the first thing they see is again the chimney, triumphantly rising above the camp.

On their first morning in Auschwitz, when a woman in striped clothes finally led them to a quarantine barracks, they had walked past one of those low buildings with a massive chimney.

'What kind of factory is that?' someone from their group had asked.

The woman did not look up, she did not move a muscle.

'Factory?' she said, nodding towards the chimney with her chin. 'That is your transport over there. Into the fireplace as we speak.'

They want to believe the rest of the family have ended up well, but each day they have not been liberated, the ovens burn up a new load. Non-stop. They are constantly reminded by the stench covering the camp grounds like a blanket and by their voice, which, as they speak their first words in the morning, sounds hoarser every day.

The days are filled with pointless work or endless roll calls. Six hours on end, sometimes twelve, sometimes around the clock, until the watery Polish sun reappears. In the first month the hairs on their arms still respond, reaching like sprouts towards the heat source, providing short-term relief as they stand there, famished, with 1,000, sometimes 2,000 people in blocks of twenty-five. But when September turns into October, a dark veil in the sky pours out one deluge after the other and soon, the rock-hard surface softens to a thick layer of stinking mud. Their clothes no longer dry and the barracks turn into damp stables in which funguses and vermin multiply at lightning speed.

**The triple** beds in their barracks are merely shelving units for stacking people. Each layer is designed for two, but because the camp is overcrowded, five to six women are lying sideways on each shelf. This adds up to eighteen shivering bodies per bed. If they are lucky, there is some straw, but often it is just the dangerously creaking wood, a sliver of a blanket and their own hand to serve as a pillow.

The tossing and turning at night is unbearable. The

bony buttocks of a stranger against your belly, always a mouthful of sores and blisters breathing in your face, the constant coughing, the crying of those who have failed to keep the thought of their children at bay. Your nose in the flaky crown of your neighbour, a knee in your back, someone else's festering wound brushing your skin. Someone is trying to pry open your hand and get hold of your valuables. A woman above you is sick and lets everything go, another one is delirious, a third one becomes aggressive.

But all discomfort pales in comparison to the itching. The maddening itching, creeping underneath your skin, crawling up your bloodstream towards your brain. It never stops. Janny often thinks more people in the camp lose their mind as a result of the itch than because of all other hardships combined. The lice, fleas, bedbugs and other creatures are everywhere: in their clothes, on their head, on their eyelashes, between their toes, under their armpits and in their crotch. Dozens, hundreds of minuscule bites all over their body, every minute, every second, in the morning, the afternoon, the evening, at night. During roll call, in the shithouse, on their beds. The bugs are so small and they are so many that it seems an invisible army is eating them alive – it drives people mad. Entire strips of skin are ripped off with fingernails, teeth or sharp bits of metal.

Skulls are scratched open and people walk around with sores on their head, which slowly work their way inside. Nothing will stop the itch and the biggest challenge is to surrender to it, without surrendering completely.

Janny keeps telling her sister: we must survive this. If only they stay together, keep their wits and look after each other. Not think of the children. Stay clean. Eat what you can. Do not scratch open your skin. And above all: do not be selected by Josef Mengele and his team of SS doctors.

The *Selektion* is a constant threat and the moment they all fear the most. Of course the main selection already took place on the *Rampe*, the platform, upon arrival. The frail, the infirm, the infants, children under fifteen: they could walk from the train into the gas chambers in one straight line. But that was not all. At random moments, SS Doctor Josef Mengele comes and selects; once a month, once a week, sometimes two blissful months go by without him appearing at all. He decides who can still work, who is interesting for his medical experiments and who has become entirely useless. He sends people to the gas chambers as if they are flies – dismissing them with a simple hand gesture. If you end up in either one of the other wretched categories, at least there is still hope.

Selections often take place immediately after *Zählap-*

*pell*, the head count. This is what happens today; after the endless wait they are not scattered around the site but instead, suddenly, there is noise everywhere. Guards, dogs, nervous *Kapos*, the shouting is even louder than usual.

'*Großer Appell! Antreten zur Selektion!*'

'*Schnell!*'

Major roll call! Line up for selection!

Fast!

The crowd disperses, everyone rushes to their own block, gets undressed. Panic sweeps through the barracks. Naked women run around, stop each other, look for their family, children, camp friends. They do not have time but anxiously inspect their bodies, turn to neighbours and girlfriends for help.

'Can you see a rash here?'

'These spots, are those sores?'

'Have I lost any more weight?'

'Press your arm against your side, you do not want them to see that wound over there.'

Someone rubs a lump of carefully kept margarine on her cheeks to put some shine on her dull skin. One woman slaps herself hard to redden her ashen-coloured face, another bites her lips and spreads out the blood. A piece of lipstick is worth a fortune, at least three daily rations of bread: a bit of colour can save you from

*Malach ha Mòwes*, as they call doctor Mengele in Yiddish. The Angel of Death.

Janny has already undressed and looks at Lien, sees how skinny she has become. Her gorgeous sister, followed around by all the boys when they were young, with her enviable figure and dark, full hair, now looks brittle and defeated, her spiked hair wrapped around her skull like barbed wire. Lien is looking at the chaos in the barracks in despair; her constant worrying takes up all of her energy. Janny has a thicker skin, is more collected, sometimes even stoic, like their mother; she is the more resilient one.

A deep blue oil slick flows across Lien's right eye, a testimony to her hot-headedness. The day before yesterday a girl in their barracks had stolen her clogs from under her head and when Lien came to demand them back the next morning, they got into a fight. They were both pulling at the same clog, shouting, and before Lien could snatch away the second one, the child hit her full in the face with it. Lien saw stars, but she did have her clogs back.

'Lientje!' Janny grabs her sister's upper arms. 'Pay attention now. We must get through this. Father, Mother and Japie are out there somewhere, waiting for us, we can*not* be selected, do you hear me?'

Lien nods resignedly but cannot find the strength

to brace herself for the showdown with Mengele. They have been on roll call for hours, she is tired and hungry and would just like to lie down on her bed. Only for a little while. When Janny shakes her up, her head bobs along like a broken tulip on a stem.

'I dreamt about Eberhard,' Lien whispers, barely audible, her eyes lowered.

Women around them begin to run outside and Janny observes her sister impatiently. Suddenly, Lien looks up.

'When they find out Kathinka is Jewish, I will never see my baby again, Janny. And it's all right for you to say Eberhard got away, but . . .'

A sob escapes her mouth and her shoulders drop even further. Janny pushes them back up and brings her face so close to Lien that their noses are almost touching. Her dark eyes flash when she speaks.

'Stop it! They are safe. And, Goddammit, we have other things to worry about!'

She is shouting through the practically deserted barracks. Janny shakes her sister again until Lien gets annoyed, tries to wriggle free and begins to scold back. Janny does not let go until Lien is livid and they are opposite each other, fighting like when they were young, red cheeks and glistening eyes. Then she takes a step back and breathes out.

'Right,' says Janny. 'Now, get outside and keep your chin up.'

The dogs go wild, SS officers are barking at the women to move on. Quick, run, bare feet through ice-cold mud, wind scraping against their uncovered bodies. They are terrified of the Great Danes chattering at them with square jaws, their foam splashing against their skin as they walk past.

Line up and go past the selection one by one. Mengele, accompanied by his medical staff, stands there waiting. He cheerfully inspects each body with his eyes. His uniform impeccable as always, his symmetrical face with shaven temples disappearing under a cap, his brown eyes filled with excitement to see what the selection will yield today. Twins in particular bring him into ecstasy, but those are a rare find in old cargos – he tends to pick them out on the platform. His zest for work is unprecedented; even on his days off he will pop up between the other doctors, hoping for a good catch.

Here, in Birkenau, he can continue the scientific research on racial hygiene that he conducted at Frankfurt University, without restrictions – and much more. Less then ten years before, Mengele, then in his early twenties, obtained his doctorate with a thesis on 'racial differences in the structure of the lower jaw'. But his Aryan fantasies have no limits and the supply of guinea pigs in Birkenau is endless. Mengele tries to make dark eyes blue and is working on an experiment to connect the bloodstreams of twins. The women have heard that he sews young twins together, veins and all, back to back, wrist to wrist. But there are also stories of him bringing the children milk and cookies. They do not know what to believe any more.

'Next!'

The fieldful of bony women moves steadily, like a conveyor belt with people. The front is inspected. Turn, the backside. Turn again and wait for his hand gesture. To the left means labour or experiment block, to the right means gas chamber. Mengele's face is soft, not tight like the faces of most other SS officers; he steps around briskly, nods here and there, his angelic face is the very model of charm.

A Russian prisoner said that Mengele once had trucks full of children under five dumped into an enormous fire pit because they were so hard to usher into the gas chambers at that age. About ten dumper trucks full of little ones drove backwards to the edge of the pit, after which SS officers, supervised by Mengele, tossed them into the flames by an arm or a leg. The burning children who tried to climb out of the pit were pushed back with long poles.

'Next!'

One step forwards. They are coming closer. It is almost Lien's turn. They cannot help but stare at Mengele's hands, giving directions like a traffic controller.

Left.

Right.

He walks a bit between the lines, friendly, his posture straight like a horseback rider. Every few seconds another silent verdict.

Left.

Right.

Everyone in the camp has lost weight, but one is worse than the other.

Is that a bump under that navel there? To the right, we do not want any pregnant women.

Is that a rash? Closer inspection, another doctor is called in and together they examine the naked girl. A nod; to the right.

A woman is pinched in her upper arm; is there any fat so she can still work? To the left.

Someone is hunchbacked. Mengele's interest is piqued; he knocks on it, traces the woman's spine with his fingers, feels her ribcage, sticking out like an open hull, and nods approvingly. To the experiment block.

You, stick out your hands, turn around. You have scabies, *Krätze*: go left, to the *Krätzeblock*. The itch mite is rampant in the camp; the tiny creature burrows into the skin to lay its eggs. It causes hellish itches and rashes, but it does not kill you. Once they have patched you up, you can go back to work. This is exactly how Anne Frank was sent to the *Krätzeblock*, separated from the rest of the camp by a high wall. Margot had pretended she became unwell, so she could follow her sister. Janny has not seen them since.

Left.

Right.

The group of women is gradually getting smaller, the crowd splits like the sea when Mengele passes through. Close up the line, Janny is a little behind Lien and keeps a sharp eye on her. The doctor walks between the women, gets closer, examines and nods, is in good spirits and enthusiastic as always.

He stops in front of Lien and starts to laugh. Janny's breath catches. Mengele has casually hooked his thumbs behind his belt. He is talking to her sister – Janny pricks her ears.

'*Was hast du gemacht?*' What have you been up to? Amused, his head tilted to one side, he looks at Lien; Janny can see the gap between his front teeth glisten. Lien does not respond. Janny sees her shoulders and neck tighten. Why is she not saying anything?

Mengele moves closer towards her, points at her face with a smile.

'*Woher hast du denn das Veilchen?*'

Lien does not understand. She pulls up one shoulder, briefly shakes her head.

A *Veilchen* – a violet? Does he mean the flower, what is he saying?

'*Ich habe keine Blumen.*' I do not have any flowers, she answers hesitantly.

Then the penny drops. She pulls herself together – Janny can tell by looking at her sister's back, which is relaxing. Lien's chin goes up and she looks at the doctor fearlessly.

'*Ach so. Ja, ich hab mich mit einem Mädchen gestritten, und sie hat mich mit einem Holzschuh aufs Auge geschlagen.*' Oh, I see. Yes, I had a fight with a girl, and she hit me on the eye with a clog.

Mengele bursts out laughing, gives her a smack on her naked bum and points to the left. Lien can go.

Janny relaxes her fists, feels her nails very slowly pull out of her flesh.

The woman after Lien is a nervous wreck by the time Mengele turns to her. The sisters know her, she is from a renowned family of frame-makers in a town near Amsterdam. She does not speak a word of

German, so when he starts talking to her too, she is almost hyperventilating. Mengele's mouth drops, he raises an eyebrow as he examines her.

'*Und du? Was hast du dann gemacht?*' And you? What have you been up to?

Displeased, he looks at her belly, not yet as caved in as most, and waits for an answer. The woman looks around in despair, unable to grasp what is expected of her, until Mengele points at her abdomen.

'*Nein, nein . . .*' she stutters, wildly shaking her head. 'I . . . *ich* . . . have . . . my little one is at home, two years.' She gestures with her hand at knee height, nodding at the doctor with large eyes, hoping he understands. He does not.

Right.

'No!' She screams, begs in Dutch, but Mengele is done with the conversation and wants to move on.

The woman begins to cry, shouts that it is all a misunderstanding, the whites of her eyes bloodshot. Janny bites her lower lip, she almost cannot control herself. Mengele takes a step back and hits the woman hard on the head. Then he beckons the guards to take her away.

A few seconds later, Mengele has passed Janny too and has given her the green light. The rows have almost dried up and there are barely any people left on the field; she should be relieved but is so furious about what just happened to the Dutch woman that she stomps around the site, fuming with anger. Then she sees a Dutch *Aufseherin*, an SS guard. Without thinking, she runs towards the woman and grabs her by the arm.

'That woman is not pregnant and you know it! She is a political prisoner, not a Jew. If she is gassed, you are personally responsible.'

Janny is small but fearlessly hisses at the woman in the face. Then she turns around and walks back to her barracks. As if by miracle, the Dutch woman is indeed dragged away from the gates of the gas chamber and they meet again later, both still alive.

# 4

# La Marseillaise

Janny and Lien fear the *Kapos* the most. These prisoners, men and women, delight in humiliating their fellow captives. They are appointed by the SS and seem to be recruited among criminals rather than teachers. In the first week, already the sisters wondered why their own *Blockälteste*, a healthy-looking Polish–Jewish girl named Rosa, would treat them so sadistically – but then they saw how Rosa was treated by the *Kapos*. If she could not compete with them, it would kill her. It will not be long before Lien incurs the wrath of one of those *Kapos*.

Ruth Feldman is a sturdy Dutch woman from their block, former head nurse of the Central Israelite Hospital. She was in their carriage from Westerbork to

Auschwitz and upon arrival passed the 'sauna' with them – the building where they were marked.

One day, the sisters and Ruth are in the shithouse, as they call the latrines: a long stone building with a row of round holes from one side to the other, in which they must relieve themselves. It smells terrible and is filthier than a pigsty, but for that same reason it is one of the few places where the SS do not come and where you can briefly speak privately. Janny and Lien have finished, but Ruth has diarrhoea and cannot get up from her hole. Before long, a *Kapo* storms in to chase them away. When Ruth does not get up – sick as a dog and worrying she will soil herself – the woman gets furious. She pounces on Ruth and tries to shove her down the hole, into the shit pit.

The women scream and shout as Ruth tries desperately to wriggle out of the hole. Without thinking, Lien takes off her wooden clog and flings it on the *Kapo*'s head with full force. The sound of a cork coming out of a bottle. The *Kapo* lets go of Ruth and the shouting fades. Lien quickly turns around and runs for her life, the *Kapo* chasing her, swearing. The woman soon loses her on the enormous site and by the time reinforcements arrive, Lien has been swallowed up by the crowd.

When she returns to the barracks much later, Janny first rages at her sister before falling in her arms – they both know that if the *Kapo* had got hold of Lien, she would have beaten her to death. And still, the incident probably saves their lives, because when they see Ruth again, she says: 'I'm signing up as a nurse and you are coming with me.'

**No matter** how hard the Nazis try to completely strip prisoners of their personality, in the barracks their last ounce of humanity is persistently standing. They impersonate an SS officer, his lower jaw sticking out like a piranha's, wobbling across the site on his short legs and jumping to attention the minute a superior walks past. They gossip about that *Kapo* with her fluffy angora jumper, short skirt, high boots and pinned-up hair. Janny fantasizes about burying that jumper in the Polish mud until the last bit of fluff is smothered.

But most conversations in the barracks involve food. They talk about meatballs and mashed potatoes with a little hole for the gravy, pasta al dente with bolognese sauce and large chunks of Parmesan, about lamb cutlets, roasted with honey and thyme. About red wine from wooden barrels, coffee made of black burnt beans and about home-made lemonade with ice cubes tinkling in the glass. They talk until the gnawing hole in their belly is filled with imaginary food.

When they seem to be enjoying themselves a little too much, the *Kapo* enters.

'*Jetzt wird nicht gefressen, jetzt wird gestorben!*' You are not here to eat, you are here to die!

And as she storms out of the barracks, a skinny woman in frayed shirt walks after her, legs wide apart, the same arrogant pose and filthy look – and they still have a laugh, three stories up in their beds.

Every day is a battle; they fight for food, for their lives; they fight for whatever has been stolen from them, for a good position at the little tap, where some women hit cups from other women's hands to get just one drop of water; they fight for the torn blanket they find on their bed after work; strips of cloth can be tied into underpants against draught crawling underneath their chemises. But at the same time, they try to lift each other up with all the fighting spirit they have left. The fury of the Italian women makes Janny laugh and she loves the inventiveness of the French. With a piece of glass and a three-pinned comb, they model their bristly heads and furry eyebrows, and with some wet soil they draw an elegant arch above their eyes. They tie a cloth around their neck and put on a coquettish smile. It is no vanity but *esprit*, as Janny explains to her sister, clearly articulating her newly acquired French word.

All the ugliness has not extinguished Lien's voice, either. Sometimes she softly sings to Janny: the lullabies she sang to the children, Yiddish songs from her repertoire with Eberhard. It takes them back in time to The High Nest, when they were afraid but not dying – and, above all: still together. It sometimes seems a lifetime ago. But when Lien sings, Janny closes her eyes and sees herself walk to the house from the tram stop at Ericaweg after a long day, the kestrel hovering high above her in the bright blue sky. The forest appears, the shell path, the gate, the red shutters – in the front room someone at the dining table waves at her. Past the shed, say hello to Japie, bent over his workbench. Lien is at the back of the garden with the three children – they are standing outside the gazebo, singing. When she stretches her fingers, she can almost touch them.

One day they are all chased out of the barracks.

'*Läusekontrolle! Alles ausziehen! Raus, raus!*' Louse check! Take off all your clothes! Get out, out!

A few hundred women drop their rags in bundles on the floor and run naked into the cold October morning. It is no roll call; they are left to their own devices on the camp site and huddle together in groups. Their barren feet sink into the mud.

'This is no louse check,' a woman in the sisters' group says. 'Clothes off means gas chamber.'

They shiver. Everyone knows the story of Mengele, who, when a typhoid fever epidemic occurred, chased 1,000 naked Gypsies out of their barracks and straight into the gas chambers. His effective approach when it came to epidemics had even earned him a medal, referred to as the 'typhus medal' by the prisoners when they were having a laugh. There is nothing to laugh about now.

They stand in silence and wait on this wasteland beneath an autumnal Polish sky, looking like martians with their twiggy bodies and large wobbly heads. Suddenly, a French woman in their group, Michelle, begins to sing. With a soft soprano voice, she sings the first notes of *'Chevaliers de la Table Ronde'*, a popular French drinking song about the Knights of the Round Table, often accompanied by violin, tambourine and guitar. The song is about tasting wine, drinking with joy and the desire to be buried in a wine cellar with one's mouth under the tap. The chorus, *'Oui, oui, oui, non, non, non'*, is usually sung along by bystanders while they link arms and whirl around. The others look up, bewildered.

Michelle sings on, confidently, and with glistening eyes replaces the lyrics with a new satirical poem on Hitler and the cowardly collaborators of Vichy – referring to the non-occupied part of France where the government sympathizes with the Nazis. As soon as she gets the melody, Lien joins in and a few other women softly hum along too.

When the last notes have evaporated, Lien starts to sing a Yiddish song. It is a cheerful tune with funny lyrics. More and more women gather around them and those who know the song softly sing along. Lien's voice drifts above the cropped heads, encircles and unites them while the *Kapos* turn their barracks upside down. Next, Lien breaks into the Yiddish Partisan song, *'Zog nit keyn mol, as du geyst dem letstn veg'* – Never say the final journey is at hand – and a few Polish women join in. They are surprised to hear the song, which only recently came up in the Polish Vilna ghetto and spread among Jews in the rest of Europe. Lien does not know all the words yet, but the Polish women help her. Before long, all the women from their barracks are standing around them, naked and shivering with cold, together in a large circle, their faces turned towards each other, singing along where they can.

Before Lien has finished, she looks at Michelle, who

taught her 'Le chant de la libération', anthem of the French resistance. Michelle nods and together they start singing the battle hymn. All the French women join in, but others, who have listened to Radio London, know it too; the BBC have started using it as their theme tune. Especially since the Nazis have banned the Marseillaise, 'Le chant de la libération' is embraced as alternative national anthem – except of course in Vichy.

Ami, entends-tu le vol noir des corbeaux sur nos
  plaines?
Ami, entends-tu les cris sourds du pays qu'on
  enchaîne?
Ohé partisans, ouvriers et paysans, c'est l'alarme!
Ce soir l'ennemi connaîtra le prix du sang et des
  larmes.

Friend, do you hear the crows' dark flight across
  our plains?
Friend, do you hear the muffled cries of our
  country in chains?
Partisans, workers and farmers, this warning is
  to say
Tonight, both with blood and tears, our enemies
  shall pay.

The song is usually accompanied by the beating of drums, perfect for marching on the spot – which they do. As they softly sing together, their knees rise in an even cadence, their feet in step with the words. For an instant they forget the chimney smoking behind them, the cold, the hunger, the number on their lower arm. Together, they are one voice and each naked foot splashing down in the mud makes their blood flow a little faster.

That day, no one is sent to the gas chambers. Even Rosa, the head of their block, normally as cold as ice, is moved to tears by the Yiddish songs and gives Lien an extra piece of bread.

A few days later, Michelle is beaten to death and a large group of French women is taken away, after all. But as the truck pulls up and drives towards the gas chambers, they can hear the banned Marseillaise, sung loudly behind the canvas of the tent.

*Allons enfants de la Patrie,*
*le jour de gloire est arrivé!*
*Contre nous de la tyrannie*
*L'étendard sanglant est levé.*
*L'étendard sanglant est levé:*
*Entendez-vous dans les campagnes*
*Mugir ces féroces soldats?*

*Ils viennent jusque dans vos bras*
*Égorger vos fils, vos compagnes!*

Come, children of the fatherland,
The day of glory has arrived.
Against us the bloody flag
Of tyranny is raised;
The bloody flag is raised.
Do you hear in the countryside
The roar of those savage soldiers?
They come right into your arms
To cut the throats of your sons, your men!

Then Lien falls ill. They all feel miserable, all the time, but as long as they can get up in the morning and stay up during roll call and work, they can plough through the fog hanging over the wetland, day after day after day. A few people attempt to escape during roll call, but it is always in vain. They are hung and the others are made to watch. Then it is back to work. They fold plastic for aircraft, they pull shoes apart with their last bit of strength and drag stones from one place to wherever the *Kapos* tell them. The purpose of neither of these jobs is clear to them. Do not ask questions, just keep going – Janny keeps repeating it like a mantra, even when the pain in her smashed ankle pulls up to her teeth. One of the girls in their group ignores the advice: she opens her mouth, complains and has to pay for it. Knelt on a large stone, she has to hold a rock high above her head for a whole day; whenever she lowers her arms one inch, the whip cracks against her skinny body.

One morning Lien is really giving up. It is still dark when they must report for roll c≠all, four or five in the morning, and they cannot be late. But she no longer cares. Lifting up her eyes is too much to ask, let alone swaying her legs over the edge of the bed and holding that feeble body up. She would rather be dead. She is hot like a stove and the energy is flowing out of her body fast; Janny knows she has to act. A girl in their barracks has scarlet fever, a bacterial infection in the throat, easily transmitted by coughing. They only noticed when the girl was covered with a red rash – on her tongue, her face, her entire body – and had perhaps already infected half the barracks. Reluctantly, Janny takes her sister to the *Krankenblock*, the sick bay, and leaves her there with a heavy heart. It is the first time they are apart.

The following days, Janny steals around the sick bay like a predator. Not at all at ease, she keeps a close watch on the doctors and nurses. Their body language, the whispers, the conversations of people leaving the barracks; she is searching for clues everywhere. The SS doctors are hunting the sick barracks too, picking the weakest for the *Selektion* – but when? Lien sleeps and sleeps and no one knows what is wrong with her. The fever is drawing the last bit of energy from her body and she has stopped speaking. A few dozen feet further, Janny lies awake at night and all she can think of are Mother's words from that last night before the transportation, when the five of them sat together in Westerbork: *You must stay together!*

On the third day, Janny intervenes. She walks to the entrance of the sick bay and speaks to a Czech doctor. The woman listens, nods and goes inside. At Lien's bed, she holds still.

'*Komm mit*, get up. Your sister is outside.'

Lien lifts up her eyelids, sighs, shuts them again. She softly shakes her head.

'Can't. I'm ill.'

The woman takes her by the shoulder, tugs at the cotton of her shirt, insists.

'Come, she is not leaving before you come with her.'

The woman stays at her bed until Lien finally slides her bony legs over the edge and pushes herself up, so the doctor can lift her under her armpits. At the entrance she hands Lien to Janny, who nods gratefully.

Her sister has not yet recovered, but the fever has subsided.

'If you hadn't got me out of there, they would have sent me to the gas,' Lien says to her sister a few days later, still weak but no longer ill.

They have heard that another selection is due. Janny shrugs. If they do not look after each other, everything is finished.

**Against the** bright beam of the spotlight, the man has faded to a silhouette, but it is him, unmistakeably. His hand behind his back, a slight smile on his face and energetic as ever, he is standing in front of the crowd like a conductor in front of his choir. They are anxiously awaiting the next gesture of his hand. Beside him, a long table with SS colleagues, pen and paper at the ready. Scales separate the women from the table. The room is filled to the brim; today's job is a big one.

Mengele nods and the next woman steps forwards. She is naked and bald. Her ribcage is a pointed roof above her caved belly, two flaps of skin are the souvenir of her breasts, vertebra swirl down her back like a string of beads. The woman behind her looks the same, and the next, and the next. On the scales. She can barely stand still, her knees buckle. Mengele's hand.

Right. Dismissed.

Next.

The woman is a copy of her predecessor, but her body seems slightly stronger. The tiniest difference.

Mengele gestures.

Left.

Next.

The group on the right grows fast. Too old. Too ill.

'I am twenty-nine!' a woman shouts at Mengele. 'And I have never had diarrhoea!'

He does not even blink.

'Right!' His voice echoes through the hall. Emotionless, as if he is organizing sports teams in the gym.

Next.

Edith Frank steps forwards. Mengele instantly gestures.

Right.

She ducks under the spotlight and quickly turns around; this is the most important bit.

'Next!'

Anne and Margot step forwards. Anne's body is covered with crusts from old scabies sores. She has only just been discharged from the sick barracks; Margot was by her side all the time. Together, they step into the beam of the spotlight and in front of the selection table. Margot nudges her sister and Anne straightens her back.

'Left!'

A pen scratches the paper. The girls pass the metal lamp and disappear in the dark on the other side. Edith gasps for breath.

'The children! Oh God . . . the children!' she shouts after them, but they are gone.

It is 30 October 1944 and the final selection in Auschwitz-Birkenau is over.

# 5

# Star Camp

A hunk of bread, a piece of sausage and a sliver of hard cheese. Move on, next platform. *Dalli, dalli.* Dogs and whips and shouting. By now they know the drill. Go, go, go. Cattle carriages waiting for them, just like in Westerbork.

'*Schneller! Hier rein!*' Faster! Get in!

Climb up, get in, that smell again. It does not matter, at least they are leaving Auschwitz, or so it seems. More people get in; they shuffle forwards. The sisters squeeze each other's hand, do not let go. The familiar feeling of strangers pressing against them – but the bodies are more angular now. Pans with water are shoved between legs and into the carriage before the door shuts, a dull thud and the curtain falls. Pitch-black. Blink as you wish, it makes no difference whether your eyes are open or not. Lientje's breath next to her. Light, thin. Janny cannot make out her face but knows that she is watching her. They are looking at each other, without being able to see.

'We're leaving,' Janny whispers, and she knows her sister nods.

**It feels** as if they are going back. Back in time, back in space, back towards the Netherlands. The swishing sound of wheels on tracks, the rhythm of the joints below them beating time. They count each bang till it makes their heads spin, until minutes, again, turn into too many hours and only the old tricks help them to stay on their feet. Stay as close to the doors as possible, gasp for air at the crack. Stand at the sidewalls; they will protect you. Snooze with your back against mine. It is different this time. They are so much weaker now than they were then. They cannot even keep up an appearance of civilization; it is each to their own now.

They stop all the time, cover a short distance before the next air raid siren sounds. First the roar of an engine starting up, then a long run-up, higher and higher, until a choir of sirens from all directions drowns out the sound of their beating hearts. Shootings, loud bangs, guards jumping off the train to take cover, while they stay in the stationary carriage, petrified, wondering what on earth is happening outside. It feels like a bomb could drop on their heads any moment. All their excitement about the Allied forces advancing has gone.

A day. A night. The first people collapse, they lie between their legs. Blankets are snatched away from bodies. Stop, door opens, a piece of bread and some water, door shuts. The air in the carriage is thick and heavy, they are short of breath, their muscles weaken and their head is pounding. They press their faces against the walls, their mouth against the cracks for some oxygen. The cold, it is so cold, but even the cold does not dispel the stench. Wheels hurtle across tracks. They do not know where to, but as long as they hear that sound, they know that they are alive.

A day. A night. They can go out, briefly. The horizon, fields, the trees next to a ditch; everything is dark and grey and wet but it is blissful. Someone says they are in Germany, they really are going back. Back in, quick, do not let go of my hand. Get in last, stay close to the door where the cracks are. At the back of the carriage, on the filthy floor, familiar faces with their eyes wide open, their lower jaw all stiff. The closing of the door and the metal bolt. Darkness. The connecting rods slowly getting back into motion.

Noise outside – they are standing still. Screeching steel of other trains around them, sharp whistles, conversations in German behind their door, laughter. Hoarse whispers from a dark corner.

'I think this is Ravensbrück.'

The women's camp near Berlin? Stories of children flung into the fire alive, babies left in empty rooms. Janny and Lien shiver and hug themselves, stiff fingers around their fleshless upper arms, a dirty horse blanket wrapped around their shoulders. A jolt, a forwards movement; the train takes off again.

A day. A night. They gasp for oxygen like dying fish. Those who are still alive press themselves against the walls of the carriage, scratching the wood with their fingernails. They did not think there was anything left to take away from them, but that was an illusion. Father, Mother, Jaap; sometimes when the sisters look up, they seem to sit next to them, alive. They can almost touch them. But when they stretch out their fingers, they are stroking a stranger. A growl, a slap.

Where are their loved ones? Did they stay behind in Auschwitz? Their cheeks are feverish, their bodies frozen and the images are haunting their minds. Their relatives gone, their families gone, the women and girls who were with them in Auschwitz gone. The carriage rocks at each switch, someone tumbles over them, they push her away. No one has spoken for hours, perhaps no one ever spoke, perhaps they do not even have a voice. No one knows who is still conscious and who has slipped away. Even the smell does not bother them any more. A pinch in a finger, are you still there? A pinch back.

And then they stop.

**Is there** anything more delightful than the smell of pine trees in autumn? It goes straight to your brain from the hairs of your nose, crisp and fresh like the start of a new day. Beds made, the cotton tucked in tightly at the foot, the first frost flowers already appearing on the window. Down the stairs and out of the kitchen door, breathing clouds, the air against your cheeks like frozen iron but not as glacial as in months to come. Take a walk on the heath with Bob, hand in hand.

A rolling landscape, shrubs under a smooth layer of fog as far as their eyes can see – it is like walking through clouds in the sky. Janny does not have to place her feet, one step follows the other. They are floating on cotton wool balls. Ahead of them is another couple, floating. Another couple in front of them, and another. An endless garland of stooped figures meanders through the heath, disappears at the purple horizon. A white sun begins to fade behind dark clouds and she feels the first drops touch her skin. She looks up. The heavens close above their heads, cover the heath with a canvas of shadow. They must get back to The High Nest before it really starts. Janny turns, someone bumps into her. The row behind them is endless too. Bob tugs at her hand, drags her along.

'Janny, come on!' Lien hisses at her sister, pulls her arm.

They walk on, tripping over tree roots and stones along the way. Her feet are numb, she must lift them higher. No floating clouds. Janny remembers where they are: Celle station, Germany. They were ushered out of the train there, barely able to stand on their feet.

'*Raus!*'

They had to drag the dead out of the carriage but were too exhausted. Their hands tugged and pulled, but the rest of them was not there. Leave the bodies on the platform, heavy and pale, feet wide apart. Move, rushed by dogs and guards.

They pull the horse blanket a little tighter, but the cold is biting their naked calves. It has started to rain. The wind picks up, but the forest air is still lovely. Lungs, heart, walk.

When they walked through the town in the first part of their journey, their blood started flowing faster, their heads shot up. Civilization. Normal people. The guards and their dogs formed a line between the procession of stumbling skeletons and the citizens. Through the gaps the sisters tried to get a glimpse of their faces, meet their gaze, street after street, mile after mile. A man, a woman, a baker, a butcher, a group of children, an elderly couple. But as soon as their eyes met, the others looked away. People passing from the opposite direction, on their bicycle, on horse-drawn carriages, gave way, pretending not to see them. Pedestrians on both sides stopped and stared. But no one spoke.

They slog on, how many miles to go? They have left Celle hours ago. The forest path they walk on ends at a stretch of heath. No more cover. Rain is lashing against their faces, runs in streams to their neck, fills the holes behind their collarbones. Gusts of wind gather speed on the open field, take a run-up and try to knock them over, someone slips. Do not stop. Knees up, step over. Those who miss one beat are lost. Drops turn into hailstones, wind turns into storm. Foul weather. Orders are barely audible. Their bodies lean forwards. Barbed wire. The camp.

Bergen-Belsen.

The sisters look at each other, hug each other tight, breathe out. Glistening hailstones fall from their hair, past their eyes, on their cheeks. When someone mentioned it at Celle station, they would not believe it, but it is true. This is good. Bergen-Belsen is good. There are no gas chambers here. This is just a camp.

They are left like animals in a corral. No roll call, no lines, no labour, no shouting. Just a foggy, barren site full of grey silhouettes in the rain, tents and shacks as far as their eyes can see. Janny and Lien sink down on a sandhill and huddle together, pulling their drenched blankets up to their noses. It feels as if they are underground; there is smoke and steam everywhere, people squat, make themselves small, walk with a stoop as if the ceiling is low. A teenager drifts about, wearing nothing but a striped shirt, his legs sticking out of the cotton like twigs. A woman on the ground grabs the hand of a passing guard and presses her lips against it – she will not let go until he gives her a push against her forehead and she falls backwards in the mud. Someone is stirring a pot above a fire. One women leans forwards, her upper body bare, while another woman empties a bucket of ice-cold water on her hair. A cloud of steam shoots up like a flash fire.

They crawl into their blankets. They no longer feel hunger; the emptiness in their stomach is a familiar block of concrete that has been there for months. But the cold in their bones, the cold that has turned their skin into pink sandpaper and is keeping their jaws locked, the cold is impossible to get used to.

A shapeless figure approaches through the rain. Two shaved heads sticking out like frozen birds. They stare at each other. A warm glow, jaws loosen. A cry of joy shoots off on the wind. They throw off their blankets and the four of them fall into each other, crying. They are Anne and Margot.

**Bergen–Belsen** was never set up as an extermination camp; it was established on the German heath for prisoners of war, including large numbers of Russian soldiers. During the war, the camp expanded and stretched for eleven square kilometres, with various subsections. Owing to poor conditions and a large number of infectious diseases, the majority of the soldiers soon succumbed. Diseases such as dysentery and typhus were passed on from neighbour to neighbour and spread further by lice and mites. As soon as someone had contracted the disease, life literally ran out of his orifices. Almost all enemy uniforms were emptied without a shot being fired.

Only one year before the sisters arrived, in 1943, the SS took over the camp administration and Bergen-Belsen also became an exchange camp for Jews. The idea was to swap these people for German prisoners of war in other countries. The chosen Jews are on the so-called Palestine List and placed in the *Sternlager*, the Star Camp. They are made to wear a yellow star on their clothes. The exchanges do not really happen, but most prisoners are not forced to work or wear prison clothing – more importantly, there are no gas chambers. And so the rumour spreads across Europe that this is one of the better locations to end up in.

This myth is debunked within a few months. In the spring of 1944, the Germans decide to pick up thousands of Polish and Hungarian women from the ghettos, and also transfer all the Jews from other concentration camps who are ill but non-terminal to Bergen-Belsen for 'recovery'. To facilitate this, extra accommodation is added: a *Zeltlager*, a tent camp, is built with large circus tents to house a few thousand women. Sometimes 7,000 people stay there at a time. There is no medical care, no sanitation, no extra water or food supply, nor any form of organization to receive them, let alone to help them to recover.

In the late summer of 1944, when the tents have only just appeared in the heathlands of Lüneburg, a logistical disaster occurs. Overcrowded trains dump their load at Celle station, ten miles away, and armies of emaciated prisoners arrive at the gates of the camp each day. Men, women, children; the influx is immense. The SS quickly orders the prisoners to build extra barracks where roll call is heard in the Star Camp for the new loads of patients they are expecting from Birkenau; some 3,000 women. The sisters' transportation was supposed to be housed in these barracks too, but they were not finished on time.

In the meantime, the tents are filled to the rafters with dying people – sometimes almost 1,000 per tent, and by the time Janny, Lien, Anne and Margot arrive, early November 1944, the number of prisoners at Bergen-Belsen has doubled. But the avalanche is yet to come.

The Red Army marches on and more and more Nazi concentration camps will be evacuated in the following months. The Brilleslijper and Frank sisters are in the vanguard of the mass evacuation; they were lucky to be in cattle carriages. After New Year, the Germans chase hundreds of thousands of men, women and children, barely able to stand on their feet, ahead of the advancing fronts in endless death marches. They die like flies along the way – exhausted, cold or shot on the spot by guards. Very few lucky ones make it to Bergen-Belsen.

In the winter of 1944 to 1945, Bergen-Belsen descends in a free fall of illness and chaos. There is no stopping it. Within a few months, tens of thousands of prisoners die and their bodies are stacked up around the camp like deadwood at the back of a garden.

# 6
# The Storm

The tents are packed. All the sleeping shelves, three layers up, are taken and the four of them spend their first days huddled together on some straw on the floor. Janny and Lien take the Frank sisters, ten years younger, under their wing; they make sure the girls wash themselves at the little tap outside every day, even when an icy wind is howling and they are very reluctant to remove their blankets and take off their thin dresses in the cold. Stay clean, eat, stay together.

When the girls found them on the sandhill, their joy was indescribable. They had come such a long way – from the Netherlands to Poland to Germany – and they had lost so many people since Westerbork already. They asked each other in which carriage they had travelled and who they had seen on the transportation. And where was their mother, Edith?

'Selected,' was all Anne said.

They are exhausted and sleep a lot, despite lice almost running off with their blankets. In this camp too, the creatures are everywhere; in clothes, on heads, in crotches. Sometimes Janny is completely mesmerized by the shaven skull of a fellow prisoner – it seems her skin is moving. Just when she thinks she has really lost it, she sees the living layer of lice crawling across the head of their hostess like a helmet.

In the daytime they are put to work in a dusty barracks, where they have to remove the soles of old leather shoes by hand. They are given a bit of watery soup and a piece of bread in return. It is hard work and their nails and fingertips soon turn into bloody stumps; people around them die of blood poisoning. Anne and Lien drop out. Margot and Janny last longer.

It is starting to rain again. Softly at first, an innocent pitter-patter on the tent, but the showers soon turn into wild waterfalls, pouring down on the canvas. The wind is howling across the grounds and tents are flapping like lashes of a whip. The floor becomes wet, the straw gets soaked and their blankets are dripping with water. On the night of 7 November, the storm really hits the camp.

Towards the evening, when everyone must find a place to sleep again, Anne and Margot are outside in the rain, bickering. The tents are full of sick and confused women. Getting in and out is almost impossible; it is as if all the visitors of a stadium are using the same entrance. Once inside, it is not easy to get out before the next morning: it is dark inside the tent and hundreds of women are packed together. Going for a pee is no option, but the latrines – open pits full of diarrhoea – are too filthy to visit in the dark anyway. Not unlike stadium visitors, they apply a range of tactics. Some are always in front because they want the best places; others just let themselves be carried by fate. Janny and Lien have always used the same strategy: they watch people pushing and fighting from a distance and when the majority has settled, they enter the tent last and quietly find a place. But tonight the Frank sisters will not wait for them. The weather is terrible; they want to get into the tent as fast as they can.

Janny and Lien stay outside in the cold, watching one stooped figure after another vanish behind tent cloths; the queues seem endless. When the tail end has gone, they slip inside. The tent is fuller than ever – masses of people are still arriving each day – and they must climb to the peak to find a place.

It is dark and the usual coughing, groaning and arguing of the women is drowned out by the storm and the rain. The entire camp seems to shake to its foundations. Gusts of wind circle around the tent, pulling and pushing the side walls, hailstones pounding on the roof. Water is soaking through the cloth, on their faces, on the floor. At places the canvas is already sagging – they can almost touch it with their fingers. Janny and Lien huddle close together. When the lightning starts, everyone falls silent. Flashes shoot through the tent and light up their faces, distorted with fear. The thunder takes a rolling run-up and explodes above their heads with a loud bang – they are expecting the earth to split and their tent to vanish into the depths below. The women lie in their beds, petrified. Then a cry, an infernal noise, the sound of cloth ripping and wood cleaving, beds falling down, a blow to their head, and it feels like sinking under water. They cannot breathe, everything is black, voices sound far and muffled. The poles have given way, the canvas is torn and the entire tent, with a few hundred women, has collapsed.

Pitch-black, flailing arms, a kick against a jaw, up, upwards, out of the canvas, oxygen. Rain batters her skull, a deep breath of air – and Janny is out. Where is Lien? Here, I am here. Away, quick, crawl over the heads and bodies, there is screaming and moaning under the tent cloth, they cannot see a thing.

They manage to reach the open field; everything is trembling, their teeth are chattering. Wounded women everywhere, more tents have collapsed; a void in the landscape where the black silhouettes used to be. Lifeless bodies in the mud. The canvas on the ground moves like a Chinese dragon as hundreds of women try to make their way out on all fours. Janny and Lien were lucky; their beds were at the top, they were not buried by others and could crawl out of the tent through a tear in the cloth.

Finally, the SS come running. Their shouting evaporates in the storm; all they can see are wide-open mouths. Those who have managed to save themselves are chased into the kitchen tent. They stand there for hours, pressed together, shivering, until the first watery sunbeams reveal the damage.

The grounds are covered with debris, wood, clothes, people. Wounded women wander around, groaning and disoriented; they had not seen the shelter in the kitchen tent at night. The entire *Zeltlager* is wiped off the map. There is no extra water or food, no medical assistance. From the kitchen tent they are transferred to the shoe barracks, where they find Anne and Margot. The girls are shivering with cold but unharmed. They embrace, stare at the mess around them: tables full of dismantled shoes, piles of rags, a thick layer of dirt covering the ground.

They have stopped believing that their move to Bergen-Belsen is their salvation.

**The survivors** of the storm night are put in a small women's camp. Guards build a broad hedge of barbed wire and straw bales, so they are cut off from the Star Camp next to them. Coming too close to the fence and speaking to someone on the other side is punishable, let alone throwing goods or food. Severe punishment awaits those who are caught; from sitting in the frosty cold for a day, holding a stone above your head, to being shot. Still, people reach out to the Star Camp prisoners, who are better off than they are. A warm jumper, a can of food, to some, is worth risking their lives for.

There are very few barracks in the new women's camp. Some women are accommodated in other parts of the camp, but new transports keep arriving and there simply is not enough space for everyone. In the evenings they just have to wait and see if they can find a place to sleep, people who cannot find a bed in time are shot. There is such chaos that Janny and Lien cannot find the Frank sisters for days.

It gets worse every day. In Birkenau, the weakest

were picked out as they deteriorated and the strongest, including the sisters, remained. Here, they must witness the deterioration, each small step in the process, until some woman breathes her last while she lies right next to them. The small crematorium roars, spitting black plumes of smoke, but it is not enough. Each night hundreds of lives extinguish all across the immense camp and each morning the bodies are piled up outside the barracks. Large groups of new prisoners report at the gate every day, but despite all the new arrivals, the camp population does not grow fast.

Rations become smaller, clean water is scarce and the pits filled with shit, shared by tens of thousands of prisoners each day, are a focus of infection; typhoid fever, tuberculosis, dysentery. The person you talked to in the evening can be outside the barracks on the pile the next day. There is no getting used to it.

One thing quickly becomes clear: you do not stand a chance on your own. Janny and Lien look for familiar faces to form a group with, and they find Anne and Margot and a few other women. From that moment on, they make sure they stay close together.

There are three pairs of Dutch sisters in the barracks: Janny and Lien Brilleslijper, Anne and Margot Frank, and Annelore and Ellen Daniel. Two more women, who were both on a more recent transportation, will join them: Sonja Lopes Cardozo and Mrs Auguste van Pels. Sonja is only nineteen years old and has been on the same journey as the Brilleslijper and Frank sisters: she was caught in hiding, was sent to Westerbork and then to Auschwitz, where she left her parents and her older brother, Matthieu, behind. She has no idea if they are still alive. Her parents are Greetje van Amstel and Lodewijk Lopes Cardozo, who lived at Kerkstraat in Amsterdam, acquaintances of Janny and Lien before the war. Sonja is a cheerful and intelligent girl, of whom they all grow very fond. She never complains and always tries to lift their spirits; she carves puppets out of bread to give to others – it never fails to make them smile.

Auguste van Pels was hiding in the annexe with the Frank girls and, already in her forties, is the oldest of the lot. Some think she is Anne and Margot's mother, because they are so close. Also in their barracks is Rachel van Amerongen-Frankfoorder, a Jewish woman with a socialist background, who worked for the resistance. She was in Westerbork camp with the Brilleslijper and Frank families, then ended up in Auschwitz too.

The women keep an eye on each other, cheer each other up, find food to share. There is always someone on the lookout for something to eat; when you are not at the front of the queue, your chance for that day is gone.

Anne and Margot share the bed below Janny and Lien, and together they try to fill the empty hours by telling each other stories. Children's stories, fairy tales, jokes, memories of Amsterdam and, of course, elaborate discourses on meals. Some women in the barracks hate it when others talk about food; it makes them nauseous and they storm out, swearing. But not the four sisters. They man a phantom kitchen like master chefs, put menus together and describe in great detail which dishes they shall eat when they get home.

One day they dream away about the stately Café Américain in Amsterdam; the four of them ordering generously from the menu in the restaurant. While the others picture themselves entering the gorgeous café with its vaulted ceilings and, eyes closed, swallow their saliva, Anne suddenly bursts into tears. She knows the chance they will ever return to Amsterdam is getting smaller every day and even the most beautiful castles in the air cannot help them to escape this reality any more.

**Towards the** end of 1944, their barrack fills up with women and girls deported from Hungary, Czechoslovakia and Russia; they are Jews, Gypsies and political prisoners. The language barrier makes it hard to communicate with them. One morning when Janny is at roll call, a Hungarian girl addresses her in broken German. She is visibly panicking, but Janny cannot make out what she wants. A little while later the girl returns with a friend and a suitcase full of things. Janny understands that their barracks is about to be deloused; the girls will have to give up everything they brought with them. Would Janny please look after their belongings? Without thinking, she takes the suitcase and hides it with Lien in the highest bed. The Hungarian girls, much relieved, return to collect their suitcase that evening and they want to pay Janny for her favour. The trade in the camp is lively; the mediums of exchange are a piece of bread or an onion, a warm jumper or underpants made from a piece of blanket. But Janny refuses; she has done nothing special and is glad she was able to help.

The hidden suitcase marks the start of an alliance with a group of Hungarian political prisoners, who will help her and Lien whenever they can. A few of the women work in the SS kitchen and slip her something extra now and again. An onion, a potato, some sauerkraut for Lien, who is suffering from diarrhoea, and even a mug of milk once. The stuff is sour and lumpy, but these are the lifelines that save them from the piles of the dead. Perhaps even more important than food is the new information the Hungarian women have. With hand gestures and in broken German, Janny sounds them out and at night she reports to her Dutch girl-friends in the barracks. The Allied forces are coming, Hitler is almost forced to his knees and if they hang on for a little, really, just a little longer, they will get out of here alive. Whether it is truth or fiction, no one knows, but they have nothing else to live on.

On 1 December 1944, Josef Kramer becomes the new camp commander of Bergen-Belsen. The sisters remember him from Birkenau. With his hulking body, his face like a broad-headed frog and his pursed lips, he was the brute beside Mengele, the delicate Angel of Death. Mengele selected with velvet gloves, while Kramer was in charge of the trip to the gas chambers. This former accountant from Munich, uninspired by keeping the books, lit up as soon as he joined the SS and, over the past ten years, had made a glorious career in the concentration camps. Starting out as a guard, he climbed the ladder, all the way up to camp commander. When Kramer arrives in Bergen-Belsen, not a single prisoner on the site could have lifted a finger against the Nazis, but he introduces a reign of terror nonetheless. From torture and setting dogs on people to executing entire groups on the edge of mass graves, Josef Kramer will go down in history as the Beast of Bergen-Belsen.

From January 1945, more than 2,000 people die in the camp per week. Each morning about 300 new bodies are piled up outside the barracks and it is impossible to burn them. Pits appear outside the camp, as large as public swimming pools, in which the victims of the dying Nazi regime will disappear; their graves anonymous but their remains forever bound to the Lüneburg Heath.

# 7

# The Party

Janny sees her sister and the Frank sisters deteriorate; their close-cut heads and protruding cheekbones look like skulls. The Hungarians say the Allies make rapid progress; they must keep themselves alive until the troops call at the gates. Janny comes up with a plan to celebrate Christmas, New Year's Eve and Hanukkah all at once on the last evening of December. Everyone is enthusiastic; the preparations alone lift their spirits. From that moment on, they save a crumb of bread each day and her friends in the SS kitchen give Janny two handfuls of potato peels. Anne fixes a clove of garlic, the Daniel sisters miraculously 'find' a turnip and a carrot, and Lien sings songs for the guards, earning some slices of bread and a spoon of sauerkraut. On the morning of the big day they all keep something of the brown morning sludge in their tin cups, to have something to drink as well.

In the evening they gather with their Dutch group on the upper beds below the roof of the stone barracks, the food displayed between them. They are all there: Janny, Lien, the Frank sisters, the Daniel sisters, Auguste, Sonja. They talk excitedly, eat and tell mouth-watering stories about the things they will do when they get home. Anne is dreaming away at the prospect already; the first thing she wants to do is eat at the posh restaurant on the corner of Leidsestraat and Prinsengracht: Dikker & Thijs. More women from their barracks gather around them, curious to see what noise is disrupting the usual downcast mood. The cold, the pain in their bones and the absence of their loved ones are briefly forgotten as they celebrate their festive dinner, sitting cross-legged on the wooden beds. Then someone begins to sing an old children's song:

The little cart drove on the old sandy road
Clear was the moon, wide was the road
The little horse walked with delight
It found its way, alone, through the sand
As the driver was sleeping so tight
I wish you safe home, my friend, my friend
I wish you safe home, my friend.

They all sing along, slowly swaying to the music on their beds. On to 'Constant Had a Rocking Horse', followed by 'Clink, Clank Clock' and 'The Little Sun is Leaving Us'. They clap along like a nursery class at singing lessons, pronounce the Dutch words as if they have never heard anything more beautiful before. Some women in the barracks are annoyed by all the merriment and hiss at them to be quiet – in French, in Russian, in words they do not know but do understand the meaning of. It does not matter; the energy that had left their bodies ages ago flows through their limbs and makes them light-headed.

Then suddenly the Czech women react more fiercely than the rest. They lean forwards from their beds, their fingers pressed against their lips.

'Shh! Shh!'

Janny and the others are startled and stop singing. They are friends with this group and do not understand what is wrong. Four Czech women begin to sing and the rest of the barracks falls quiet too. It is beautiful. They sing in four-part harmony, the melody perfect, the Dutch broken:

*Constant had een hobbelpaard*
*Zonder kop of zonder staart*
*Zo reed hij de kamer rond*

*Zomaar in zijn blote. . .*
*Constant had een hobbelpaard*

Constant had a horse to rock
It had no head nor tail
He was riding through the room
Just in his naked. . .
Constant had a horse to rock

And so they sing on. The tension in the room is broken and the Dutch group below the roof bursts out crying, relieved they no longer have to bear up.

**It is** early 1945, Death is wielding his scythe and all Janny can do is put out fires with thimbles. She and Lien try to save anyone who can be saved. Almost everyone in their small women's camp has become too sick, too weak to work. Anne, Margot, Sonja, Auguste – they stay in the barracks, hotbeds of bacteria. Lien feels ill too. At night, ice water leaks through the roofs on their beds, and in the morning they wrap the dead in their own wet blankets and throw them on the pile outside.

Janny has volunteered to work as a nurse again and, without asking, raised Lien's arm too when the SS were looking for more candidates: they are now nurse and nursing assistant. They get to wear a white band around their arm, have access to the camp pharmacy and can move around the site more freely. Janny walks around like a busy working ant, gives orders, delegates. Her body is shrinking and her head feels heavier each day, but she holds on to the promise she made to her mother and her children: she and Lien will make it out of here. They need water for the sick to drink and also to wash bodies and clothes with. The pump is no safe place – too much chaos, too many people – and on the way back to the barracks, others may hit the water out of their hands. Janny puts together an escort of women to accompany her, so she can safely get water. They walk up and down with mugs and cups and pans, keep people clean, try to rinse the dirtiest clothes and dry them outside in the freezing cold. There is a typhus epidemic, but they have nothing to fight the disease. To give her patients at least some sense of humanity, Janny steals handfuls of smelly stuff from the pharmacy to get rid of lice and fleas.

One morning Lien asks her sister to come along to a small block in their own part of the camp, which has just been filled with new arrivals. To Janny's surprise, the women squeezed together are all Dutch. There are some old people and a couple of very young children too. She knows a few of them, such as Marianne 'Sis' Asscher and her three little ones. The children are in a bad way and some of the women can no longer stand. There is no moaning, no crying, just staring with large eyes that barely register a thing.

It turns out this is not a new transportation; the women say they were in a different part of the camp before, with their husbands. All of them are relatives of diamond merchants who have been in Bergen-Belsen for some time but had put their fates on hold by paying. When they had neither diamonds nor gold left to bribe the camp commander and his officers, their men had been put on transportation. So far they had survived because they were together, but when the families were torn apart, the whole set collapsed like a house of cards. Their will to live has gone; it has left with their men on the trains.

The sisters immediately get to work. Women are sent away to fetch water, the old people are helped onto a bed, the children are washed outside in the freezing cold, then rubbed dry firmly with rags. They try to find them some food. Sis Asscher is apathetic; her two sons, little Bram and Jopie, hang around her; and her daughter Truusje, born in Westerbork towards the end of 1943, lies in a filthy pram like a doll, her limbs spread wide. Janny catches Lien's eye and knows they think the same. Liselotte. Kathinka. They shake off the thought and carry on. There is no time to lose.

The new women and children are in such a bad way that Janny and Lien are appointed as full-time carers of the small barracks and move in with them. They ask Anne and Margot to come along, but Margot has diarrhoea and is not allowed to leave the block owing to risk of typhoid fever infection. Anne tries to nurse her older sister as well as she can, and Janny and Lien keep an eye on the girls. The Brilleslijper sisters are now responsible for the sick and the dead in their new, small 'diamond barracks', and they must get water and food for everyone and keep the barracks clean; for hours on end they pick lice from blankets and clothes, hoping to provide some relief.

The group of diamond women also includes a Mrs Henriëtte van Amerongen. Janny and Lien tell her there is a Van Amerongen in their previous barracks too: Rachel. This turns out to be her daughter-in-law. They quickly get Rachel and although the reunion clearly does Mrs Van Amerongen good, it is not enough; she is too sick to recover and passes away shortly after. Janny and Lien close her eyes and carry her to the pile. They take her fur coat and wedding ring – before some stranger does – and give them to Rachel later that day.

Each day at roll call, Janny has to tell the SS guards how many people really cannot walk or stand any more. At one such occasion, a female guard leans over Truusje

Asscher's pram and jumps right back again. The little girl's belly is swollen like a balloon, her arms and legs sticking out like twigs. The startled guard writes out a coupon for a daily gallon of milk porridge. Truusje stops breathing that same afternoon, but Janny uses the coupon to feed many other children.

In another barracks, the Germans have set apart Dutch children who might not be fully Jewish. Janny and Lien try to cheer up the Frank sisters and ask Anne and Margot to help them look after these children. Read to them, play with them, cut their nails, their hair – anything to drag the little ones through the day. Anne and Margot come along a few times, sing Dutch children's songs and tell some fairy tales, but they soon feel too sick to leave their barracks. Margot can no longer stand on her feet and Anne is not leaving her sister's side.

In a final attempt to breathe some life into the girls, Janny and Lien take Jopie and Bram, Sis Asscher's remaining children, to Anne and Margot, but the sisters will not play with them. They have withdrawn into a shadow world and are too weak to respond to the toddlers.

Lien and Janny collect food to bring to the girls when they can, but one day they find their beds empty; Anne and Margot have been transferred to the sickbay. This is bad news; they will not receive any treatment there, but they will be exposed to more bacteria. Everyone in the sickbay is terminally ill with dysentery or typhoid fever.

Lien and Janny go to see the girls, try to convince them to come with them, but to no avail. The sickbay is heated, so they are warm and they are allowed to share the same bed. Anne says she wants to stay with Margot. Margot does not speak any more.

# 8
# City of Dead

Janny stands at the edge of an enormous pit looking up at the stars above the Lüneburg Heath. A waxing moon is shining on the corpses below. She stands there, her shoulders hanging down, clasping the blanket between her fingers – it has just released the bare body of a woman, she must take it back – her short-cropped head lifted up towards the heavens. The smell of decay is pungent; it enters her nose even when she presses her lips and holds her breath. Flocks of birds circle above the bodies then dive into the pit. Janny stands still, stares at the sky and looks for a sign of the stars.

Death marches still bring in masses of people, more than the camp can contain. In a barracks designed for eighty soldiers, over 1,400 women are crammed. Newcomers must fight the other prisoners for a place on the dirty ground. Many simply give up, allow their bodies the rest they so crave and fall to their knees on the spot.

The body lice were always a problem, but owing to a lack of control and an abundance of new prisoners, the floodgates really open and a serious plague takes over the camp. Hundreds of thousands of tiny creatures go round the barracks to suck up human blood and spin a web of typhoid fever around each shack. There is no escaping the disease. It starts with a headache, nausea, pain in all muscles and glowing fever. After a week, a bright red rash covers the body and most patients will sink into a delirium. They end up in a mist between life and death, and in the winter of 1945, there is hardly anyone who makes it to the bright side of this haze.

Lien too is sick and in bed. Margot has been ill for a while and is rapidly deteriorating. Janny paces between the barracks, tries to do what she can, and in between shifts checks in with the Frank sisters. Margot has a high fever and can only whisper. Anne does not leave her side, but she is feverish too, with glowing cheeks and large eyes. She tries to take care of Margot, but Janny can tell she has one foot in another world already. There is so little she can do to help them.

Janny feels that she herself is sick too – the glowing cheeks, the blurry sight. It is a race against the clock. She must go on, rushes from one barrack to the next, tries to keep Lien clean, cuts off frozen fingers and toes, fetches water for the endless row of sick, pre-chews stale bread, but lives slip away like sand between her fingers. A woman in their barracks dies with her living baby in her arms. It is like working in an assembly line; she shuts eyes that no longer see, removes whatever other prisoners can use and carries bodies to the pits. A Sisyphean quest. Corpses are scattered across the camp like brushwood, limbs reaching for the sky. There is silence in the barracks and on the grounds, although the camp population has risen to the size of a small town.

Suddenly, Anne appears before Janny. She wears nothing but a blanket wrapped around her bony shoulders. It is freezing, the snow has only just begun to melt between the trees. Janny draws her closer.

'What are you doing here? Where are your clothes?'

'Margot is so very sick.' The girl can barely speak. 'And the lice . . .' She twitches her head and tickles with her fingers, thin as a spider's legs.

'Everyone is sick, Anne. Come here,' says Janny as she begins to gather clothes and presses them into Anne's hands.

There is almost no food any more; sometimes the camp staff refuse to give them anything for days, but she hands Anne some of the last bread she had saved for Lien.

'Take this and stay in your barracks. I'll come see you as soon as I can. Now go.'

Shortly thereafter, Margot falls from her bed and hits her head on the concrete floor; she does not wake up any more. Anne already assumed her father and mother were dead, and with her sister gone, she has no more reasons to stay. She lets go too.

When Janny and Lien check in on the girls a few days later, they find their bed empty. They search between the piles of corpses outside and find their lifeless bodies. With the help of two other women, they wrap the sisters in blankets and carry them to one of the pits, where they lower them into the depth one by one.

**Everything is** blurred, as if the retina has been stripped from her eyes. Colours have disappeared and all she sees are silhouettes wandering across the field in shades of grey. Janny's head is constantly pounding and feels too heavy for her neck. Days and nights melt into one, weeks and lives pass.

Lien is slightly less ill, but Janny can barely stand on her feet. The camp is a runaway fair of insane, sick and dying people. From time to time the air raid siren sounds – it wails from the trees across the field but nothing happens, so prisoners have stopped looking up to see if the Allies have arrived to save them. Dead bodies everywhere, no one has the energy to clear them away. They are lying in gutters, on paths, in the barracks; hundreds of them, or thousands – there is no one who keeps score.

Most people lie apathetic on their beds, hang against walls, or simply sit outside on the cold ground. There is hardly any food left – sometimes some turnip in water: hot, cold, often rotten. The Hungarian women tell Janny the craziest stories. That the Brits are already here but too afraid to enter the camp because of all the diseases. That the Germans have put explosives under the camp to blow it up with all of them in it. Nothing happens.

It is less cold outside, or perhaps this is the fever warming up her bones. Janny steals aspirins from the pharmacy and eats them all; she must stay on her feet to get water for Lien and herself. Lien is her only chance to survive – without her sister she does not want to go back home.

Another air raid siren, aircraft, shooting from all sides, they do not know if it comes from the Germans or the Allies. Guards flee and suddenly it is completely silent in the camp. A couple of prisoners take a look in the SS barracks and soon reappear in the doorway; they are gone! People begin to scream, run, portraits of Hitler are ripped from walls. Janny can barely move any more, she is watching it all from a distance. Two towering mountains of turnip are discovered, starving prisoners pounce on them and all the vegetables are gone within minutes. The notion that they really are about to be liberated unleashes a beastly fury in some. Fires are lit everywhere, red flames shooting up in a grey landscape. Prisoners put SS jackets on to get warm and are swiftly attacked by others.

Suddenly more shooting, someone calls: the Krauts are back. The whistle for roll call, followed by the usual shouting of guards, urging them to hurry. In a dream-like state, Janny drags herself to the roll call place. Her head is spinning and light – it feels as if she is floating.

Camp commander Josef Kramer is there. He and his men are suddenly wearing white bands around their upper arms and are acting kind in a very strange way. Prisoners approach from all sides, distrustful, and try to hear what he has to say. Kramer steps on a platform, beckons them, grimacing; *Kommen sie her, kommen sie, meine Damen.* Come here, come, my ladies. There is whooping, someone calls: This is no roll call, the Brits are at the gate, stop listening to him!

Janny just stands there, people running past her at all sides. Kramer is beaten and kicked by people in uniform, his white cuffs are ripped off and he is thrown into a jeep. As Janny sees it happening, she feels a warm glow spread across her body from her belly. Moon men in rubber suits are moving towards her. Then she passes out.

It is 15 April 1945. The British liberate Bergen-Belsen. Across the camp site they discover 60,000 emaciated prisoners and 13,000 unburied corpses in various stages of decay. Emergency hospitals are set up at lightning speed to start a rescue operation for the survivors; in the following weeks another quarter of them will die.

# 9

# The Final Journey

Janny leans her head against the window and looks outside, takes in everything she sees and tries to breathe. They enter Amsterdam from the south. Spring adorns the streets with colours she had almost forgotten existed. Violet, fuchsia, apple green and an infinitely blue sky. She stares up, sees the faces of Father, Mother and Japie appearing in the heavens, the red bricks, between leaves on the trees. There is no escaping it. This is the season they love. The city waking up from hibernation. Windows are opened, cotton sheets flutter in the breeze, Waterlooplein is buzzing. Work was always easier for Joseph and Fietje when the sun reappeared. Would they be elsewhere in this city, staring at the same sky? A stabbing pain at her temple, her sight gets blurry. She presses her eyes shut and forces the image of her parents and Japie away. Do not think about it. Not now.

*Noorder Amstellaan, Apollolaan.*

The stately houses on Apollolaan, the broad avenue around the corner from the posh Jansen sisters – would they be alive still? A succession of robust wooden front doors on both sides of the green flashes past the car window. Bob and Eberhard in their Sunday best, visiting the Jansen sisters for the lease, The High Nest, their life in the forests, the resistance work in Amsterdam, the failed assignment at Roelof Hartplein, the betrayal. She remembers standing at the three-forked road: Van Baerlestraat, J.M. Coenenstraat, Roelof Hartstraat. Her brisk pace, Robbie clinging to her hand. It was a beautiful day then, too. It seems like one hundred years back in time, a flash of a film she once saw. Not her, not her own life, less than a year ago.

Janny glances at her hands, resting on her skinny legs. Blue veins pushing against translucent skin, the space between her thighs could fit a football. The car zooms on. Her stomach tightens, she feels sick but she cannot swallow.

*The crossroads of the axes Apollolaan-Stadionweg, the steel and glass of the Social Security Bank, the building is still there.*

The Tower of Labour. German searchlights on the rooftop. Janny looks at her sister, catches her eyes and knows they are thinking the same. Lien sits bolt upright beside her, wearing a warm rabbit fur coat, swapped for her daily ration of cigarettes in the refugee camp in Soltau, near Bergen-Belsen. Her hands lie motionless in her lap. Neither of them is able to speak.

*Turn right, onto Beethovenstraat, cross the water, second to the left.*

They sway from one side to the other, along with the car. Their shoulders touch briefly and they both back away. The city feels different – emptier, quieter – but when they drive over bridges it seems nothing has changed. The water has kept on flowing as if the world were not standing still. They have heard about a hungry winter claiming thousands of people's lives. Severe cold, no heating, the west of the country cut off from the rest. But the water in Amsterdam still flows.

*Jacob Obrechtstraat. Narrow houses with arched windows make way for wide blocks with rectangular frames.*

Janny shifts on the back seat, moves her feet, her fingers rubbing hard over her palms. She tries to swallow again but her mouth is dry as dust. She can see the little square in the distance, she can make out the Concertgebouw, almost. 'To the right,' she hears her sister tell the driver. He turns the wheel. 'Number 26.' She points.

*Johannes Verhulststraat 26. Haakon and Mieke.*

The car stops. Narrow houses, their entrances under an arch, balconies supported by heavy ornaments. Janny cannot move, stares up at the stairs leading to the front door, black spots dancing in front of her eyes. The car door slams shut, Lien runs up the steps, rushes down again with a note in her hand, turns a quarter, sprints across the pavement and stops a few doors further. Janny cannot take it any more. After what seems like an eternity, Lien reappears with a second letter in her hand, runs back to the car and falls down next to her. She shoves the paper into Janny's face. Letters move across the page. Janny pushes it away.

'Can't.'

'Let me.'

The man behind the wheel reaches into the back and takes the letter.

'There was a note for us on the door,' says Lien. 'In case Lientje and Janny come here; three doors down, with Jopie Bennet, is a letter for you from Eberhard.'

Lien is gasping for air as she speaks. She has not fully recovered yet, neither of them has. They weighed less than four and a half stone when the British came. The driver reads out: 'Bob lives at Amstel 101 with the two children, I live in Oegstgeest with Mr Blomsma.'

Lien grabs Janny's hand and squeezes it. The corners of her mouth go up, trembling.

'There you go, Sis.'

Janny tries to smile back but she cannot. Her body has shut down.

*Amstel 101. Why? Whereabouts is that? She cannot think.*

The man does not know the way; he is not from here. They have met him in Enschede, just across the German border, where they were accommodated in an old school building. They were not expected there and not welcomed – yet another miserable step along the long journey home. So many people on the road. So many trucks going everywhere and nowhere. Only twenty miles per day. Stop, delouse, register. It was as if the Netherlands did not want them back.

One day the Dutch tricolour was pressed into their hands and when their vehicles crossed the border, they all burst into the national anthem. Everyone in the truck was weeping and finally, yes, finally, they were given a warm welcome. Children cheering on the side of the road, waving flags. But it was not for them; it was for the soldiers crossing the border in similar lorries with lollipops, chocolate and other sweet treats. The children slunk off with long faces and they just stood on the truck with the flag in their hands.

In Enschede they were deloused for the hundredth time and registered for the thousandth time. Then they were put in a room with Dutch Nazi women. When one of them started yelling at the sisters, Janny had had enough and she called the people in charge to order: 'Welcome to Enschede? You take us to a stinking, empty school, make us sleep on straw, again, and what, for goodness' sake, do you feed us? Turnip! Enough of this, dammit!'

But it did not make a difference; going in or out

of North and South Holland was forbidden owing to infectious diseases. It was late May already, but they were not allowed to go anywhere. Things sped up a few days later when they ran into an acquaintance of Jan Hemelrijk. They got permission to leave on Sunday and this man, a dentist looking for a lost relative, was kind enough to take the sisters and two other women home.

They first dropped off an older lady in Harderwijk, then a young woman in Hilversum. It was early afternoon when they arrived in Harderwijk. The street was silent, and the four women sat in the car, all tensed up, nervous about the welcome. But when the family saw the older lady, the street exploded with joy. Next stop, Hilversum. At the address of the second woman everything was dark; her house was empty. Husband, children – gone. The look on her face was unbearable, but the sisters wanted to move on. To Amsterdam. Janny with a white bear and a pillowcase full of raisins and marzipan on her lap, her jaw locked. Lien beside her in her Sunday best. She gives the dentist directions from Johannes Verhulststraat.

'First you go back to the Berlage bridge, then we can drive down the Amstel from there.'

The man accelerates. The house of Mieke and Haakon glides out of sight.

*Follow the same way back, cross the water, Apollo-laan, straight ahead, Noorder Amstellaan. Past a bench. She sat there with Bob once.*

Bob. She had tried hard not to think of him and the children, afraid she would tumble into a bottomless well. But in recent weeks, images of the children and Bob kept coming up. Liselotte's face under a woollen hat with under-chin ties. Robbie laughing out loud, skipping through leaves in the forest. Bob coming home from work, bicycle in his hand, or sitting opposite her in his chair, reading to her in the evening. Would he even recognize her? Janny's hand shoots up to flatten unruly wisps of hair. 'No! Don't cut it!' she had screamed when the Swiss nurse found another louse. As weak as she was, at least she had managed to prevent that. No shaven head any more.

How sick she had been. Unconscious for over fourteen days; she had opened every door between life and death. But each time there was something worth coming back for. Clean sheets on her broken skin. Bones warmed by a sunbeam shining through the window. The sweet voice of a nurse. Doctor Jim, the ginger Irishman, exuding a sense of 'all shall be well'. He asked her the same question each day, but she was too weak to answer.

'Where are you from?' Sparkling eyes, a cheeky smile.

'Amsterdam,' she finally managed.

No sound, he had to read her lips.

'I'll go find your sister,' he had said. 'If you promise to eat, I'll go find your sister.'

But Janny could not eat, she had so many sores in her mouth that she could not swallow. A cord was tightened around her chest, she could not breathe, she had to eat, or he would not look for Lientje. In her coma, snatches of conversations between the nurses about decomposing corpses, countless sick people, still hundreds of deaths per day, mass graves. She had to find Lientje in time, but she could not move, her mind was disconnected from her body.

*Daniël Willinkplein, where the three Amstel avenues connect in a Y, its striking centrepiece: the twelve-storey house.*

Janny looks up as they pass the building. The concrete skyscraper with its iron balconies. She and Lien used to giggle, wondering who on earth would want to live up there. *That Lientje must be dead.* She still hears the nurse whisper it to Doctor Jim; it was as if someone injected ice water straight into her veins. Her body was cold and numb, feet falling limply to the side, the palms of her hands pointing helplessly towards the ceiling, but inside she was overflowing. Tears streaming across her cheeks, they kept on coming, and she could do nothing to wipe them away.

*The skyscraper at their back, they cross Rijnstraat. Very few people on the street. Tram 8 stopped running in 1942. Onwards via Amstellaan, the bridge in the distance.*

Lien gestures to the nice man: straight ahead. Janny dreamed of her at night, walked barefoot across the camp site in her nightgown, searched piles of bodies, rummaged through limbs and always woke up to the face of the nurse above her bed, an apologetic look in her eyes; no news. She saw Lientje's silhouette everywhere; she saw her through the window at the end of the ward, she saw her walking between the beds, she heard her voice, so familiar it seemed to come out of her own body, and she raised her hand. A primal scream, an embrace as if they could dissolve into each other and never be separated again.

'I am taking you out of here, I won't leave you behind again ever, I'm taking you with me!' Lien whispered in her ear.

She arranged for two strong women to help carry

Janny from the sickbay, quickly, before anyone would see them, to the barracks where Lien was staying. But she was so weak, she could not eat. Lien pre-chewed the food, gently pressed it into her mouth. It did not work. Janny was lying on the lower bed and all she could do was cry. So sick. Lien fed her like a little bird, *go on, you have to eat, the plane to the Netherlands is leaving soon, come on,* but Janny almost choked and was rushed back to the sickbay.

The plane left without them.

*Berlage bridge. The threshold to Amsterdam.*

Dutch people along the way told them that Canadian troops had entered the city via Berlage bridge a few days after the liberation. What a sight that must have been. As they approach the bridge, Janny notices the tower on the central pillar, sticking out above the rest of the bridge. When you approach the bridge from the city centre, via Amsteldijk, you see the sculpture on top of the tower: Genius of Amsterdam. The patroness rises out of the water, the afternoon sun shimmering on her crown. Ever since they were young, Father pointed out such details to them; she must have paid better attention than she thought.

*Cross the bridge. Rhythmic thumping of tram tracks below the tyres, like rails.*

Janny holds her breath and squeezes her buttocks, tries not to feel the joints, not to hear them.

*Away from that bridge.*

After a week they did get permission to leave – with a tube of pills for her chest pains. Doctor Jim was worried, but her heart was still beating and that was all that mattered. They sat on wooden benches at the back of lorries with strangers, everyone feeling equally miserable and excited, worried what they might find at home, who was still alive, whether their houses were still there. They covered fifteen miles per day, no more, but it was enough, because they had survived where they came from and were not sure if they could bear what was awaiting them. Lientje put on a brave face, but she felt wretched; she secretly took Janny's heart pills and they almost killed her. Emergency hospital, stomach pumping, but they were on a freight train the next day. Everyone wanted the doors to stay open, but this was not an option.

'Left here,' Lien says to the dentist.

*Weesperzijde. Amstel 101 – why are they there? Nieuwe Achtergracht is at right angles to Amstel, would they perhaps, all of them, together . . . Bob, the children, Father, Mother and Japie, in a new home?*

Janny's body presses heavily into the seat as if she wants to stop the car, slow it down. The riverbank and the water blend, perhaps they will drive into the water. Dip down slowly. She sees Bob, Liselotte and Robbie in the water, knee-deep, she sees them from the hill, just behind the forest, where the IJsselmeer opens up like a picture book at your feet. Perhaps they will not recognize her. No hair. No fat on her bones. A few lives older. She turns around as if fleeing is an option. Genius with her sun crown is watching them from Berlage bridge, her hand raised as if to greet and cheer them on.

Janny bursts out crying. Loud sobbing with snot and tears. She cannot stop. The dentist glances anxiously over his shoulder; they continue on Weesperzijde and Janny is bawling in the back seat. Lien gets furious.

'Be happy, *mensch*, we're almost there! I still have to go all the way to Oegstgeest, goddammit.'

But Janny keeps crying and Lien keeps getting angrier. She turns around in her expensive coat and has a go at her sister.

'Are you out of your mind? Finally, we are going

to Bob and the children, and you just sit here weeping! What is this all about? You have really lost it, haven't you?'

She curses and rages as Janny so often did to her in the past months.

'You stupid fool! And now you stop it, do you hear me?'

Through her tears Janny begins to laugh. The dentist drives full speed ahead and feigns an interest in the stately Amstel Hotel as the sisters argue in the back.

The car has to slow down for the narrow part of the street, the water on their left, canal houses on their right. Just before Carré Theatre, they fall silent. Their parental home lies on Nieuwe Achtergracht on their right. As the car slowly passes the narrow street, they both look – as if there were something to see. As if Joseph were waiting there, his arms open wide, his chest puffed up. No one. The street is empty. They pass Carré, the car crawls up the bridge. Then Lien grabs Janny's arm.

'Look! Those are your curtains from The Hague!' She points at the house on the corner, across the bridge. 'I can see Bob!'

The dentist has not even stopped before Lien flies out of the car. Janny does not dare to look up, she just sits there, lowered head, hands in her lap; her body has stopped working. Bob comes running outside, pulls open the door, lifts her up like a feather and carries her inside. Robbie is dancing around them, shouting with joy.

'See? My mother is back! Come see, everyone, my mother is back!' He follows them inside, runs back to the street. 'You guys, everyone, look, I have my own mother! My mother is back again!'

The boy trips over his own feet through the front door, falls into his mother's arms and looks at his father.

'Dad, I told you; Mummy promised me that she would come back.'

Everyone is standing in the hall, crying, embracing each other. The dentist, Bob, Lien and Janny. Robbie is holding his mother's pillowcase and hands out raisins to passers-by.

'My mother is home! Come see, everyone, my mother is home!' he shouts across the river.

Janny has pulled herself together somewhat and is looking for Liselotte.

'Where's my girl?'

She finds the perplexed child hidden in one of the bedrooms, her eyes wide. Janny lifts her up from under the bed and gently presses her daughter to her chest. Robbie snuggles up too and so the three of them sit together on the floor in their new house at Amstel 101.

'Why don't you stay here tonight?' Bob suggests to Lien, but she shakes her head.

'I want to go to Oegstgeest, to Eberhard,' she says. She looks at the dentist questioningly.

'Come,' he says without any hesitation.

**Piet Verhoeve** and Haakon Stotijn tune their instruments and get ready. It is one of their last house concerts with the Blomsma family at Emmalaan in Oegstgeest and they are looking forward to it. Haakon will first play an oboe concert, then Piet will do a piano concert by Beethoven, then there will be a sonata for piano and oboe and they will finish with the wedding cantata by Bach. No stiff, religious piece full of sadness and atonement but light-hearted lyrics sung by a soprano comparing the blossoming of love with the announcement of spring. Mrs Kramer will do the arias.

The house fills with guests, the mood is cheerful. The concerts have become popular in and around Oegstgeest; in the hungry winter they have been a comfort to many. No one is aware that Piet, as these people know him, has been in hiding with the Blomsma family for almost a year now.

They play beautifully and have almost come to the end of the concert. Mrs Kramer begins to sing her last arias, accompanied by both Haakon and Piet. Her clear voice is twirling through the liberated streets on the cheerful notes of the cantata:

*Und dieses ist das Glücke,*
*Daß durch ein hohes Gunstgeschicke*
*Zwei Seelen einen Schmuck erlanget,*
*An dem viel Heil und Segen pranget.*

And this is good fortune,
When through a lofty gift of fate
Two souls obtain one jewel,
Resplendent with health and blessing.

A car drives through Emmalaan, slowly, hesitant. Curious faces appear behind windows; they have not seen a passenger car in months, there were only military vehicles these past years. The high whistles of Haakon's oboe reach far beyond the house on this silent Sunday afternoon. The car stops abruptly. The door swings open and someone runs up the path.

Piet lets his fingers dance on the keys; his upper body is swaying along to Bach's folk music. He looks contently at the living room full of people enjoying the music with their eyes closed. Then suddenly a face appears behind the window. Two large brown eyes, black spiky hair. Mrs Kramer sings on, but his hands freeze above the keys. He jumps off his stool, dives over the grand piano, through and over the audience, runs to the front door and takes Lientje in his arms. They kiss and they cry and they almost squeeze each other to death. Lien is so skinny; Eberhard can feel it in his own bones. They go back inside, together, hand in hand. Everyone has got up and is standing there, glistening eyes, handkerchiefs, excited about this miraculous reunion. Lien is welcomed with a standing ovation. Haakon, too, presses Lien to his chest; the concert is finished.

'No, no, carry on!' Lien takes her place on one of the seats and looks at her husband expectantly. 'It's been so long since I heard good music, please continue.'

They look at Eberhard questioningly – a short nod and they resume their positions. Mrs Kramer is so upset that she keeps sniffing between notes, but as Haakon introduces the final aria with his solo, her voice does not waver and Eberhard's fingers do not miss a key. A deafening applause fills the house and the street; they all rise and clap till their hands hurt. Only Lien stays on her chair, too exhausted to get up. Eberhard kneels before her and cups her small face in his hands.

'I'll pick up Kathinka at Cilia and Albert in Wassenaar tomorrow, and we'll all be together again.'

Outside, a car pulls off and drives out of the street. Lien would have loved to thank the dentist for all he did for them, but he quietly left. They never found out who he was.

# Epilogue

The traffic on the highway whizzes in the distance, withered leaves crunching below my feet – otherwise, all is quiet and deserted. The light between the trees drops onto a tomb resembling an old child's bed: rusty bars, a gravestone as a headboard. Weeds grow between the bars. I walk towards it, try to make out a name, part of a year – nothing. Next. A sagged stone with a young Christmas tree growing in front of it. I push it aside to see the letters. Faded. Onwards, along decapitated angels and crumbled pillars clearly defined against the sky. I walk cautiously through the thick layer of leaves, scooping them up with each large step I take. It seems like autumn, but this is the hottest day of the year: 37 degrees. Heatwave in the Netherlands.

I spent the first half hour searching the Roman

Catholic Cemetery. I came via the service road, the busy junction, and walked straight to this vast field; the graves were clearly visible from the street. The cemetery looked well maintained, with shiny tombstones and framed footpaths. An elderly lady with a watering can was tending her husband's grave; one morning each week, she entrusted me. There were few trees there – the sun pounded on my crown and sweat ran down my temples. Yet in the corner of my eyes I saw the woman pacing back and forth across the grounds, towards the tap.

I walked and read, row after row, tombstone after tombstone. Years that reminded me of grandparents and years that reminded me of friends. I skipped the years that reminded me of my children and after a while I just stood there in the middle of the cemetery, slowly turning around. Everything seemed too new to me, too just-dead. I remembered an article about the shortage of space in the Netherlands, the reusing of graves. My heart sank. The elderly lady had been keeping a close eye on me all the while and could no longer bear it.

'Who are you looking for, child?'

We stood opposite each other, separated by ten rows of tombstones. I explained and she thought, stared into the distance as the full watering can stretched her arm. I felt bad. Of course this woman did not know where I should be looking, but I had made her an accomplice.

'Have you been to the Old Cemetery yet?'

I sprang up.

'Isn't this it?'

She laughed and shook her head.

'This is the Catholic Cemetery, *that* is where the Protestants and the Jews are.'

She pointed at a place behind us, between the trees.

'The Old Cemetery of Naarden?'

She nodded and as I thanked her, I began to walk, excited by this new possibility. Although I was not expecting to find much in that small blind spot, wedged in by a residential area and the junction of the Jan Tabak Hotel.

'I'll walk with you.'

A little further on, the woman walked in the same direction, parallel to me, the watering can still in her hand. We met at the gate.

'Look . . .' She pointed to a path that disappeared between the trees. 'When you walk up that path you will see a fence on your left. That's the Old Cemetery of Naarden. I don't know if you can get in.'

I thanked her again and walked up the path, into the

thicket. The trees closed behind my back and suddenly I found myself surrounded by foliage. A large steel gate between sagged pillars. Closed. A smaller gate to its left. A push, the sound of scraping steel and I was inside.

It is huge, perhaps three times the size of the place where I just was, and it is beautiful. A central avenue lined with lime trees stretches out in front of me. A mishmash of overgrown monuments on both sides. Bluestone surrounded by wild grass, wooden crosses decorated with garlands of ivy. Broken marble covers stones with velvet moss growing out. Organized chaos, divided into blocks by yew hedges.

I wander between corroded fences and wild bushes, stop at a neo-Gothic church on a family grave, discover mini chapels and timeless ornaments. It feels as if I have discovered a secret spot at one of the busiest junctions in this area.

I cannot remember being this surprised by a place in these surroundings before. Yes, I suddenly realize, I can. Once before: the first time I drove up the forest path towards The High Nest, when the house and the garden revealed themselves to me.

The way the house stood on that hill, majestic and timeless, its back towards the residential area that had been built around it, its gaze towards the forest and the water, unperturbed by the everyday hustle and bustle – I was speechless. A safe haven. A place inviting you to climb and laugh, or sit quietly on a bench, stoking a fire. The spontaneous plan to go looking for the grave on this Friday afternoon was inspired by procrastination and weariness from the heat. It was no indispensable step in my research, not really, but suddenly it makes perfect sense.

**The grave** that I am looking for belongs to musical wunderkind Dirk Witte, a songwriter born in 1885 who wrote one of the best-known songs in the Netherlands, much loved in all sections of society and performed by voices from each generation: *'Mensch, durf te leven'*, 'Remember: life is for living'. Dirk composed the song during his time in military service and although he never fights, he is a stretcher-bearer; the war and the massive influx of refugees make a deep impression on him. The song has a spirit of resistance, encourages critical thinking and is rendered brilliantly; it becomes a huge hit in post-war Holland.

Shortly after its release, Dirk takes the plunge and quits his job to devote himself completely to his artistic life with his partner, Dutch cabaret artist Jean-Louis Pisuisse. He marries above himself with the beautiful, well-to-do Doralize 'Jet' Looman from Bussum, and in 1920 they commission an architect from Zaandam to build their dream house. On a fairy-tale site in the middle of a nature reserve in Naarden, where the heathland meets the forest, a robust country house emerges. Large windows offer unobstructed views in all directions, even as far as the Zuiderzee. Seen from the sky, the house flows into its surroundings; the large garden is enclosed by oak trees merging into the forest, and the roof is covered with the entwined stems of the same yellow reed growing along the nearby stream.

On a bright summer day in 1921, Dirk and Jet, their newly born daughter Doralize in a pram, proudly pose in front of their new home: The High Nest. Witte had no way of knowing that twenty years later, when another World War puts humanity to the test and many people in the Netherlands wonder what to do, his battle cry will so literally come to live in his house, as if the soul of the song has been built into the walls.

**And so,** I find myself looking for Dirk Witte's grave – the final, but first, piece of my puzzle to reconstruct the history of The High Nest.

Dirk's wife, Jet Looman, had the first verse of his signature song 'Remember; life is for living (memento vivere)' engraved on his tombstone:

Life's full of beauty and wonderful things
Don't hide in a cage, but instead spread your wings
Remember: life is for living!
Keep your head high, stick your nose in the air
What others are thinking, why would you care?
Keep your heart warm, with love it will sing
Wherever you go, you shall be king
This gift to yourself keeps on giving
Remember: life is for living!

It is said that the grave was neglected to such an extent that the text was no longer legible in 1971. In 2005, Dirk Witte was buried in the Loomans' family tomb, with the love of his life, Jet. I have been searching for this grave for over an hour, but without any luck.

I sit down on a bench shaded by the trees and think about the long road that took me here. After we moved into The High Nest in 2012, I studied the persecution of the Jews, the concentration camps and the political situation of that era. I charted each individual war year and followed the route of the Brilleslijper family. I tried to make my own 'dotted map' of Dutch Nazis around Naarden, learned more about the role of the Dutch elite and looked for patterns in the resistance. Each year on 4 and 5 May, Remembrance and Liberation Day, I placed a table in front of The High Nest with a guest book, in which I briefly described the war history and put a request for information about that period.

In Steven Spielberg's USC Shoah Foundation archives I found pictures of children hiding in The High Nest, playing in our garden. Via American universities I found anecdotes about the house and the underground activities. I contacted experts, biographers, relatives and friends, developed a close connection with the children of Janny and Lien, and was told stories no scriptwriter could ever imagine. I got access to Janny's personal documents at the Anne Frank archives, where I found letters of the sisters and their loved ones, and Janny's handwritten statement that Anne and Margot Frank had died with her in Bergen-Belsen.

I travelled through Israel and found more information on The High Nest than in the Netherlands. But, above all, the people I met there had an urgent message for me: tell this story, because it is different from the many stories the world knows. The Jews did not go to their deaths willingly – indeed, there were Jewish resistance fighters. Female ones at that.

The children who hid at The High Nest are now in their seventies. They came back to the house from various corners of the globe to see the places where they had played during war, and where my children now play in freedom. The desk where this book is written is right above the hatch where all the important papers were quickly hidden when Jew hunters surrounded the house.

I realize that the true restoration of The High Nest was not about repairing its walls but about reconstructing the exceptional events that took place between them.

**The sun** has almost gone now. The graves are sunk in dark shadows; warm air hangs between the trees. I get up and resume my search. A few miles from here the kestrel and a cold beer await me, but I am not leaving before I have found Dirk.

Between the leaves I suddenly notice a shiny grey surface sticking out above the ground, not dilapidated, not overgrown; it is as if someone was expecting me and just gave it a quick wipe. I draw closer and there he is, in the Loomans' family tomb: Dirk Witte, 1885–1932. The rest of the stone is empty – his famous battle cry is gone.

It does not matter. I would have liked to tell Dirk how Janny and Lien have brought the house he built to life. The memory of the war seems to fade, but their fearlessness is carved into the stones of The High Nest for ever:

What others are thinking, why would you care?
Remember: life is for living!

# After The High Nest

- Joseph Brilleslijper, born 27 February 1891, arrived in Auschwitz-Birkenau on 6 September 1944, almost certainly gassed immediately upon arrival.

- Fijtje 'Fietje' Brilleslijper-Gerritse, born 14 January 1891, arrived in Auschwitz-Birkenau on 6 September 1944, almost certainly gassed immediately upon arrival.

- Rebekka 'Lien' Rebling-Brilleslijper, born 13 December 1912, died 31 August 1988. Moved to East Berlin in 1952 and therefore lost her Dutch nationality. When she came to the Netherlands for the wedding of her niece Liselotte in 1964, she was closed in by the Aliens Police. Janny was furious and called every influential person in her circle of friends to free her traumatized sister and let her have a Dutch passport – with success. Lien performed around the world with a repertoire of Yiddish and resistance songs her entire life, often accompanied by Eberhard and her daughters, Kathinka and Jalda.

- Marianne 'Janny' Brandes-Brilleslijper, born 24 October 1916, died 15 August 2003. Janny, Bob and the children stayed in the house at Amstel 101. After the war, Janny, with Bob, fiercely kept resisting the ongoing public anti-Semitism in the Netherlands, devoting her life to the recognition of war victims. She was involved with the Auschwitz Committee, the Anne Frank Foundation and the Foundation '40–'45, among others. Each year during the commemoration of the February Strike, Janny had a large pan of lentil soup on the fire for people on their way back in the cold from around the corner of her house, where the dock worker monument still stands.

- Jacob 'Jaap' Brilleslijper, born 7 June 1921, arrived in Auschwitz on 6 September 1944, died there after 15 September 1944 but before 1 October 1944.

- Eberhard Rebling, born 4 December 1911, died on 2 August 2008. Eberhard was one of the first Germans to receive Dutch citizenship after the war. He became a musical editor at communist newspaper *De Waarheid* (The Truth). He moved to East Berlin in 1952, therefore losing his Dutch citizenship again, and became director of the conservatory there. Recognized as Righteous Among the Nations by Yad Vashem.

- Bob Brandes, born 20 February 1912, died 27 September 1998. Bob worked at the Municipal Giro Bank, among other places. Until his death, he was a great support to Janny in dealing with the lifelong effects of the war years and the loss of so many family members. Bob suffered from a severe form of epilepsy and needed a lot of medication. Janny often said: 'If only Gerrit [Kastein] were alive; he would help him after the war.'

- Kathinka Rebling, born 8 August 1941. Kathinka moved to the German Democratic Republic (GDR) with her parents as a child. She was given violin lessons from a very young age. She went to the conservatory in Moscow when she was eighteen and obtained her doctorate in Musicology, just like her father. Kathinka returned to Berlin to teach, giving concerts and master classes around the world.

- Jalda Rebling, born 13 February 1951 in Amsterdam, moved to the GDR with her parents and her sister, Kathinka, one year later. She went to the Berlin drama school, became an actress and singer, and specialized in European Jewish music. She is a chazzan and spiritual leader of the Ohel Hachidusch congregation in Berlin.

- Robert Brandes, born 10 October 1939. A visual artist, he lives in the Netherlands. A major theme of his aquarelle paintings and etchings is the city of Amsterdam and its canals, inspired by the view from his house at Amstel 101, where he has lived for most of his life.

- Liselotte Brandes, born 6 September 1941, lives in the Netherlands.

- Jetty Druijf, born 16 January 1919, was deported to Theresienstadt on 31 July 1944 and Auschwitz on 28 September 1944, where she died on 3 October 1944.

- Simon Isidoor van Kreveld, born 27 January 1921, was deported to Theresienstadt on 31 July 1944 and

Auschwitz on 28 September 1944, where he died on 3 October 1944.

- Pauline (Puck) van den Berg-Walvisch (sometimes spelt as Paulina or Walvis), born 26 May 1924, was deported to Auschwitz-Birkenau on 3 September 1944 and on 27 October 1944 to Libau Camp, which was liberated by the Russians on 8 May 1945. She returned to the Netherlands on 11 June 1945. Present situation unknown.

- Abraham 'Bram' Teixeira de Mattos, born 31 May 1888, arrived in Auschwitz-Birkenau on or around 6 September 1944, almost certainly gassed immediately upon arrival.

- Louise 'Loes' Teixeira de Mattos-Gompes, born 12 August 1890, arrived in Auschwitz-Birkenau on or around 6 September 1944, almost certainly gassed immediately upon arrival.

- Rita (Grietje) Jaeger, born in 1920, stayed in Westerbork as cleaner until the camp was liberated in April 1945. Died 30 November 2015.

- Chaim Wolf (Willi) Jaeger, born 17 March 1914, stayed in Westerbork as a baker until the camp was liberated in April 1945. Died in 2006.

- Jan Hemelrijk, born 28 May 1918, died 16 March 2005, was a professor of Statistics at the University of Amsterdam after the war. The characters of Herman and Lidia in *The Evenings* by Gerard Reve are based on Jan and Aleid Hemelrijk. Together with Bob van Amerongen, Jan founded the famous 'PP resistance group', named after the fantastical beasts Porgel and Porulan from the *'Blauwbilgorgel'* poem by Cees Buddingh. Loes Gompes and Sander Snoep made the documentary *Fatsoenlijk land* (*Decent Land*) about this group. At the death of Jan's father, Jaap Hemelrijk, in 1973, the forest path leading to the Buerweg – where Janny and the rest of the family were hiding – was renamed: het Hemelrijklaantje, Hemelrijk's Lane.

- Aleid Hemelrijk-Brandes, born 16 December 1914, died 28 November 1999.

- Leo Fuks, born 29 December 1908, died 12 July 1990. Leo taught Modern Hebrew and Yiddish at university after the war.

- Louise Christine 'Loes' Fuks-de Betue, born in 1905, died in 1962.

- Maarten 'Mik' van Gilse, born 2 June 1916, was executed by firing squad on 1 October 1943.

- Jan Hendrik 'Janrik' van Gilse, born 5 June 1912, was shot by SD officers as he attempted to flee them on 28 March 1944.

- Jan van Gilse, born 11 May 1881, died 8 September 1944.

- Gerrit van der Veen, born 26 November 1902, was executed by firing squad on 10 June 1944. After the war the SD headquarters and Euterpestraat in Amsterdam were named after him: the Gerrit van der Veen School (now Gerrit van der Veen College) and Gerrit van der Veenstraat.

- Dirk Uipko Stikker, born 5 February 1897, died 23 December 1979. He was a director of Heineken from 1935 to 1948. After the war, among others, he became the first chairman of the conservative-liberal political party VVD (People's Party for Freedom and Democracy).

- Frits Reuter, born 19 February 1912, died 8 November 1985. After the war he was a member of the Lower House for the Dutch Communist Party and a union leader.

- Rhijnvis Feith, a neurologist in The Hague, his date of birth and death are unknown.

- Gerrit Kastein, born 25 June 1910, died 21 February 1943. The room at Parliament Square (Binnenhof, The Hague) where Gerrit jumped out of the window was named after him on 20 June 2017: the Gerrit Kastein room.

- Karel Emanuel Poons, born 14 August 1912, died 12 March 1992. After the war he was a co-founder of the National Ballet and a director of the Scapino Dance Academy.

- Marion Pritchard-van Binsbergen, born 7 November 1920, died 11 December 2016. After the war she worked for the (predecessor of the) UN in the United States of America, where she continued to live, had a psychology practice and gave lectures on the Holocaust until her death. Recognized as Righteous Among the Nations by Yad Vashem.

- Fred Lodewijk Polak, born 21 May 1907, died 17 September 1985. After the war he became a director of the Centraal Planbureau (Bureau for Economic Policy Analysis), a member of the Dutch Senate, a university professor and the founder of educational broadcasting company Teleac.

- Grietje Kots, born 7 January 1905, died 13 May 1993. She worked as mask, puppet and marionette maker, painter and sculptor after the war.

- Anton Mussert, born 11 May 1894, was sentenced to death on 12 December 1945 and executed on 7 May 1946 on Waalsdorpervlakte.

- Eduard 'Eddy' Moesbergen, born 26 June 1902. He was prosecuted after the war and sentenced to death in November 1948. Later pardoned by Queen Juliana in 1949; punishment turned into life sentence. Pardoned again in 1959; punishment shortened to twenty-three years (the longest punishment of all members of the Henneicke Column). Released in

1961, he emigrated to New Zealand, to his wife and four children. Died 8 November 1980.

- Willi Lages, born 5 October 1901, died 2 April 1971. He was prosecuted after the war and sentenced to death, later granted a pardon, which was turned into a life sentence. His sentence was deferred for a maximum of three months in 1966 on 'humanitarian grounds' (he had bowel complaints). He departed to Germany, underwent surgery and from that moment on lived as a free man because he could not be extradited.

- Harm Krikke, born in 1896, was prosecuted after the war and sentenced to death, later granted a pardon, which was turned into a life sentence. Date of death unknown; a family announcement in the *Friese Koerier* newspaper on 15 July 1969 mentions the death of one Harm Krikke on 12 July 1969.

- Willem Punt. A detective at the Amsterdam Police during the war, he was subsequently charged after the war. Date of birth and death unknown.

- Annie Bochove, born 9 July 1913. Immediately after the war, in early 1946, the Bochove couple applied for emigration; they intended to move to the United States of America. Their papers did not arrive until 16 July 1949 and Annie died on the same day. She was posthumously recognized as Righteous Among the Nations by Yad Vashem.

- Bert Bochove, born 1 October 1910, emigrated to the United States of America after the war, where he died in California on 13 August 1991. Recognized as Righteous Among the Nations by Yad Vashem.

- Eva Besnyö, born 29 April 1910, died 12 December 2003. She made her name as a photographer after the war.

- Mieke Stotijn-Lindeman, later Riezouw-Lindeman, born 15 December 1914, died 23 April 2009. She was politically active after the war (Communist Party Holland and later PvdA, the Dutch Labour Party) and a founder of the Vondelpark-Concertgebouw area community centre in Amsterdam.

- Haakon Stotijn, born 11 February 1915, died 3 November 1964. He was a solo oboist in the Concertgebouw Orchestra after the war.

- Kurt Kahle, born 18 October 1897, died in a car crash in 1953. He was a film- and documentary maker after the war.

- Marianne Gerritse-Lootsteen (mother of Fijtje), born 28 May 1858, died 23 December 1916.

- Jacob Gerritse (father of Fijtje), born 19 August 1858, died 27 December 1936.

- Isaäc Gerritse (brother of Fijtje), born 5 May 1882, died in Auschwitz 27 August 1943; five of his six children died in concentration camps.

- Mozes Gerritse (brother of Fijtje), born 15 August 1895, died in Jawischowitz labour camp (coal mine), near Auschwitz, 1 January 1944. His wife and both of his children died in concentration camps.

- Debora Beesemer-Gerritse (sister of Fijtje), born 7 January 1898, died in Sobibor on 21 May 1943. Her husband and three of her four children died in concentration camps.

- Alexander Gerritse (brother of Fijtje), born 10 November 1900, died in Auschwitz in 1942 or 1943.

His wife and three children died in concentration camps.

- Trees Lemaire, born 15 January 1919, died 10 December 1998. After the war she ran her own art gallery in Amsterdam, was head of the documentary department of the socialist broadcasting association VARA and a member of the Lower House for the Dutch Labour Party, PvdA. Trees and Janny were best friends for as long as they lived.

- Carolina 'Lily' Biet-Gassan, born 20 July 1913, died 14 October 1975.

- Anita Leeser-Gassan, born 17 September 1935, was a lawyer and juvenile judge after the war, and the vice president of the district court, Amsterdam.

- Edith Frank-Hollander, born 16 January 1900, died 6 January 1945. When Anne and Margot are sent to Bergen-Belsen by the end of October 1944, they mistakenly believe that their mother was sent to the gas chambers. Shortly thereafter Edith dies of sickness and exhaustion in Auschwitz, after all.

- Otto Frank, born 12 May 1889, died 19 August 1980. On 27 January 1945, the Russians liberate Auschwitz. Otto returned to the Netherlands, where he searched for information on the fate of his daughters day and night. The Red Cross referred him to the Brilleslijper sisters. In July 1945, he visited both Lien and Janny, and they told him Anne and Margot died in Bergen-Belsen.

- Margot Frank, born 16 February 1926, died in February or March 1945 in Bergen-Belsen.

- Anne Frank, born 12 June 1929, died in February or March 1945 in Bergen-Belsen.

- Ida (Simons-)Rosenheimer, born 11 March 1911, died 27 June 1960. She was deported to Westerbork in September 1943, where she played in the camp orchestra as a pianist. She was deported to Theresienstadt in 1944, brought to Switzerland in February 1945 and returned to the Netherlands in the summer of 1945. After the war she made her name as a writer. Her novel *Een dwaze maagd*, A Foolish Virgin, published in 1959, became a bestseller.

- Alexander de Leeuw, born 15 May 1899, went into hiding from time to time during the occupation until he was arrested in 1941 and put on a transportation to Auschwitz in July 1942, where he was gassed on 4 August 1942.

- Kees Schalker, born 31 July 1890. He was arrested at an underground Communist Party meeting towards the end of 1943 and executed by a firing squad at Waalsdorpervlakte on 12 February 1944.

# Acknowledgments

This extraordinary story could only be told with the help of others and I am deeply indebted to many. Thank you to the residents of the neighbouring villages who delved into their memories, left old documents and pictures in my letterbox, came to the door, or sent me emails full of personal stories.

To the relatives of the war victims who had the courage to rake up the past and kept encouraging me despite their own pain and sadness.

To the authors and historians whose knowledge I could draw from and who inspired me, including the late Evelien Gans, to whom I owe so much and would have so wanted to give a copy of this book.

To the archivists of newspapers, libraries and concentration camps in archives both at home and abroad, who enthusiastically helped me in my search and provided more information on their own initiative.

To all the neighbours of The High Nest who lovingly accepted our family, supplied me with pictures, information and anecdotes, and kept an eye on things from time to time: Fransje Sydzes-Westerman, Frans Bianchi, Randi and Alois Stas, Oma Aartje and Opa Lambert Kruyning, Maria Wesselius, the Kos and Westland families, Marijke and Nico Buijs – and many others.

To the Dutch Foundation for Literature, the employees of the Anne Frank Foundation and the employees of Yad Vashem, among whom are: Loes Gompes, David Shneer, Co Rol, Sylvia Braat, Louise Paktor, Buck Goudriaan, Marise Rinkel Bochove and Paul Schiffers.

To Willy Lindwer and Ad van Liempt, master craftsmen, who encouraged me at critical moments.

To the entire team at Lebowski Publishers and Overamstel, and to capo Oscar van Gelderen, 'my jaunty publisher with an impish smile'.

To my editor and buddy Jasper Henderson, a man who, when you are about to chuck all your work out of the window, tells you to sit down, relax and just eat a banana first.

To the children of Janny and Lien, who welcomed me into their family with so much love, and gave me their trust, their memories and access to all the personal documents of their mothers; I can only hope I have done you justice.

To my dear family and friends, who have been so supportive and understanding during my physical, and often mental, absence.

And finally, to my first and, hopefully, also last love, Joris – the Marlin to my Dory and sometimes also the Creed to my Rocky. To my bonus daughter, Anne, and my children Josephine, Duc and Cees who, in trying times, showered me with kisses, hugs, omelettes with mayonnaise and bags full of sweets; you make me happier than you will ever realize.

Immersing oneself in the details of the Holocaust for a long period of time profoundly changes a person, but the strong will, courage and humour of the Brilleslijper sisters I can draw on for the rest of my life. To end with the words of that other resistance fighter, Albert Camus: 'In the midst of winter I, at last, discovered that there was in me an invincible summer.'

# References

This story is based on numerous sources, part of them *oral history*. I have been able to check almost all stories with multiple sources or against official documents. There is uncertainty about one thing: Janny Brilleslijper has always said she first saw the Frank family at Amsterdam Centraal Station, although she did not know them personally at the time. However, the Frank family and Janny Brilleslijper do not appear on the same date on the lists of the Amsterdam–Westerbork transports of the Dutch Red Cross. This can mean two things: either Janny did not see or remember it correctly, or there was an administrative error in the lists, which happened more often. Since I follow Janny's memories throughout the story, and she was always very consistent and detailed, I chose to stick to her version.

## Personal Documentation and Interviews

Brandes-Brilleslijper, J. *Voltooid en onvoltooid verleden tijd; memoires voor besloten kring* (Past and present time; memoirs for a private circle), 1986

Brandes-Brilleslijper, J. *Eberhard Rebling: 90 jaar! memoires voor besloten kring* (Eberhard Rebling: 90 years! memoirs for a private circle), 2001

Jaldati, L. and Rebling E. *Sag nie, du gehst den letzten Weg, memoires van Lin Jaldati en Eberhard Rebling* (Sag nie, du gehst den letzten Weg; memoirs of Lin Jaldati and Eberhard Rebling), Berlin, Buchverlag Der Morgen, 1986

Personal documentation of Eberhard Rebling and the Brilleslijper family in the Yad Vashem Archives.

Personal documentation of Janny Brandes-Brilleslijper and the Brilleslijper family in the Anne Frank Archives.

Personal conversations with Kathinka Rebling, Jalda Rebling, Rob Brandes, Willy Lindwer, Ad van Liempt and many others involved.

Registered conversations with Janny Brandes-Brilleslijper, Lien Rebling-Brilleslijper, Eberhard Rebling, Karel Poons, Marion Pritchard, Bert and Annie Bochove, Jan Hemelrijk and many others involved.

Filmed testimony of Janny Brandes-Brilleslijper, USC Shoah Foundation, the Institute for Visual History and Education, 1996.

Filmed testimony of Janny Brandes-Brilleslijper, *De laatste zeven maanden van Anne Frank* (The last seven months of Anne Frank), documentary by W. Lindwer, 1988.

Filmed testimony of Jalda Rebling, Yiddish Book Center, 11 dMarch 2014.

Slesin, A., *Secret Lives: Hidden Children and Their Rescuers During World War II*, documentary, 2002.

Police interviews, witness statements, transport lists, et cetera, National Archives.

Correspondence and documents of the Dutch Red Cross.

Building plans, permit application and notarial acts of the architect during the construction of The High Nest, 1920.

## Archives and Websites

*Adolf Eichmann's Testimony in Jerusalem about the Wannsee Conference*, Haus der Wannsee-konferenz, Gedenk- und Bildungsstätte

*100 jaar Joods Bussum*, Joodse Gemeente Bussum, online archief (*100 years of Jewish Bussum*, Jewish Community Bussum, online archives)

Anne Frank Stichting (Anne Frank Foundation); information source: <https://www.annefrank.org>

Archief *De Vrije Kunstenaar*, Vakbeweging in de oorlog (Archives *The Free Artist*, trade unions in wartime); information source: <https://www.vakbewegingindeoorlog.nl/documenten/vrije-kunstenaar>

Archief Eemland (Eemland Archives); information source: <https://www.archiefeemland.nl>

Archieven.nl, afdelingen erfgoedgids, kranten, personen (Archieven.nl, sections, archives, historical associations and museums, newspapers, people); information source: <https://www.archieven.nl>

*Art Is My Weapon: The Radical Musical Life of Lin Jaldati,* Media project by David Shneer; information source: https://www.david shneer.com/art-is-my-weapon.html

*Artistiek Bureau,* online magazine by Nick ter Wal, information on Gerrit van der Veen, Mik van Gilse and others; information source: <https://www.artistiekbureau.com>

*Auschwitz Bulletin,* Nederlands Auschwitz Comité (*Auschwitz Bulletin,* Dutch Auschwitz Committee); information source: <https://www.auschwitz.nl/nederlands-auschwitz-comite/onze-activiteiten/auschwitz-bulletin/>

*Beeldbank WO2,* NIOD, (Image Bank WW2, NIOD; Institute for War, Holocaust and Genocide Studies); information source: <www.beeldbankwo2.nl>

Beleidsnota Bestuur Gooise Meren, Beheervisie Oude Begraafplaats Naarden, 2004 (Policy Memorandum,

Gooise Meren Council, Management Vision Old Cemetery Naarden, 2004)

De Theaterencyclopedie, Bijzondere Collecties (UVA) en Stichting TIN (The Theatre Encyclopedia, Special Collections (University of Amsterdam) and Theatre in the Netherlands Foundation); information source: <www.theaterencyclopedie.nl/wiki>

Dodenakkers.nl, archief van de Stichting Dodenakkers, Funerair Erfgoed, o.a. over de dood van Jan Verleun en luitenant-generaal Seyffardt (Dodenakkers.nl, Archives of the Dodenakkers (Graveyards) Foundation, Funerary Heritage, among others on the death of Jan Verleun and Lieutenant-General Seyffardt)

Drenthe in de oorlog, Lourens Looijenga en rtv Drenthe, www.drentheindeoorlog.nl ((The province of) Drenthe in wartime, Lourens Looijenga and rtv (radio/television) Drenthe); information source: <www.drentheindeoorlog.nl>

Encyclopaedia Britannica, Inc. 2010; information source: <www.britannica.com>

Herinneringscentrum Kamp Westerbork, archief en collectie van Kamp Westerbork (Memorial Center Camp Westerbork, archive and collection of Camp Westerbork); information source: <www.kampwesterbork.nl>

Het 'Illegale Parool'-archief 1940–1945 (The 'illegal Parool' (underground newspaper) archives 1940–1945); information source: <www.hetillegaleparool.nl>

Het Verzetsmuseum Amsterdam, collectie en bibliotheek van het museum (The Amsterdam Resistance Museum, collection and library of the museum); information source: <https://www.verzetsmuseum.org/>

Historical Papers, krantenarchief van Wits University (Historical Papers, newspaper archive of Wits University); information source: <http://www.historicalpapers.wits.ac.za>

*Holocaust Survivors and Remembrance Project,* Holocaust Rescuers; information source: <https://www.isurvived.org>

Humanistische Canon, Humanistisch Verbond i.s.m. Humanistisch Historisch Centrum (Humanistic Canon, Humanistic Association in collaboration with Humanist Historical Center); information source: <https://www.humanistischecanon.nl>

Jewish Virtual Library, American–Israeli Cooperative Enterprise (AICE); information source: <https://jewishvirtuallibrary.org>

Joods Monument, Joods Cultureel Kwartier (Jewish Monument, Jewish Cultural Quarter); information source: <https://www.joodsmonument.nl>

Kranten Regionaal Archief Alkmaar (Newspapers Regional Archives Alkmaar); information source: <https://kranten.archiefalkmaar.nl>

Krantenviewer Noord-Hollands Archief (Newspaper viewer North-Holland Archives); information source: <https://nha.courant.nu/>

Nederlands Instituut voor Oorlogsdocumentatie (NIOD), Instituut voor oorlogs-, holocaust-en genocidestudies (Netherlands Institute for War Documentation (NIOD), Institute for War, Holocaust and Genocide Studies); information source: <https://www.niod.nl>

Nederlandse vrijwilligers in de Spaanse Burgeroorlog, database van het Internationaal Instituut voor Sociale Geschiedenis (Dutch volunteers in the Spanish Civil War, database of the International Institute of Social History); information source: <https://www.spanjestrijders.nl>

Notulen van de Wannseeconferentie, d.d. 20 januari 1942, Haus der Wannsee-konferenz, Gedenk-und Bildungsstätte, en Yad Vashem, The World Holocaust Remembrance Center (Minutes from the Wannsee Conference of 20 January 1942, Wannsee conference house, memorial and educational site, and Yad Vashem, The World Holocaust Remembrance Center)

*Nuremberg Trials Project*, Harvard Law School Library; information source: <https://nuremberg.law.harvard.edu>

*Onderzoeksgids oorlogsgetroffenen WO2, terugkeer, opvang, nasleep.* Het Nederlands Instituut voor Oorlogsdocumentatie (NIOD) en het Huygens Instituut voor Nederlandse Geschiedenis (Huygens ing) (*Research guide for WW2 war victims, return, relief, aftermath.* Netherlands Institute for War Documentation (NIOD) and the Huygens Institute for Dutch History (Huygens ing)); information source: <https://www.oorlogsgetroffenen.nl>

Parlementaire enquête regeringsbeleid 1940–1945 (Parliamentary inquiry into government policy 1940–1945); information source: <www.parlement.com>

Stichting Joods Erfgoed Den Haag (Jewish Heritage Foundation The Hague); information source: <www.joodserfgoeddenhaag.nl>

Stichting Oneindig Noord-Holland (Foundation 'Infinite North-Holland'); information source: <https://www.onh.nl>

The Holocaust Education & Archive Research Team, h.e.a.r.t.; information source: <https://www.holocaustresearchproject.org>

Toespraken van Reichsführer-SS Heinrich Himmler in Poznan op 4 en 6 oktober 1943, (Speeches by Reichsführer-SS Heinrich Himmler in Poznan on 4 and 6 October 1943); Harvard Law School Library, Nuremberg Trials Project

United States Holocaust Memorial Museum, archieven en

interviews (United States Holocaust Memorial Museum, archives and interviews); information source: <https://www.ushmm.org>

Wallenberg Lecture 1996, Marion P. Pritchard, 16 October 1996.

World Holocaust Remembrance Center Yad Vashem, The Holocaust Martyrs' and Heroes' Remembrance Authority; information source: <https://www.yadvashem.org/>

## Books

*De laatste getuigen uit concentratie-en vernietiging-skampen, een educatief vredesproject*, Brussels, Uitgeverij Asp, 2010.

Agamben, G., *Remnants of Auschwitz*, trans. D. Heller-Roazen (New York: Zone Books, 2002)

Block, G. and Drucker, M., *Rescuers: Portraits of Moral Courage in the Holocaust* (New York: Holmes & Meier Publishers, 1992)

Braber, B., *Waren mijn ogen een bron van tranen: Een joods echt paar in het verzet, 1940–1945* (Amsterdam: Amsterdam University Press, 2015)

De Jong, dr. L., *Het Koninkrijk der Nederlanden in de Tweede Wereldoorlog* (The Hague, Sdu, 1969–1991)

Enzer, H.A. and Solotaroff-Enzer, S. (ed.) *Anne Frank:*

*Reflections on Her Life and Legacy* (Illinois: University of Illinois Press, 1999)

Fischel, J., *The Holocaust* (Westport, Conn.: Greenwood Press Guide, 1998)

Fournet, C., *The Crime of Destruction and the Law of Genocide; Their Impact on Collective Memory* (Farnham, Surrey: Ashgate Publishing, 2007)

Hoeven, L., *Een boek om in te wonen: De verhaalcultuur na Auschwitz* (Dissertation, Hilversum: Verloren, 2015)

Keller, S., *Günzburg und der Fall Josef Mengele: Die Heimatstadt und die Jagd nach dem NS-Verbrecher* (München: Oldenbourg, 2010)

Kershaw, I., *Hitler*, trans. M. Agricola (Amsterdam: Spectrum, 2011)

Klemperer, V., *Tot het bittere einde. Dagboeken 1933–1945* (Amsterdam: Atlas, 1997)

Land-Weber, E., *To Save a Life: Stories of Holocaust Rescue* (Illinois: University of Illinois Press, 2006)

Lee, C.A., *Anne Frank 1929–1945: Het leven van een jong meisje, de definitieve biografie*, trans. M. de Bruijn (Amsterdam: Uitgeverij Balans, 2009)

Lee, C.A., *Anne Frank 1929–1945: Pluk rozen op aarde en vergeet mij niet*, trans. M. Benninga et al (Amsterdam: Uitgeverij Balans, 1998)

Levi, P., *If This is a Man*, trans. S. Woolf (London: The Orion Press, 1959)

Liempt, A. van, *Aan de Maliebaan. De kerk, het verzet, de NSB en de SS op een strekkende kilometer* (Amsterdam: Uitgeverij Balans, 2015)

Liempt, A. van, *Frieda: Verslag van een gelijmd leven* (Hooghalen: Herinneringscentrum Kamp Westerbork, 2007)

Liempt, A. van, *Kopgeld* (Amsterdam: Uitgeverij Balans, 2003)

Lindwer, W., *De laatste zeven maanden van Anne Frank* (Meppel: Just Publishers, 2008)

Lindwer's documentary by the same name was released in 1988

Minney, R.J., *I Shall Fear No Evil: The Story of Dr. Alina Brewda* (London: Kimber, 1966)

Pollman, T., *Mussert & Co: De NSB-Leider en zijn vertrouwelingen* (Amsterdam: Boom, 2012)

Presser, J., *Ondergang. De vervolging en verdelging van het Nederlandse jodendom, 1940–1945* (The Hague: Staatsuitgeverij, 1965)

Rol, C., *En nu een gewoon Hollandsch liedje. Leven en werken van Dirk Witte (1885–1932)* (Zaandijk: Stichting Vrienden van het Zaantheater, 2006)

Romijn, P., *Burgemeesters in oorlogstijd: Besturen onder Duitse bezetting* (Amsterdam: Uitgeverij Balans, 2006)

Schütz, R., *Achter gesloten deuren: Het Nederlandse notariaat, de Jodenvervolging en de naoorlogse zuivering* (Amsterdam: Amsterdam University Press, 2010)

Schütz, R., *Kille mist: Het Nederlandse notariaat en de erfenis van de oorlog* (Amsterdam: Boom, 2016)

Seymour, M. and Camino, M., *The Holocaust in the Twenty-First Century* (London: Routledge, 2017)

Went, N., *Hoe de Leider voor volk en vaderland behouden bleef* (Bussem: Autonic, 1942)

Würzner, H., *Österreichische Exilliteratur in den Niederlanden 1934–1940* (Amsterdam: Rodopi, 1986)

Zee, S. van der, *25000 Landverraders, de SS in Nederland / Nederland in de SS* (The Hague: Kruseman, 1967)

## Magazines/Newspapers/Articles

Bruggeman, H., 'In memoriam: Jannie Brandes-Brilleslijper (1916–2003), Verzetsvrouw', *Auschwitz Bulletin*, no. 3, September 2003

Flap, H. and Tamme, P., 'De electorale steun voor de Nationaal Socialistische Beweging in 1935 en 1939', *Mens & Maatschappij*, vol. 83, no. 1, 2008, pp. 23

Gompes. L., 'Fatsoenlijk land', *Rozenberg Quarterly Magazine*, 2013

Meyers, J., 'Mussert in mei veertig', *Maatstaf*, vol. 30, 1982

n.n. 'Mensch durf te leven', *De Omroeper*, vol. 19, no. 2, 2006, pp. 75–80

Rolfs, D.W. and Professor Schaberg, 'The Treachery of the Climate: How German Meteorological Errors and the Rasputisa Helped Defeat Hitler's Army at Moscow', *Special Topics in History; World War II*, 2010

Shneer, D., 'Eberhard Rebling, Lin Jaldati, and Yiddish Music in East Germany, 1949–1962' Oxford University Press, 2014

Articles by D.J. Zimmerman (chairman of the Military Writer's Society of America), Defense Media Network, Military History

*Delpher* (regional newspaper archives and online newspaper archives)

*De Huizer Courant* (newspaper)

*De Jacobsladder* (quarterly publication of the Historical Society 'Otto Cornelis van Hemessen')

*De Typhoon, Dagblad voor de Zaanstreek* (newspaper)

*De Zuidkanter* (newspaper)

*De Groene Amsterdammer* (weekly magazine)

*De Omroeper, Stichting Vijverberg*

*Historisch Nieuwsblad* (magazine)

*Leeuwarder Courant* (newspaper)

*Maatstaf* (magazine)

*The New York Times* (newspaper)

*Nieuw Israëlietisch Weekblad* (magazine)

*Ons Amsterdam* (magazine)

*Over Oegstgeest* (biannual magazine)

*Vrij Nederland* (Dutch magazine)

**ROXANE VAN IPEREN** is an award-winning author and journalist. Her novelistic eye, combined with her rigorous research, result in a hugely compelling portrayal of courage, treason and human resilience. *The Sisters of Auschwitz* is a truly unforgetable book and winner of the Opzij Prize for Literature 2019.

# HARPER
# LARGE PRINT

We hope you enjoyed reading
our new, comfortable print size and found it
an experience you would like to repeat.

**Well – you're in luck!**

Harper Large Print offers the finest in
fiction and nonfiction books in this same larger
print size and paperback format. Light and easy to read,
Harper Large Print paperbacks are for the book lovers
who want to see what they are reading without strain.

For a full listing of titles and
new releases to come, please visit our website:
**www.hc.com**

## HARPER LARGE PRINT

**SEEING IS BELIEVING!**